Religious Minorities in Iraq

Religious Minorities in Iraq

Co-Existence, Faith and Recovery after ISIS

Maria Rita Corticelli

I.B. TAURIS
LONDON • NEW YORK • OXFORD • NEW DELHI • SYDNEY

I.B. TAURIS
Bloomsbury Publishing Plc
50 Bedford Square, London, WC1B 3DP, UK
1385 Broadway, New York, NY 10018, USA
29 Earlsfort Terrace, Dublin 2, Ireland

BLOOMSBURY, I.B. TAURIS and the I.B. Tauris logo are trademarks of
Bloomsbury Publishing Plc

First published in Great Britain 2022
This paperback edition published 2024

Copyright © Maria Rita Corticelli, 2022

Maria Rita Corticelli has asserted her right under the Copyright, Designs and
Patents Act, 1988, to be identified as Author of this work.

For legal purposes the Acknowledgements on pp. xi–xii constitute an
extension of this copyright page.

Series design by Adriana Brioso
Cover image © Zaid Al-Obeidi/AFP/Getty Images

All rights reserved. No part of this publication may be reproduced or transmitted
in any form or by any means, electronic or mechanical, including photocopying,
recording, or any information storage or retrieval system, without prior
permission in writing from the publishers.

Bloomsbury Publishing Plc does not have any control over, or responsibility for, any
third-party websites referred to or in this book. All internet addresses given
in this book were correct at the time of going to press. The author and publisher
regret any inconvenience caused if addresses have changed or sites have ceased
to exist, but can accept no responsibility for any such changes.

A catalogue record for this book is available from the British Library.

A catalog record for this book is available from the Library of Congress.

	ISBN:		
	HB:	978-0-7556-4134-5
	PB:	978-0-7556-4136-9
	ePDF:	978-0-7556-4133-8
	eBook:	978-0-7556-4135-2

Typeset by RefineCatch Limited, Bungay, Suffolk

To find out more about our authors and books visit www.bloomsbury.com
and sign up for our newsletters.

To my mother
To José María
And to all who shared this journey with me

Contents

List of figures — viii
Foreword by Father Dr Ghazwan Yousif Baho — ix
Acknowledgements — xi
List of abbreviations — xiii

Introduction — 1
1 The Kakais of Iraq: Origins, history and religion — 13
2 Hope and resilience: Christians in Iraq — 45
3 Survival: Yezidis and the power of testimony — 97
4 Unheard Muslim voices: The Sunnis — 123
5 The challenge of statehood and modernity for the Kurds: Baghdad vs Erbil — 137
Conclusion — 163

Glossary — 167
Notes — 171
Bibliography — 183
Index — 195

Figures

2.1	Rabban Hormizd Monastery. Source Wikimedia Commons.	64
2.2	Courtyard of St George Church, Teleskof, October 2018.	79
2.3	Chaldean Catholic Cathedral of Saint Joseph (Mar Yousif) in Ankawa, Arbil. Source, Wikimedia Commons.	85
3.1	Celebrating the Yezidi New Year on 18 April 2017, Lalish. Source, Wikimedia Commons.	98
3.2	View of Shrines of Sheikh Adi, Sheikh Hassan, and Sheikh Bakr at the Yezidi holy site of Lalish in Kurdistan Region. Source, Wikimedia Commons.	120
3.3	Yezidi women (18 April 2017) celebrating the start of the new year which begins the following day at Lalish. Source, Wikimedia Commons.	120
4.1	Refugee children in Camp Garmawa near the city of Dohuk in Northern Iraq. Source: Getty Images, Ullstein Bild.	127

Foreword

Father Dr Gharzwan Yousif Baho

I am so glad to introduce this book, written by someone coming from the other side of the world who chose to write about our religious minorities and their situation in Iraq. It was Palm Sunday on April 2019 when the crew of programmes for BBC World Service arrived in Alqosh with our friend Maria Rita Corticelli.

The world has changed since the proclamation of the new so-called Islamic state (ISIS). More than three years of war changed the lives of those who lived only fifteen kilometres from the border with the so-called caliphate. During those years, around two million people from Mosul and the Nineveh Plain among them, Christians, Yezidis, Shabaks, Shiites and Sunnis, who refused to give in to this jihadi interpretation of Islam fled to seek refuge in Erbil while ISIS troops destroyed ancient cities and villages.

Maria Rita starts her journey through some of the most prominent religious minorities struggling for their survival in the country. She manages to unveil the origins, history and religion of the Kakais community in Iraq by explaining the sacredness of the Zagros Mountains from where they originate and by introducing to the reader the Saranjam, Kakais' holy book. Reading this book, I could also appreciate Kakais' fight for recognition in this very challenging historical moment for Iraq. Their courage and resilience set an example for all of us.

Maria Rita also presents the history of Christians in Iraq, their contribution to the culture and social development of the Nineveh Plain along the centuries before exposing their current situation after the war with Islamic state (ISIS). She recounts the history of Alqosh, the City of God, the only village spared by ISIS's fury as if somebody from above was protecting it. With its three-thousand-year history, Alqosh incarnated the hope for the other Christian villages Telesqof, Baqosfa, Batnaya, Batalla, Karmles and Qaraqosh. Maria Rita did not forget Ankawa, the largest Christian enclave in the Middle East situated in Erbil.

Reading her book, I felt the power of testimony when the author talks about Yezidi women victims of ISIS who have become the protagonists of the introduction of the values of human rights both in Iraq and Kurdish regional government. Equally important is the analysis of the positive consequences of the internationalization of the Yezidis' case. Thanks to their gained knowledge of similar traumas suffered by other women around the world, Yezidi women have been able to share their experience and to bring about important changes in their own community.

It was very inspiring the presence unheard Muslim voices from the Sunnis and of the Shaback communities. Their insertion in a book of this kind does not have to be taken for granted. Usually, because of all the suffering religious minorities had to endure, the idea that Muslims can also be victims of violence is hard to understand. However, during this tragedy and in its aftermath, some Muslim communities have not been spared and a dialogue with them is pivotal in order to change the future of all our communities.

I want to finish this presentation of this wonderful book with my memory of the visit of Pope Francis to Iraq in March 2021, a ray of light not only for Christians but also for all the religious communities in the country. I was with him praying for the victims of the war in Hosh al-Bieaa (Church Square) in Mosul only six years after ISIS proclaimed the caliphate from this very place. In opposition to ISIS's words of intolerance, Pope Francis restored our communities' dignity, fairness, equality and respect with these words:

> If God is the God of life – for so He is – then it is is wrong for us to kill our brothers and sisters in His name.
> If God is the God of peace – for so He is – then it is wrong for us to wage war in His Name.
> If God is the God of love – for so He is – then it is wrong of us to hate our brothers and sisters.

Acknowledgements

The origin of this book lies in a two-year work experience between 2016 and 2017, in Erbil, the capital of the Kurdish semi-autonomous region in the north of Iraq. I worked there as university lecturer and as Director of the Center for Genocide Studies. It was during that time that I met all the people without whom it would have been impossible to write this book.

I am extremely grateful to Farhad al-Kake for introducing me to the Kakai community and its sacred land of Hawar. I am also grateful to his family for their hospitality and the affection they always showed me. Within the Kakai community, I would like to thank Rashid Luqman for sharing with me his knowledge of the Kakai religion and, in particular, for sharing with me unpublished, fascinating stories from the Saranjam, the Kakais' sacred book, and for introducing me to their rites. The insight and the commitment he showed were pivotal for the completion of this book. I also thank Leyla and Shadmo for their help and for sharing their life experiences with me. I am grateful to Adel Kakay for sharing his knowledge of the Kakai religion and culture and for the translation of part of the notebook written by the dervish, Rashid of Hawar, for the British diplomat, C. J. Edmonds. My thanks also go to Ako al-Kake for his hospitality during our visits to Halabja and Hawar.

I am grateful to Ranin Taher from the Shlomo Organization, Erbil, and her family for their help and hospitality. From the same organization, I also thank Faris Yousif Jeojo. My thanks also to Vian Ako and Nozad Polis Akim for their help and hospitality. I would also like to express my gratitude to Father Ghazwan, Father Ammon, Father Behnam Benoka, Father Noel Kosso, Archbishop Michaeel Najeeb and Archbishop Bashar Matti Warda for their invaluable contribution to this research. My thanks also to John Neill for his help in Erbil and Suha Rassam for her availability.

In addition, I am grateful to Khadher Domle for his availability and support during the collection of information about the Yezidi community and for providing me with the testimony of his own experience in saving Yezidi women from captivity. I also wanted to thank him for his time and commitment to my research in Erbil and during the writing of this book.

I would like to acknowledge with thanks Eve Streeter for producing the series *Iraq's Religious Minority Exodus and Extinction* broadcast by the BBC World Service in 2019, and cameraman, Dominic Byrne, for producing a short film on the Kakai community in Hawar.

A number of institutions were important for their support and I want to acknowledge them with gratitude. First, I thank Stephen Smith and the Shoah Foundation at the University of Southern California, where I was Scholar in Residence in 2017. It was an invaluable experience which allowed me to learn how to gather and assess testimonies from the victims of genocide. I thank Tali Nates, Director of the Johannesburg Holocaust and Genocide Centre, for her support in hosting a conference on minorities in Iraq. For the same reason, I thank Emmanuel Cortney from Yahad-In Unum in Paris. I also thank Debbie Usher, archivist at the Middle East Centre Archive, St Antony's College, Oxford University, for granting me access and reproducing parts of C. J. Edmonds papers.

I am grateful to Dr Yael Simon for reviewing my manuscript, and to Dr Matthew Hone for revising the proposal for this book. I also thank Dr Mitchell Belfer and the Euro-Gulf Information Center.

My life in Erbil would not have been so meaningful without my friendship with Nazdar Balder and her good sense of humour and irony.

I would like to thank all the volunteers of the Centre for Genocide Studies at the International University of Erbil, in particular Swan, Ferman, Rawa and Mai for their enthusiasm and commitment.

I want to remember also all the families that both in cities and villages opened their doors to me. I will never forget their warm hospitality.

Abbreviations

AM	Assyrian Movement
ADM	Assyrian Democratic Movement
CDO	Civil Development Organization
CRSV	Conflict-Related Sexual Violence
GFIW	General Federation of Iraqi Women
HRW	Human Rights Watch
IDP	Internally Displaced Person
ICTR	International Criminal Tribunal for Rwanda
ICTY	International Criminal Tribunal for the Former Yugoslavia
ISIS	Islamic State of Iraq and Syria
IMK	Islamic Movement of Kurdistan
KAS	Konrad-Adenauer-Stiftung
KDP	Kurdistan Democratic Party
KRG	Kurdish Regional Government
NPA	Norwegian People's Aid
PUK	Patriotic Union of Kurdistan
OTT	Open Think Tank
TAL	Transitional Administrative Law
TCCDR	Tribal Criminal and Civil Disputes Regulations
UNDP	United Nations Development Program
UNESCO	United Nations Educational, Scientific and Cultural Organization
UNHCR	United Nations Refugee Agency (United Nations High Commissioner for Refugees)

Introduction

The literature about religious communities in Iraq usually suffered from the same sectarian attitude affecting parts of Iraqi society: Westerners in general tend to treat them in isolation, as though Christians, Kakais, Yezidis and other communities were closed inside watertight compartments without any interaction between them. Two years of fieldwork carried out between 2016 and 2018, show that the reality on the ground is very different. Without compromising the richness inevitably originating in diversity, all these groups interact in a very dynamic way and are animated by the same desire for a new, more tolerant society. This book aims at showing the lacunae left by both media and academia with a fieldwork which offers a more nuanced and deeper investigation into the way the communities live and cope with past and present intimidations. In their own words, members of these communities tell stories of resilience against oppression, creativity in the darkest moments, hope amidst death, the final affirmation of faith in life against violence. All of them are now reunited in a common, almost heroic effort of reconstruction and peace-building, impossible to realize without a newfound interfaith dialogue.

In over two years, I have interviewed more than a hundred people between representatives of the religious communities, academics, activists, politicians, policy-makers, citizens and refugees. Among them were victims and perpetrators, men, women and children, who have been overwhelmed by the tragic events of the past few years. Through these religious minorities' narratives and archaeological sites, I travelled to the remotest villages of Mesopotamia to find out how, after centuries, the monasteries and Christian churches still mark the rhythms of the villages destroyed by the Islamic State of Iraq and Syria (ISIS) and now only partially reconstructed; and I visited the sacred places of the Kakais in the Zagros Mountains, almost unknown to most travellers and that only a few Westerners have reached. I visited Lalish, the sacred place of the Yezidis, to listen to how the community is coping with the last wave of deadly violence. I talked to Sunni Muslims about the discrimination they endured, and who from perpetrators have become victims of violence and intolerance.

Thanks to a privileged access to the communities, this book offers the reader a unique insight into the micro-history of the flourishing religious minorities living in Iraq and of their persecution. The book relies on the consultation of chronicles and archives, and archaeological and art history, as well as local culture and narrative to portray how their faith has helped them to survive and preserve their identity during the various moments of rupture and continuity in Iraq's history. It offers the reader the unique opportunity to embark on a fascinating journey to the land of the Christians, Chaldeans, Yezidis, Sunni Muslims and Shabbak, but also of the Kakais, the most secretive religious group of Iraq, who have revealed to a Western audience their sacred places, faith, rites and efforts for recognition. It examines the relationship between religious communities and civil society and how they have woven networks of aid and protection that have been little studied so far. I am aware that not all the minorities currently present in Iraq are treated in this book. This is because I did not want to fall into the temptation of writing a compendium of religions. By choosing specific groups, I wanted to focus on communities that are questioning their past and their present and are rebuilding their future in a not always peaceful confrontation with political powers and within themselves.

Iraq occupies most of the territories once called Mesopotamia, known in the West as the cradle of civilization. This region is also the birthplace of all monotheistic religions. Due to its strategic geographical position on the route between West and East, this region has traditionally been the receptacle of different faiths and ethnicities which have coexisted for centuries, united by a thread that has been understudied and often misunderstood. All these communities have experienced various degree of persecution, marginalization and violence which affected their views, their faith and also their vision of the future. However, in the past few years, they have shown a constructive interest in each other's existence and in the pursuit of their religious and civil rights. This book discusses how the experiences of hostility and politics of annihilation imposed by the different powers who have controlled the region have raised their awareness and shaped their ideas of a new society based on a harmonious coexistence.

It is very difficult to talk about the fate of minorities in Iraq without first referring briefly to the legacy of Saddam Hussein's regime. As Charles Tripp observes in his book, *A History of Iraq*, the level of violence experienced by all the minorities living in the country was not unknown before him (2014). On the contrary, his power was based on the traditional tribal organization of the society which always prizes belonging to different clans or families. The emergence of Saddam Hussein and his construction of a dictatorship demanding obedience and using violence on a scale unmatched in Iraq's history were the dominant themes of the politics of this period. The factors which made it possible, as well as its consequences for Iraq's political life, did not suggest a radical break with the past. On the contrary, the methods Saddam Hussain used, some of the values he espoused and the political logic of the system that he established in Iraq, were all prefigured in previous regimes to various degrees. Indeed, in many ways, they epitomized some of the distinctive characteristics of the Iraqi state itself, as process and as structure. It could be argued that had this not been the case, had the regime not rooted itself in important social networks and had it not taken account of the associated expectations, its power would have been much more limited, whatever the ambitions of its leader (ibid.). It is in this context that Tripp explains the success of the narrative of the Iraqi state as a vehicle for the perpetration of the limitless power of a state based on 'exclusivity, communal mistrust, patronage and the exemplary use of violence were the main elements, woven into a system of dependence on and conformity with the will of a small number of men at the centre in the name of social discipline and national destiny' (ibid.).

Tripp does not only provide an explanation of the strategies put in place but also of how Saddam Hussein was able to keep himself and his acolytes in power for such a long time, but he also indirectly offers a partial answer to the aspirations of the representatives of the minority groups currently working in Iraq. Tripp traces a continuous thread between past and present, stating that violence perpetrated by one group against another weaker one has always been part of history. However, if we consider the history of the past two decades, this interpretation, even if useful, does not take into account how this history of violence is perceived and interpreted on the ground by the different communities who actually suffered it.

A wider awareness, together with the dramatic experiences of the past few years, have led all the communities to offer a different approach to their past and present history. This reading is very seldomly told either in private or can be traced in very rare documents collected by volunteers and local NGOs in the heroic effort to fight against the daily loss of documentation on the crimes consistently committed against minorities and to preserve their memory. In some cases, the legacy of division still permeates these communities that are always at the mercy of bigger and destructive powers. However, the experience of massacre, indiscriminate killings, abductions and, in some cases, genocides, as well as the public internal and international exposure, in particular after 2014 and the advent if ISIS, have favoured among the minorities a new vision of a collective shared tragic past. This involves the recognition of a shared land, in particular the Nineveh Plain as well as the need for a coexistence. The idea of coexistence is slowly replacing the old violent idea of revenge and it is the minorities, with their everyday struggles, who are pushing for a change in the mentality as well as in the policy of the country.

It is probably very difficult for the Western audience, whose time and space are regulated by the certainty of scientific analysis, to understand the persistence in these communities of a chronological time which does not always coincide with ours. It is true that the secularization of our societies has forcibly obscured the exemplary force of these tales, however, this does not mean that we have to underestimate their importance, because they have inspired, and still do inspire, these peoples' behaviour and thinking for many generations. These tales constitute an unbreakable link which connects their past and present permeating their perception of the world, their way to interpret their history, their faith and their society.

This book aims at providing a solid historical background, and revealing the importance of the interfaith dialogue of religious minority groups who have been able to transform historic tragedies into strategies for survival and chronic displacement into a quest for a new identity and a proactive role in shaping their future. The Kakais are one of the most ancient religious groups in the Middle East. Theirs is a monotheistic religion which originated in the Zagros Mountains, their sacred land. Kakais are better known as Yarsan, and the majority of them live in what it is now Iran. This is the most secretive community in Iraq. The fieldwork for this is one of the rare occasions in which the community opens its doors to external glances, revealing their sacred places and the origin and the content of its sacred scripts. They talk openly about their cultural continuity and how they have interacted with other religious communities and with the state throughout the history of Iraq. Historians, activists and members of the community talk about how they were able to survive for many centuries in a hostile environment. This group is also of particular interest because it offers the unique opportunity to observe a passage from an oral to a written tradition.

While investigating the origins of their sacred scripts, it was possible to trace some of them in the personal papers of the British diplomat Cecil J. Edmonds, kept at the Middle East Centre Archive, St Antony's College, Oxford University. C. J. Edmonds was an adviser to the British Ministry of the Interior in Iraq between 1935 and 1945. In two little notebooks, one on the Kakais, a religious man explains in almost indecipherable old Gorani Kurdish the core of Saranjam, their sacred book. These notebooks were not the only sacred texts of the Kakais, and something very fascinating was going on within the community in Iraq. Some younger Kakai intellectuals have embarked on the effort to renew their faith by recovering ancient texts with the purpose of translating them into modern Kurdish and Arabic to make them more available to their faithful. In the process, they are questioning some of the previous interpretations offered by dervishes who misrepresented them. The access to an English translation of the Saranjam constitutes a strong limitation, nevertheless, and in order to enter their world, I did not have any other alternative but to listen to their voices, however broken and feeble, because they had not been recorded previously, at least not in the shape they take in the narrative proposed specifically for this book.

Despite this apparent lack of reliable sources, together with members of the community and in particular with Rashid Luqman, it was possible to establish a few firm points. The first one is chronological. Because of the strong influence of Iranian politics over the Yarsan community in Iran, the version of the Saranjam that appear in this book is that which had been published before 1980 and the Islamic Revolution of 1979, led by Ayatollah Khomeini. This is because the Iranian Revolution had a strong impact on the Yarsan community in Iran, part of which, after this date, started to identify with the Shi'as. In addition, the content of the translation into English has been revised by an English-speaking religious man of the community. The stories, the prophets, the people as well as the locations of old and new temples mentioned in the Saranjam, offered the opportunity to make historical, cultural and religious connections with the geographical region and the civilizations that shared it throughout the centuries. Trapped between two souls, one fighting to act in secrecy and the other battling for recognition, the voice of the Kakais can now be heard thanks to the efforts of activists and the establishment of civil organizations that represent them. The Chraw Organization for Documentation, Erbil, is currently documenting and denouncing the persecutions and killings perpetrated by ISIS and other militias, in particular in Iraq's disputed territories.

Chapter 2, which is dedicated to Christians, talks about the religious beliefs and practices that have led this minority to resist culturally and politically against repeated waves of violence. The advent of ISIS had a devastating impact on the most ancient Christian community in the world. From around 2 million before 2014, they were just 140,000 in 2021. ISIS not only destroyed most of their historical villages, churches and monasteries, but it also destroyed the whole infrastructure that allowed the community to survive. Besides testimony from refugees from the affected areas, this book also includes the testimonies of Father Michaeel Najeed and Bashar Matti Warda, the archbishops of Mosul and Erbil, respectively, as well as of Father Ghazwan Yousif Baho, the parish priest of Alqosh, Amar Abona, the parish priest of Qaraqosh, and Father Behnam Benoka, the parish priest of Bartalla. I also talked to the founders of the Shlomo Organization, a local NGO that works incessantly to document the testimonies of the victims and to record the material and cultural destruction of Christian heritage in the Nineveh Plain. This chapter will talk about how all of them, in different ways, link the dramatic events of the past few years with their past and how do they see their future in the country.

According to the Yezidis, they survived seventy-two genocides. Despite the world's interest in their tragedy after ISIS, very little is known about how the Yezidis are really coping with the last tragedy. It looks as though, in the vortex of all the attention they have been subjected to, their voices have been heard but not listened to. This chapter is based on a series of interviews carried out between 2016 and 2020 with survivors, religious people and activists who talk without the pressing presence of the media, about the new organization of their lives and the new ties which link past, present and future. Some of the interviews have been carried out in Lalish, their religious centre. However, contrary to what happened in other writings on this now famous religious group, I wanted to offer the reader the opportunity to hear the voices of Yezidi women not as victims, but as active bearers of a deep change in the way they live their faith, culture and social organization. In their testimonies, Yezidi women reveal the coping strategies adopted by the community and how these have changed their way to rethink their values in the face of the legacy of ISIS. Their testimonies reveal the degree of sensibility to the changes in their role within and outside their own community. This awareness links them in unexpected ways with the history of women's fights for their basic rights in past and present Iraq. By doing this, Yezidi women started a dialogue with their own community, questioning its traditional values, but at the same time strongly confirming their belonging to Yezidi religion. It is a dialogue that inevitably questions the customary isolation of the group and inaugurates an important passage from a religious group that is almost closed to the world to one whose members are actively struggling to rebuild their trust with other sectors of the society.

An interfaith dialogue cannot be successful without also engaging with the Muslim community. This is for two main reasons: the first one is that tolerance comes from the knowledge of the other; the second is because, in the permanent state of war in which Iraqis live, perpetrators can become victims of the same violence in which they collaborated. In 2014, after eleven years of social and political vacuum, the intervention of ISIS gave Sunnis an opportunity for revenge and redemption, again transforming them from victims into perpetrators. However, since the conquest of Mosul, ISIS attacked all those Sunni Muslims suspected of collaboration with the Shi'a-led Iraqi government and with the Kurds forcing them to seek refuge in the Kurdish Region. Abandoned by both the Iraqi and the Kurdish governments who branded them as extremists, and unable to return to their lands because of the still very real threat posed by remnants of ISIS, these refugees have again been pushed into a kind of civil and social limbo, which threatens to spark a new destructive sectarian civil war between the Shi'a and Sunni. To meet the Sunnis, I travelled to the Garmawa Refugee Camp in the Dohuk Governorate, where some of them still lived in 2018, remembering their lives in the now destroyed Mosul. Among those who suffered the consequences of ISIS's violence are also Shabak, who, in Iraqi history, were never saved from persecution. In search of a universal consensus for their cause, the Ba'ath Party first, Saddam Hussein later, and most recently ISIS, killed, imprisoned and tortured whoever they perceived to be their potential enemy, regardless of their ethnic, religious or political affiliations. Will they ever be able to knit the thread of tolerance with peaceful coexistence interrupted by yet another war? Will they be able to participate fully in the efforts for an interfaith dialogue without which peace will be impossible?

This is not a historical or political account of post-Saddam Iraq and for this reason history and politics will be touched upon only in relation to the past and present state of the minorities. The focus is on how and if a culture of human rights developed in Iraq and in particular in the Kurdish Region. It is not the purpose of this book to offer a history of the constitutions, either Iraqi or Kurdish. However, for the sake of the argument, it is useful to compare both of them in order to understand the basis on which any analysis of the development of human rights in Iraq has to take into account the difference between Iraq and the Kurdish Region.[1] The secular character of the Kurdish Region caused the development of a civil society which expresses itself through organizations representing minority groups. No researcher who has spent more than two weeks in the region and had the chance or the intellectual curiosity of getting in touch with the communities outside of the traditional academic or political circles can ignore this reality.[2] Local NGOs and civil organizations, in particular after 2003, started to operate in the Kurdish Region thanks to the favourable security situation offered and to its culture of tolerance toward minorities.

However limited this progress can be, it means a lot in terms of the relationships among the different groups. Also, it allowed all the minorities to live together and to come and discuss together the challenges of their coexistence.

Between October 2011 and April 2012, a report entitled, *The Minorities in Iraq: Seeking Justice, Equality and the Fear for the Future*, was released by the Civil Development Organization (CDO) and the Al-Mesalla Organization for Human Resources Development supported by the Norwegian People's Aid (NPA). The purpose of the report was to analyse the state of minorities in different provinces in Iraq: Baghdad, Erbil, Sulaymaniyah, Nineveh, Kirkuk and Duhok. The findings of this exercise were very interesting: on the one hand, it was clear that after 1992, and in particular after 2003, members of the minorities 'were able to open their own cultural centers, and the freedom of religion became more protected; besides guaranteeing their political rights were significantly emerged as they run political seats and various responsibilities in the Kurdish Regional Government [KRG], and they had members of parliament' (CDO 2012). On the other hand, it was clear from the answers given by the interviewees that their perception of the protection given to their rights changed depending on the geographical area but remained in general negative regarding the will or the possibility of the state to protect them from attacks, despite the 2015 Minorities' Rights Law issued by the KRG. However, a culture of tolerance that the KRG wanted to promote did not permeate the whole region and attacks on Christians and other minority groups by Muslim Kurds were and still are a reality in the Kurdish Region. In 2011, Muslim Kurds incited by hate speech in one of the mosques in Zakho attacked Christians shops.[3] This was a very frightening episode that made some Christians flee the area to seek refuge abroad or in other cities of the region.

The problem of hate speech causing violence and pulling apart society is felt in particular now as a consequence of the ideological legacy left by ISIS. In 2018, Kurdish society remained deeply religious, and one in which Islam is practised by the majority of the population. In the three KRG governorates of Erbil, Sulaymaniyah and Dohuk alone there are 5,537 mosques, while Mosul and Kirkuk, belonging to the disputed territories between the KRG and the central government in Bagdad, count around 3,000 mosques for a total of 10,000 imams.

In this context, the religious intolerance preached and practised by ISIS found fertile ground in the areas it occupied as well as in some of the most extremist Muslim population in the rest of both Iraq and the Kurdish Region. A renewed religious intolerance reflected in the recrudescence of hate speeches delivered by different imams in the mosques was also supported by some of the media. This situation alarmed both religious minorities that feel threatened by the possibility of renewed violent attacks against them, and also the most moderate sections of Islamic representatives who are working for the establishment of a more stable and peaceful society through a constructive inter-religious dialogue.

In the end, minorities in Iraq are generally still fighting for their religious, cultural and educational rights. No Yezidi has held an important position in the government and there has not been a Mandean minister or leader, while their situation is considered as catastrophic by most of the humanitarian agencies (Mandeans claim to be the last Gnostics). In addition to this situation, the KRG did not make an effort to efficiently integrate minorities into the life of the region, embarking on what has been defined as a 'Kurdification' of the areas. Tensions between the KRG and the religious minorities are very real despite the efforts mentioned above. The reasons are multiple and depend on the situation in the region, but also on its dependency from the laws promulgated in Baghdad. The application of Shari'a law across the whole country has direct consequences on individuals. It is very difficult to enforce any law in defence of religious minorities when these laws do not apply to everyone. According to Shar'ia law, and specifically to Article 26 of the Constitution, Muslims cannot convert to any other religion, however, the contrary is possible.

In addition, the same law provides that a child born to one Muslim and one non-Muslim parent is automatically listed as Muslim. In a country where religious affiliation is written on identity cards, this can cause a lot of misunderstanding in the future. This law has been strongly criticized by the representatives of the other religious minorities for the consequences it has on the efforts being made for coexistence among communities. This law de facto has caused Muslims who want to convert to face violence from police and security services.[4] The fear of the religious minorities is also that these laws can actually unsettle the already fragile equilibrium established among the communities in the Kurdish Region. One of the main fears that minorities have is that a non-pluralistic society can prevail in the near future. During meetings with the representatives of the different religious minorities, this argument always surfaced as a real possibility despite a superficial analysis of the political and social situation, combined with the set of laws for their protection provided by the KRG which gives the opposite signal. If we take into consideration the current difficult economic and social climate, however, these fears are not completely unfounded. The resurgence of religious extremism is also affecting the Kurdish Region, where episodes of violence against minorities have been denounced, in particular in the areas where they reside in their majority.

Within the past few decades, the history of the minorities living in Iraq has been particularly violent, also in comparison with other countries at war. In this chronic instability, the different communities sharing this land have been most of the times left alone in their struggle to survive the various mass killings they have been subjected to. The process of rebuilding communities after the physical, moral and economic upheaval in the wake of every war has been most of the time the responsibility of individuals fighting to preserve their memory. The fragmentation of society, together with the political instability, makes it very difficult to gather information and preserve the reminiscences of the genocides committed against Kurds, Christians, Yezidis, Kakais, Mandeans and other groups, a violence of which ISIS is perhaps the latest and cruelest but not the only expression.

The grip of Saddam's dictatorship was felt until the end. Despite Saddam abandoning the Kurdish people to their destiny, it was not easy for the newly established region to embark on a path of real change. The economic situation was extremely weak, with the government in Baghdad cutting civil servants' salaries and with an international community almost deaf to the Kurdish question and with most international agencies, including the United Nations Development Program (UNDP), being unable to fulfil the recommendations proposed in their 1991 diagnostics and plans for the development of the region (McDowall 2000: 382–3). All this had a very detrimental effect on the internal politics of the newly born Kurdish Region which, despite the commitment to a democratic process proposed in its draft constitution, fell into what McDowall in his book defines as 'neo-tribalism'. After the elections held on 19 May 1992, the two main parties, the Kurdistan Democratic Party (PDK) and the Patriotic Union of Kurdistan (PUK) with Massoud Barzani and Jalal Talabani did not work for a unified Kurdistan but for the supremacy of their respective parties. The loss of international credibility due to the two different agendas followed by both Barzani and Talabani constituted one of the reasons for the tepid international response to the Kurdish cause. One of the Kurdish politicians, Mahmood Uthman, interviewed in London on 11 November 1992 by McDowall denounced this lack of unity:

> They [Barzani and Talabani] do not trust each other. If you visit one all he can do is talk about the other. They are obsessed with their party rivalry ... they do not work out of a common strategy. There is no strategy at all, except of get ahead of the other party.[5]

Just two years after the elections of May 1994, this rivalry exploded into a four-year civil war which saw both parties looking for allies in Baghdad and in Teheran, respectively.[6] The economic and human cost of the civil war was incalculable, with thousands dead and displaced. In addition, the rivalry between the two parties sparked the military intervention of the Islamic Movement of Kurdistan (IMK) which, under the leadership of Mulla Uthman al-Aziz of Halabja, backed by Iran, was promoting Kurdistan as a ground ready for an Islamic revival, conquering territories in particular in the area of Halabja (McDowall 2000: 386–7). A war between 'obscurantists' and 'atheists', an aspect of the war that has not been studied properly but of which divided people and territories, and which refer us back to the status and participation of religious minorities in the Kurdish Region.

During the first elections held in May 1991, only two main minorities were officially recognized: Turkmans and Assyrian Christians. Other minorities were not recognized, or they did not present themselves at the elections as independent parties. Both Turkmans and Assyrian Christians suffered greatly under Saddam's regime and both of them came with a different agenda. Turkmans were asking for the inclusion of Kirkuk into the Kurdish Region without a precise idea of how to negotiate their status with the Kurdish authorities in the future. On the other hand, Christians voted separately from the Kurds. Assyrians had worked with the Kurdish national movement since the 1960s. One of the most famous Peshmerga commanders was an Assyrian woman, Margaret George Malik, killed in 1966. Crudely described, Assyrians tend to fall into two categories: those who live in the countryside and who identified with the Kurdish movement, and the town-dwellers who tended to identify more with the Arab population.[7] Victims of the policy of divide and rule established by Saddam, when the Kurdish elections took place, 'the only Assyrian party of note was the Assyrian Democratic Movement (ADM), founded in 1979.'[8]

It is clear from what McDowall says about the scant participation of the minorities in these first elections that in a country oppressed by dictatorship and on its knees due to the continuous wars and genocides committed against its own citizens, minorities in general tended to hide in order to avoid persecution and death. The case of the Assyrian Christians is very interesting in this sense. The idea of identifying themselves with the Arabs instead of with the Kurdish people is the result of the process of forced Arabization carried out by the Ba'ath Party and Saddam Hussein. In addition, identifying with the Arabs in most cases meant saving your life. A strategy which very rarely was successful. It is not surprising, though, that only few Christians at that particular moment in time felt safe to identify themselves with the Kurdish cause. However, what it is clear from this short information about the role of the Christians in the establishment of the KRG, is that their partial identification with Kurdish nationalism paid off in terms of representation and influence in the parliament of the KRG, where Christians, together with other religious minorities, have a representation. This situation is far from being wholly accepted, in particular after the advent of ISIS and the renewed dispute between the KRG and the Iraqi government for control of the liberated areas.

Despite the Kurdish Region's success in reuniting different forces and ethnicities in a common goal, the presence of minoritized groups within its borders meant a revision of what being Kurdish really means. The Kurdish people inherited a region replete with wars and still dealing with large-scale genocides committed against them by the Ba'ath Party and Saddam Hussein. However, throughout the years, and in particular after 2003, the Kurdish Region and its institutions had to deal with an increased awareness about their faith and ethnicities present within its borders and in particular in the territories disputed with the central government in Baghdad. Article 140 of the 2005 Iraqi Constitution provided for a referendum which had to solve the dispute, once and for all, by 2007. The central government never agreed to the referendum, which was held unilaterally and without the support of the international community in September 2017. Among the territories disputed is the Nineveh Plain where most of the minorities live, Assyrians/Christians, Yezidis, Kakais and Shabak. And it is on this stretch of land that faith and ethnicity are discussed in a way that is undermining the Kurdish claim on those lands. The fact that until now the Kurdish Region is the only region in a federal state is due more to historical and political reasons than to legal ones. This exclusivity created a constant confrontation between the KRG and the central government in Baghdad, resulting in the use and misuse of minorities on the battlefield. This reverberates also in the Kurdish element living as a foreign one, compromising the survival of Christians and other minorities in the region by Kurdifying the population and changing the demography of the Nineveh Plain to its advantage by appropriating Assyrian and Christian history and by adopting policies directed at the demographic change in the area.

In each chapter, it will be clear that throughout the centuries, despite all these communities maintaining close links with their neighbours, mistrust between ethnic and religious groups did not vanish, because the relationship between groups and tribes has always been affected by the same violence that allowed people to change their identity and religion according to the political convenience of the moment. This shifting identity of groups and individuals seems to prevent the birth of an idea of a country and unifying the citizenship of all the souls in the country. At least until now.

1

The Kakais of Iraq

Origins, history and religion

The sacredness of the Zagros Mountains

Kakais belong to Yarsanism, a very ancient religion whose members now live mainly in Iran. The name Yarsanism is the combination of two words: Yar = God and San = Beloved. During their long history, the followers of the Yarsani faith have taken on many names: Ahl-e Haqq (People of the Truth) or Kakai' (Brother), but they call themselves Yarsans. They are among the most ancient religious groups in the Middle East. Theirs is a monotheistic religion which originated in the Zagros Mountains, an extended mountain range that forms an artificial border between Iran and Iraq. According to their belief, the Angels were created before Adam and for this reason their religion is older than the first man created by God. Angels have the power to reincarnate not only among themselves but also in other beings, humans and even non-humans. In the Kakais' version of history, the same soul in charge of renewing humanity's faith in God, reincarnated in Moses, Jesus, Mohammed, Plato and others who, with their thinking, changed the world. In Iran, the Yarsan community is estimated to be between 4 and 6 million. However, it is the community that was artificially separated from its brothers on the other side of the border, in today's Iraq, by the European powers in the aftermath of the First World War[1] who are the subject of this chapter. The number of Kakais is estimated at around 200,000. They currently live mainly, but not exclusively, in the areas of Khanaqin, Erbil, Sulaymaniyah and Halabja.

The roots of the word 'Kakai' is of very ancient origin as a number of the ancient rulers of Kurdistan were dubbed the nickname *kaka* or *kika*. The ancestors of the Kashion Kurds ruled the present-day Lorestan region, and one of their kings, Akum Kak Remi, was able for the first time to rule Babylon, as he seized the opportunity of the Hittite invasion and established his rule there in about 1590 BCE. Also, one of the rulers of Khopushkia Province was named

Kakai and ruled during the beginning of the first millennium BCE. The word 'Key', reminiscent of Kakai, also preceded the names of Median rulers (700–550) such as Keyxesrew and Keykawis, with the meaning of 'great' or 'noble'. As history Professor Jamal Rashid Ahmad states, the word Kakai is an Aryan word mentioned in the Assyrian texts referring to the concept of uncle or maternal uncle. Today, it refers to elder brothers, and it has become a name for a Kurdish clan to denote the fraternal relations that bind its members to one another. The origin of the word 'kaka' goes back to the word *aaka*, present in the Avesta, the Zoroastrian holy book, with the meaning of 'great' or 'chief'. Since the appearance of the word Kakai long precedes the emergence of the Zoroastrian religion, it is very likely that also the ancient Aryan word 'Zardasht' was borrowed from the language spoken by the ancestors of the Kashite, Kakai and Medes Kurds.

In the past few years, new generations of Kakais realized that the only way to preserve their religion, culture and memory was to embark on a difficult recovery of the old sacred texts. This is because only a fresh approach to their heritage could allow them to liberate the Kakais' original religious message from the inevitable interferences it suffered due to succeeding wars and persecutions. One of the main challenges of the new generation of reformers is to translate from the old Gorani Kurdish dialect in which they were written, into the modern Kurdish and Arabic Kakais' sacred book, the Saranjam, whose content has remained obscure for most of the Kakais for many decades. This constitutes a major effort aimed at recovering the link with their ancestral culture and beliefs, compromised by long centuries of secretiveness. The main reason behind the choice of studying the Kakais of Iraq instead of including the whole of the Yarsan community in Iran are multiple: the first one is that, after 2003, a new generation of more educated members of this small community saw the opportunity to reaffirm its religious identity despite new and old persecutions.

The second reason, a corollary of the first, is that in order to obtain local and international recognition, this group of reformers embarked on the difficult operation of reestablishing the links with their community lost because of the successive wars and destruction that dismembered Iraq in the past few decades. Wars, genocides and persecutions have shaped this area and left the small community in Iraq for many years almost oblivious to its history and religious identity. The Kakais' sacred books, hidden for centuries, were in the hands of the dervishes who were in charge of keeping the community united in the most adverse circumstances. To make sense of themselves and of their historical role in Iraq and in the international community, the Kakais had to go back in time and rewrite their own history by recovering the sacred texts kept secret to the world and to most of the Kakai faithful. The reading and interpretation of these texts introduced them and us into a world in which political boundaries become extremely blurred; in a world where the landscape is populated by unexpected divine presences, where nature and the cult of the dead meet in sacred places hidden in caves and entangled in the vegetation. But also where an urban sacred world in which these same presences reappear in temples dedicated to other gods of the present and the past.

Despite this new movement, the Kakais are not particularly easy to approach. It is necessary to win their trust and what is the best way is to accept to be drawn into a world apart, in which our Western vision of life, faith and history assumed outlines completely unknown to us. A world in which our society, our way of thinking, our perception of time is challenged everyday by the acceptance of the presence of angels and ancestors. Presences that linger on each conversation and impact on their daily lives. A mystery born among those nomad pastoral populations occupying the lands that stretch from the Nineveh Plain and enter the Zagros Mountains, and whose life is still an enigma for us.

On the Zagros Mountains, the emergence of a pastoral society can be traced back to prehistoric times.[2] Its semi-nomadic character probably resulted in the discontinued relationship the inhabitants of the mountains had with the empires, Elamite, Akkadian, Sumerian, Assyrian and Persian who, due to the almost complete inaccessibility of the area, always had to exercise an indirect control over its population through local leaders. Very few travellers dared to journey into these mountains. Even Alexander the Great never gained complete control of the area. It is plausible, even though archaeology does not help us, to identify the Kakais as an ancient Kurdish group belonging to these mountains. It was probably this independence from the main powers of the region that led to the peoples of the Zagros developing religious practices and beliefs that do not involve the construction of temples or statues to represent the divine, but which are expressed by the closeness and symbiosis with the nature that surrounds them.[3] This is a very important detail to keep in mind because one of the most striking features of the Kakais, probably inherited from their ancestors during many centuries of repression and persecution, is their ability to dissimulate.

It is on the Zagros Mountains that, according to their holy book, the Saranjam, their first Jam took place. It happened on the banks of the Sirwan, a strong river that runs from the mountains in Iran to a region called Hawar, the sacred land of the Kakais. The river is mentioned in Herodotus' *Histories* under the name of Gyndes. According to the historian, the river slowed down considerably Cyrus' military advance. 'Because the Gyndes was too deep to be fordable,'[4] the Persian king took the unfortunate decision to cross it using boats. However, after one of its sacred white horses plunged into the water and died, dragged by the strong currents of the river, Cyrus reacted 'with fury'[5] and 'he swore so to enfeeble the Gyndes that in future even a woman would be able to cross it easily and emerge with her knee perfectly dry'.[6] He fulfilled his promise by diverting the river by digging 360 channels, an enterprise which lasted the whole summer. The river returned to its former proportions after the channels disappeared under the sand. Parallel to the history narrated by Herodotus, the Saranjam reports another sacred history which sees as the protagonist the birth of the Sirwan River, the same waterway of 'brutal arrogance' encountered by Cyrus on his way to conquer Babylon.

According to the Saranjam, there was a village in the mountains called Tashar. One day, their inhabitants invited Sultan Sahaq to visit it. On his way to the village, already deep in the mountains, he saw many women singing holy welcoming songs for him. Despite them being forced to walk long distances to reach the closest source of water, their voices sounded very happy because it was the day on which Sultan Sahaq would arrive to bless them and the whole village. When Sultan Sahaq appeared, accompanied by other men and women, who at first did not recognize him, the village women stopped singing out of fear. He saluted them and asked them why they were so happy even though they were walking without shoes and their feet were bleeding. One of them answered, 'You do not know, but today we are receiving God in our village. We are carrying water from that river because its water is pure and sweet and with it, we are going to make a pomegranate juice for him and his friends.' He asked them why they were going so far to draw water and the women told him that the village was far away from any source of water. The Saranjam says that after Sultan Sahaq heard this, he hit the ground three times with a stick and water flowed out of the soil. From that day on, there was water in Tashar. When the women saw this, they recognized him and ran back to the village to announce his coming. From that day, the river flows very strong and its waters are sweet. From that moment, it is considered a holy and healing water. The Saranjam says that whenever you want to see angels during your holy gatherings, you should prepare a juice with this Tashar water from the pomegranate.

Religious men in Hawar say that there is a holy place called KaliGaKuzna, which means the 'first sacrifice'. It is believed that the first sacrifice from the Kakais to God took place in this very region. This is also the water that every child should drink during baptism. But the most interesting feature of this story is that this information is used by the Kakais to verify that the person they have in front of them is actually a member of the community. To the question, 'Which water do you drink?' the person has to answer, 'Tashar,' all in their original language. Unfortunately, this is a region which lies in the unstable border area between Iran and Iraq and is currently highly militarized. In 2021, the religious men still living there reported that the Iranian military destroyed their ancient shrine along the river on purpose with the excuse that a new road had to go through it.

Evidence has been found of loose earth by the Sirwan River in the area, which supports the hypothesis of the construction of a road that threatens the existence of one of the most sacred places for the Kakais.

Saranjam: The holy book of the Kakais

Saranjam means 'The Conclusion' or 'The Discourse' and it is the Kakais' main religious text. Kakais believe that the Saranjam is the book of divine guidance and direction for humankind and consider the text in its original Gorani language to be the very word of God. According to the sources, the Saranjam consists of nine hundred books, of which only 35 are accessible while the rest are kept secret. However, despite the limitations, based on the texts available and the fieldwork and interviews with dervishes and historians, it was possible to trace its origins. The divine verses of the Saranjam were passed down orally and then in writing through the generations and their composition can be divided into three phases: Pre-Pird-i War, Pird-i War and Post Pird-i War. Pīrdwer is a shrine built between the fourteenth and fifteenth century in Kermanshah Province in Western Iran, and is now the destination of pilgrimage for both Yarsans and Kakais.

Some of the faithful believe this is the grave of Sultan Sahaq, the last incarnation of God and the last reformer of the religion, who lived in the fourteenth century. The first phase of composition belongs to the mythical era of SajNar, before the Big Bang. On that occasion, God and the Angels together presided over the creation of all living beings. According to the Saranjam, it was the Angel Pīr Musi, in charge of recording human deeds, who was the first author of Kakais' sacred book. The chronology of the second and third phases is more reliable. According to the Saranjam, the era before Sultan Sahaq and Pīrdwer can be calculated as between 2000 and 2700 years, during which the reincarnation that preceded Sultan Sahaq contributed to the update of the Saranjam. The protagonist of the second phase of the composition of the Saranjam is Sultan Sahaq, the last reformer of the religion whose teachings constitute a main religious guidance for the Kakais. According to the Saranjam, Pird-i War was a fortress/shrine that for the first time made manifest the presence of the Kakais in the area sanctioning the passage from a secretive religion to one openly committed to countering the military, political and religious advance of Islam in the area.

Starting from this moment, the Saranjam also records the deeds of the Kakais against Islam and their epic struggle for survival in an increasingly hostile environment. Sultan Sahaq is the protagonist of one of the stories of resistance against Islamic forces that took place in another sacred place for the Kakais: the Marano Cave on the Shirnawa Mountain, overlooking the Saraw Dudara Temple in Hawar. When Sultan Sahaq and his followers were attacked by Muslim groups, they hid in the Marano Cave for three days. During the time of Sultan Sahaq, seven dervishes set out to join him. When they arrived in the mountains and realized that nobody was there to receive them, they acted with arrogance. 'How can it be? We have been praying, fasting for Sultan and Yarsan/God and now nobody is respecting and receiving us.' When Sultan Sahaq heard of their pride, he decided to punish them, unleashing a severe snowstorm that forced the dervishes to find refuge in a cave without food or drink. After three days, Dawūd went to talk to Sultan Sahaq, asking for mercy. The Diwān, the council of the Yarsani religion which included Sultan Sahaq as well as the seven angels, sent Angel Mustafa, who has the power of fire, to melt the snow and open the cave. The dervishes were finally released and then received by all the villagers, who gave them food and drink. To commemorate this event, the Kakai community fast during Qawltas to remember the importance of the third pillar: humility.

Few of the Kakais are aware that a British diplomat called C. J. Edmonds mentioned them in a short paragraph in a book he wrote after his visit to Hawar at the beginning of the twentieth century. They knew that a local religious man called Sofi Rashid from Hawar had produced a text containing the basic principles of the Kakai religion and had it translated for him during one of his journeys during his time serving as an adviser to the British Ministry of the Interior in Iraq between 1935 and 1945. In 1957, Edmonds published with Oxford University Press a book entitled *Kurds, Turks and Arabs: Politics, Travel and Research in North-Eastern Iraq 1919–1925*. He quotes as his primary source Vladimir Minorsky, who, in 1920, in the *Revue du Monde Musulman*, published an article that was republished the following year as a book in Paris by Ernest Leroux, in which he presents the sect known as Ahl-Haqq. This name means, 'The Ones Who Worship the Truth', even though he probably did not know exactly what he meant. Edmonds says that his conclusions differ from his main source but that it is thanks to him that he could acquire his current knowledge. However, he decides to rely on informants from the place with a brief excursion beyond the Persian border. It is difficult to estimate if Edmonds already detected a change in the community due to the new borders between Iran and Iraq being drawn arbitrarily by the winning European powers. The fact is that he decided to base his research on three 'authorities': a small pamphlet or Tazkara prepared for him by Sofi Rashid of Hawar, several poems in the Goran dialect and records of conversations with 'a dozen or more adepts'.

In the beginning, Edmonds' intention was not to delve into the Kakais' religious beliefs, because they also did not allow him. Edmonds talks about their organization and the origins of their religion despite declaring that he did not have access to their ceremonies or esoteric beliefs, thereby avoiding overcoming the 'the boundary which I have set myself'. After talking about the presence of their villages in different parts of Iraq, he lingers on one specific place, Hawar. He talks about it very briefly, only at the end of the chapter contributing to the mystery of the place, by reporting on a brief visit he made 'many years later', in 1941. He starts to report about his experience, saying that this is 'probably the most interesting settlement of all, the isolated village of Hawar, situated in a secluded valley eight miles east of Halabja and distant only five as the crow flies from Pird-i War itself'. He goes on to say that, 'this is the last and only Kakai community left in what I may call their Holy Land where the Founder walked and talked, and the place may thus have housed the adepts continuously for over six centuries'. Edmonds also offers a very precise geographical description of the place, but, more importantly, he mentions the main places of worship, some of which we can still appreciate today: Weyzar, the *chardirgá* or camp site of Sultan Sahaq himself. However, currently, none of the Kakai community is able to identify with certainty the location mentioned by the British diplomat and, at the same time, it is difficult to know if this is due to the fact that the real location of the whereabouts of Sultan Sahaq's camp has, in some mysterious way, been lost in translation. Nevertheless, the Kakais in 2021 think of Edmonds' informant, Sofi Rashid, as a very reliable source. They were able to contact one of his grandsons, who confirmed that Sofi Rashid was one of those religious men who through dreams had the power to vaticinate the future. This is the reason why, today, some Kakais consider the content of the Takzara as part of the Saranjam.

In 1969, Edmonds published another article, almost unknown, but with the power of shedding a new light on his travels and his relationship with his informants and in particular the parallels and gaps between the personal information he recorded during his journey and the Takzara. The urge for writing this new article came from the fact that only now, after a detailed account of their beliefs had been published in Teheran, he felt compelled in finally publishing what he retained out of respect for more than three decades. The article entitled, 'The Belief and Practices of the Ahl-I Haqq of Iraq', is an interesting read, but it also leaves some open questions. The first one is the role of the informant, who wrote the Takzara specifically for him in 1933, in pencil and in a very small hand, in which he uses 'a more legible Kurdish translation', made by his friend Colonel Taufiq Wahby. Edmonds claims that it is from this document that he had access to the most secret dogmas and ceremonies as well as to Gorani verses. He calls this informant 'a venerable Sofi of Hawar'. The article is a comparison between the revealed truth of the Takzara and his own personal notes but it does not really explain the Kakais' religious life in details.

This is a turn of events that is very difficult to accept for any researcher, also because, in both of the articles published by Edmonds, no sacred text is ever mentioned. It is difficult to understand why a sacred man from the community did not trust him with this information. However, it is understandable that he felt the need to protect the community and its heritage from possible retaliation from the Islamic community. In the nine years which separates Edmonds' first visit to Kurdistan and the writing of the Tazkara in 1933 and his first visit to Hawar in 1941, the situation in the country had changed notably. Iraq was struggling to establish itself as a unified country.

The seventy-two angels are also the seventy-two Pīrs that Sofi Rashid of Hawar describes to Edmonds during his visit to Hawar: information that Edmonds never shared in full with the English-speaking public. He neither included this information in the short chapter dedicated to the Kakais in his book, nor did he include it in his more detailed article published in 1969, in which he limited itself to comparing his notes with some of the information he was provided. It was only by looking at his private papers kept at the Middle East Centre Archive at St Antony's College, Oxford University, that, after almost eighty years during which the notes were available in the archive, no one researched them and so the material is unknown. To our knowledge, nobody took on the long and difficult task of going through them and trying to translate the notes that were written for hm in old Gorani Kurdish. One of the booknotes, now fragile and with a black cover, can put off any reader because of its minute calligraphy. These documents and the secrets they contain assume an invaluable importance for the Kakais as well, while providing us with something else on which to base the description of the Kakais' beliefs besides Edmonds' article, the interviews with Kakai historians in 2019 and the few insights that the religious men offered us regarding the content of their sacred book.

This notebook bears only a few lines in English, at the very beginning, presumably Edmonds writing to remind himself what the small black notebook was about. He writes: 'This small manuscript was given me by Soi Rashid of Hawar. The Latin transcription by Wahbi.' On the opposite page are just a few lines: 'Given to me by Sofi Rashid of Hawar.'

According to the translators who, with difficulty, managed to decipher the handwriting, this book is based on the Saranjam and contains the names and description of the seventy-two Pīrs.[7] This is a very important detail toward the reconstruct of the basic concepts of the Kakai religion. First, as we heard, they represent the religions created by God and which have to live in harmony and peace until they are reunited under a single one. Second, the Pīrs are the reincarnation of the original angels and constitute the relationship between God and humanity. The four angels were present at the time of creation and their names were: Jebrā'il, Mikā'il, Esrāfil and Ezrā'il, who will be known later as Benyāmin, Dāwud, Pīr Musi and Mostafā, respectively.[8] But the little notebook given to Edmonds reveals something more about the Pīrs.

The notebook states that, through a series of reincarnations, Pīrs/Angels also provide an historical and religious continuity between past and present. In the notes written by Sofi Rashid from Hawar, the angels present themselves with all their reincarnations, overcoming its historical, religious and geographical limitations. One by one, the Pīrs/Angels introduce themselves. All of them were responsible for something. All of them mention their past lives, introducing the guarantee of their presence along history:

> *I am Pīr Dajadin and I was the angel Pourtas before the creation of the earth. In Kerbala my name was Nordeman. With the prophet Mohammed my name was Sleim Ben Abdullah. In Luristan my name was Deiash. I was responsible for the capital and bringing people to the religion.*
>
> *I am Pīr Ahmed and before the creation of the earth my name was Seuan. During the time of Prophet Mohammed my name was Kardah. During the Persian empire was Nahim. I was responsible for finding the fire.*
>
> *I am Pīr Aziz and I was in the city of Basrah. When they created earth my name was Zakhara. With Mohammed my name was Kassim. During the Persian empire my name was Gazhar. I was responsible for teaching the animals.*

> *I am Pīr Rstm. My name was Komsa before the creation of the earth. My name was Ghazi during Mohammed. My name was Mandil with prophet Dawud. I am responsible for teaching our culture.*[9]

The angels existed before the creation of Earth and all of them reincarnated during history. All of them have a specific role in the religion and they will always be with us. With the return of the angels, it was imperative to collect the writings which until then spread across different parts of the region. However, it is interesting that these Pīrs/Angels ensure that their audience knows about who they were, in particular during the Persian period and when Mohammed founded Islam.

Religious men of the community confirmed to me that the texts included in Edmonds' notes are actually extracts of their sacred book, presumably written in the thirteenth century, because they mention Sultan Sahaq's efforts to reorganize the religion and put an end to centuries plagued by the spiral of hatred and oppression which forced the Kakais into hiding after the advent of Islam. According to the Saranjam, only after a long period of darkness, in which the mountains would have been covered in blood, will the Kakai religion break the long silence into which this event had plunged it. The Kakais believe that the Angels have the power to reincarnate, not only among themselves but also in other beings, human and not human. With time, the message and the main core of religion is lost by the deeds of human beings and needs to be renewed. According to the book, the last update happened with Sultan Sahaq from his base in Pird-i War in the Shekhan area, also home to the Lalish Yezidis' most sacred shrine. Sultan Sahaq, the last incarnation of God according to the Saranjam, came with two very specific purposes: renewing religion and reaffirming the presence of God among men and countering the violent advance of Islam.

Purity via 1,001 reincarnations

According to the Kakais, reincarnation is an incontrovertible proof that God exists. However, reincarnation does not happen all the time. According to the Kakais, the lower souls are handed over to the rulers, who place them in new bodies. Once reincarnated, these people go through multiple lives until they are purified and can join God in its entirety. According to holy texts, death is just a transition from one body to another. Reincarnation reminds us of the Gnostics. The difference between them is that at the end of the cycle of reincarnation,

Gnostic souls go through multiple lives until they are redeemed and gain salvation. For the Kakais, human beings will be reunited again in one common religion after the last update. When will that be? When you hear the tambour playing again, it means that the Angel came back to life. The Angel will announce itself as a bird and will have the speed of lightning.

The idea that all prophets have actually brought the same message throughout the centuries also belongs to the Gnostic tradition. However, contrary to Zoroastrianism, Gnostics and Manicheans believed in the reincarnation of a single soul carrying the same message and foretelling the future.

Since the Kakais never try to convert their audience to their own faith, their beliefs still carry the freshness and spontaneity of an original message. Reincarnation is, for them, the proof of the existence of God. It is the way in which their universe is linked with the past, present and future. It is the way in which to explain good and evil. It is the source of understanding their own presence and role in a much wider and more complex view of reality. When they talk about his experience of a past life, it is not just a story, what they are trying to communicate is a perception of a past impression through which comes the knowledge of past lives.[10]

According to the Kakais, in cosmic time and the process of rebirth, each one of us has been one's mother, father, sister, brother or a good friend in the vast cycle of rebirths. This awareness has a measurable effect on the Kakais' lives since this assumption militates against prejudice, allowing them to see beyond gender, ethnicity, religion and nationality in a communion which includes not only human beings but also all of creation. They are used to seeing their lives as part of a wider, cosmic narrative. Their souls, through the cycle of rebirths, is constantly looking for perfection, a no-predetermined route which contemplates no guilt or eternal punishment but a continuous process toward bliss through the exercise of free will. Reincarnation for Kakais and the narratives associated with it constitute a template for behaviour. A Kakai should never talk about another person's wrongdoings. This is not because, as in the biblical tradition, whoever is without sin, let them cast the first stone. It is because good and evil are present in the same individual and only the cycle of rebirths can restore balance in his or her life, since this life is not his or her only opportunity to make amends.

The Saranjam contains many stories explaining how reincarnations play a crucial role in the interpretation of historical cycles. For example, one whole Saranjam is dedicated to Abadeen, a Muslim who lived between the thirteenth and the fifteenth centuries. the Kakais respect this man because God spoke directly to him. Abadeen was a mollah in the mosque, and he used to torture Kakai people until he converted to the Kakai religion. To his former co-religionists who tried to win him back to Islam he said: 'After I saw Diwān, the counsel of angels and Mawla (God), I am not going back because we Muslims hate each other, and we are cutting trees. Nature is the proof of reincarnation, but you cannot see it because you are blind. Every spring, the same grass on the ground will grow to die and to grow again. In the same way, every time we die, we come to life again.' A woman, Nargiza, was in love with him and Abadeen's enemies convinced her to seduce him back to Islam. After talking to him, Nargiza asked him, 'You are a different person, before you were angry and unhappy. Now you are like an angel, a very wise man. What happened to you?' 'I am like this because I have found my God, this is my way and all human beings should behave this way,' he replied. Once, Nargiza stepped on the branch of a tree and he said, 'Be careful, do not hurt the tree because the tree has a soul.' But Nargiza told him that he was a fool to think that a tree could have a soul. Finally, they killed him, but not before, according to the Kakais' holy book, he warned Muslim people: 'You will fight each other, you will never find peace on earth. I will let black and white[11] killing each other because you are not respecting God, the ground, the soil, the rain as gifts from God. There will be no mercy on you.' He continued, 'the first thing I will do when I am back will be to show respect to the moustache. I will make you torture each other.' The Saranjam also mention the initials of the person he was going to reincarnate in S. H. When Saddam Hussein took power, he touched and grew his moustache more than seven times, saying that they should be sacred, 'Later on, I will be killed and betrayed.' When he rose to power, the Kakais knew that it was coming.

Divination is strictly linked to their way of living the past, present and future. Through dreams, the dervishes warn the community of an imminent threat. Not all of them are important to them. The dreams can talk about a fact regarding the past, however, more often, through dreams, God will send the community a sign or a message. Only the dervishes and pure people can see these dreams from the Mawla. They live isolated in the mountains, fasting, most of them in Hawar. The Kakais believe in the divination power of dreams. Just before the advent of ISIS and their attack on Kirkuk, the Kakais living in the area had planned a ceremony, when, before scheduled date, dervishes contacted them with a message from God. They had to postpone the event for three days because something very serious was going to happen. Nobody in Kirkuk believed them until one early morning, ISIS entered Kirkuk and remained in control of the city for three days. In 2014, just before ISIS attacked Mosul, the dervishes warned the Kakais living in the area to be ready to flee their houses, leaving everything behind. As a result of this premonition most of them survived.

Resistance and persecution

In March 1988, Halabja made the headlines about the chemical attack ordered on it by Saddam Hussein and carried out by his cousin Ali. Within a few hours, 5,000 people died in front of the incredulous eyes of the international communities and the media. It was probably one of the few times when such a serious act of genocide has been recorded and broadcast live on TV and reporters from all over the world were present. Images were broadcast of civilians caught in the last spasms of life. Men, women and children lie next to each other, frozen in their last attempt to escape their tragic destiny. Some of the witnesses remember the roar of engines. At first, they did not know with certainty where they came from, and only later did it become known that they were helicopters and airplanes. Some of the survivors reported their ordeals to the *Financial Times* in 2002. Among them was Aras Abed Akra, 20 years old at the time of the events:

> We could smell something strange like rotten eggs. Down in our shelter we felt short of breath. A soldier went out and next door he saw that the birds in the cage of our neighbor were all dead. We stayed in the shelter until evening, but then I just wanted to escape. We wrapped our faces in wet towels. It was hard to breathe. One friend became blind immediately when he removed his towel. We were confused and lost; we couldn't see more than a meter ahead.[12]

At the time of the attack, Halabja was a Kurdish district that belonged to Sulaymaniyah governorate and its population was roughly 75,000. Situated 16 kilometres inside Iraq from the Iranian border in Southern Kurdistan, its control was disputed between Iraqi and Iranian forces at the culmination of the Iran–Iraq War (1980–8) wanted by Saddam Hussein. During the war, on Sunday, 13 March 1988, Iranian forces began shelling Iraqi military positions in and around the city of Halabja, and by Tuesday, 15 March, Iranian advance forces already reached the Zalim River, 5 kilometres south of Halabja, where they started destroying the bridge there in order to prevent the Iraqis from returning. At the same time, the Iraqi government started cutting the electricity, water and telephone lines from the city, making the citizens even more vulnerable to the attacks that were to follow. With the town completely isolated and disarmed, Saddam's forces counterattacked the next day, first with napalm then with conventional bombs and artillery and finally with gas, killing 5,000 and wounding 15,000 civilian Kurds.[13]

Kaven Golestan, a Pulitzer Prize Winning Iranian photographer, witnessed the Iraqi MiG-26 sortie from outside Halabja: 'it was not as a nuclear mushroom cloud, but several smaller ones: thick smoke'. Golestan then entered the city after the bombing with a gas mask and protective suit to cover the story via military helicopter. After the attack, only ghosts remained. It was not the first time that the Iraqi Army had used chemical weapons against its own population. Secret memo no. 7371, dated 31 March 1987, and discovered after the fall of Saddam's regime, sent from the General Military Intelligent to the Headquarters of Military Staff, showed that this happened before in the areas of Siyosinan, Askar Goptapa, Balisan and Shaikh, setting a dangerous precedent. But in memo no. 153 sent from the Office of the Chief of Staff to the Headquarters of the 1st Corps, signed by Brigade General Staff Nazar Abdul Karim Faizal al-Khazraji that years later legal investigations would discover, showed that the person directly responsible for the massacre was Saddam himself (Ihsan 2017).

When they escaped from the attack on Halabja in 1988, the Kakais living in the city were probably not aware that they were following Sultan Sahaq's traces. They still remember how they had no food or water in the caves where they sought refuge. A few of them were able to read a kind of divine intervention in the fact that only two members of the Kakai community were killed in the attack. It was also a sign that the time had come for their faith to save others and to transform the mountains full of blood into a renewed sacred place. It was time to go back to the origin of their religion and tradition and rediscover Hawar after a large number of the community were executed by Saddam Hussein during the Iran–Iraq War.

For the Kakais who escaped from Halabja seeking refuge in Hawar, the road was difficult and access to the area was almost impossible, however, they found their way. All of them had heard stories about Hawar. Some of the oldest among the Kakais kept going to the mountains when the war and the conditions made it possible to take care of the place. However, all the temples and places of worship mentioned by Edmonds during his brief visit in 1941 were now a shadow of their former selves. Most of them had been destroyed by the incursions of the Iranian and the Iraqi armies and had fallen into oblivion, including the Marano Cave in the Shirnawa Mountain. This situation lasted until after 2003, when the Kakais started to rediscover their sacred places and to restore their shrines.

The unpretentiousness of their places of worship surprised even Dominic Byrne, the cameraman who, in April 2019, was part of the crew that reached

Hawar to record a radio programme on the Kakai for the BBC World Service. At a first, superficial glance, the Kakais seem to have a recognizable material culture, almost 'nothing to show'. Their little shrines are small constructions painted in green which blend with the surrounding landscape. The cameraman's reaction was an anticipation and a revelation of how difficult it would be to talk about the sacredness, the holiness and the faith in God of the Kakais starting from this remote place to a wider audience who could not see first-hand the divine immensity of the surrounding mountains. All other religions in this part of the world, including the Yezidis, can rely on a very rich material culture. The Kakais were much more difficult to understand. Their reticence to open themselves to others is not exclusively due to their historical need to hide themselves from almost certain persecution. After listening to their stories, I believe that it also depends on the will to preserve their mystery, their special relationship with God and through Him with the rest of humanity.

The shrines in Hawar did not have any writings, but were surrounded by trees or built on the banks of a stream, the graves of ancestors. We were allowed to enter, silently, into one of them, almost hidden at the end of a narrow path which winds along a stream, at the bottom of high mountains. We took off our shoes in the courtyard and entered the small building. The grave is in an inner room, surmounted by a small altar. Only a few objects are there to honour the memory of the ancestor. A bigger cemetery, centuries old, is just in front of this shrine, leading to a new construction used for religious gathering. This is the most visible shrine in this area. We are so used to seeing material proof of humanity's relationship with God, that this apparent lack of material culture is quite surprising. Usually, temples, even in the remotest parts of the world, are full of writings, images and sculptures which talk about the people who built them, about their faith and the way they see the world outside of them.

In Iraq, due to the continuous threat to their community, the Kakais have learned to hide their shrines by making them pass for Islamic places of worship by raising a green flag or changing its original Kakai name into an Arab one. This stratagem, as we shall see, is a double-edged sword, however, as it allowed the preservation of these shrines for future generation. The Kakais' fears are based on reality. In 2017, a book written by Abbas Shamsadin entitled, *Faked Shrines (Al-Maraqid al-Muzayfa)* was published in Baghdad. This book saw three different editions in just three years and affected the Kakai because it made public the names and locations of some of their shrines. As a result, the Kan Ahmed shrine in Khanaqin was attacked three times. The original Kakai name of this shrine is Bawa Mahmi. Bawa means 'father' in the original language of the

Kakai, and is still used by children to address their fathers. When this word precedes the name of a person, as in the case of Bawa Mahmi, it indicates an important religious figure, belonging to one of the highest religious authorities.

There is another danger looming for the Khanaquin shrine. Being officially a Shi'a shrine, it can receive endowments from the government for its maintenance. However, this possibility is very difficult to accept for the Kakais because, by officially claiming it for themselves, they expose it to further attacks or, on the other hand, by accepting protection from the Shi'a, they risk losing it forever. This is perceived as very detrimental for the next generation of Kakais because losing one of their main shrines means compromising their heritage and identity. However, it is the Saranjam that can keep the memory alive. In it, there is a blessing dedicated to this particular shrine which testifies to its importance for Kakais.

The old name of the city of Kirkuk testifies to the ancient presence of this community in the city. Bawa Gurgur was the name of one of the Kakai dervishes who lived there between the seventeenth and the eighteenth centuries. According to the Saranjam, just before he died, he asked to be buried in a specific area and invited people to visit his tomb after a few months, saying that they would find a black liquid coming out of his grave. The first visitors found that the structure of the tomb had collapsed and that a black liquid was coming out of it. Being Kirkuk, it is easy to guess that the black liquid was actually oil. Only recently was it possible, by comparing different sources, to identify Bawa Gurgur's tomb with the Baba Gurgur[14] oil well. Back in the 1920s, driven by a shortage of oil suffered during the First World War, Great Britain decided to resume the project of extracting oil from the area interrupted by the war. Kakai sources locate Bawa Gurgur's tomb in the Kaywan area, a former Iraqi Air Force base captured by US forces in 2003 and renamed K1.

In Kakai language, Kaywan means 'Mars', and they say that, in the summer, it is possible to spot the red planet. They also have a saying which mentions this: 'Bawa Gurgur, I am coming with eagerness to visit your grave and I am asking you that my first child is a boy.' Until now, the Kakai community never made public the identification of their ancestor's tomb at this specific place. However, their claim is not to be ignored. In the biography dedicated to his father Mike who worked as a geologist in the Middle East for the British Oil Company and then for the Iraqi Petroleum Company in the 1920s, Michael Quentin Morton wrote:

> The presence of gas at Baba Gurgur had been evident for thousands of years. Baba Gurgur means 'the father of underground rumblings', and it was well

known for its burning gases escaping through faults in the structure of the earth. Visitors to Kirkuk were encouraged to visit the fires at night, when the effects of the flames were at the most spectacular.[15]

The author also offers the opportunity to verify the sacredness of this place. As an introduction to his father's biography, Michael Quentin Morton identifies Bawa Gurgur with the biblical 'burning fiery furnace' from Daniel 3.21, where the three Jews, Shadrach, Meshach and Abednego, emerged unharmed from the fiery furnace they had been thrown into for refusing to worship Nebuchadnezzar's idol. This biblical story is also immortalized by the British painter, William Turner, in 1832 in a painting now at the Tate Gallery in London.

Plutarch, in his biography of Alexander the Great, reconstructs the episode, indicating Adiabene, today's Erbil, as the theatre of the event:

> Next, he attacked Babylonia, and soon subdued the whole country. What he found most astonishing there was the chasm of fire in Adiabene, where flames constantly shoot up into the air like a fiery fountain, and the stream of naphtha which is so extensive that it forms a lake quite close the chasm. Naphtha is basically similar to asphalt, except that it is so sensitive to fire that it is ignited, even before a flame has touched it, just by the radiance around the flame, and often sets fire to the intervening air as well. In order to demonstrate its qualities and power, the Babylonians lightly sprinkled the street leading up to Alexander's quarters with the substance, and then stood at one end of the street and applied their torches – for night was drawing in – to the moistened spots. The first spots caught fire straight away, and the fire spread too quickly for the eye to follow; as quick as thought, it shot down to the other end until there was an unbroken wall of fire all the way down the street.[16]

In this episode, the young Athenophanes volunteers to try on himself the igniting power of this mysterious substance, but contrary to what happened to his Jewish predecessors, no God saves him from death.

In the summer of 1927, the Turkish Petroleum Company, which would become the Iraqi Petroleum Company just a year later, established its headquarters in Tuz-Khurmatu. On 27 October of the same year, Well No. 1, a single derrick well, was built in the wadi called Baba Gurgur. Nobody would have suspected what was going to happen when:

> Like an eruption from Hell, first with a rumble and then with a deafening roar, oil burst out of the ground and rose above the derrick, raining down black crude and rocks on the surrounding wadi and filling nearby hollows with poisonous gas.

> Oil was struck at 3 a.m. on 15 October 1927. Next day, from 20 kilometres away, the huge spraying column of oil looked like a clump of trees in the distance. To the people of Kirkuk only eight kilometres away, crowding the roof tops for a view, it looked like the vengeance of an angry God.[17]

After this event, all the search for oil concentrated in this area, transforming Kirkuk and the adjacent areas into one of the most disputed territories in Iraq.

There is a shrine, 10 to 15 kilometres away from Erbil called Pīr Dawūd, clearly a Kakai shrine. This one was not renamed, probably because being very close to the capital of the Kurdish Region, the area was considered safe from attacks and also because it was actually a graveyard. Only very recently did Kakai people interested in their history start to visit the area in order to visit their ancestors. In April 2020, the area was targeted and attacked and the Kakai people were deterred from recognizing it as theirs.

Rhythm, harmony and soul

It is already dark when the Kakai musicians summoned from Iran by the community enter the private house in Sulaymaniyah where they are going to play exclusively for the BBC World Service crew I came with. It was April 2019. The musicians placed themselves at the end of the room, surrounded by other Kakais, informed of their arrival. They are men of all ages and slowly they start to prepare their tamburs. Somebody tells us that two women musicians were stopped at the border with Iraq. The border control saw them with the instruments and denied them entry. It is a pity because, in Kakai culture, women play a very important role. One of the members of the heptad is Rabzan, a woman. Also, the Kakais have seventeen Sufi women in their ranks. For this reason, music groups are usually mixed because in the Kakai tradition men and women are created equal. Music means a lot to them because it links them directly with the moment of creation. According to the Kakais, after God created Mashe/Adam, he was just a simulacrum, unable to move. It was necessary to provide him with a soul, but in order to do this, God needed the help of the Angels. On the subject of creation, the Saranjam tells that when God created Adam, there were fourteen angels, seven bad angels and seven good ones, each one with a specific role. The seven bad angels already entered the body; however, their lone presence was not enough to create a soul. When God ordered the good angels to join the bad ones in the body, they refused. Then, God entered the body and tricked them into following Him. Later, God came out from the belly button and made a knot to keep all the fourteen angels inside. A fight started between the good and bad angels, so fierce that Adam was not able to stand up. It was then that God ordered the good angels who remained outside the body to play the tambur to calm Mashe/Adam's soul. Only thanks to the music of the tambur was Mashe/Adam able to gain control of his soul.

The idea that music is an element that can provide harmony to the soul connects directly to the Kakai tradition with the history of ancient music. Since antiquity, an undeniable thread supported by archaeology as well as by ancient literature ties different cultures through music and beliefs because:

> The art of music has been found to be a powerful presenter of the sacred in almost all religions. The beautiful sounds of music – gripping rhythm, haunting melody, special qualities of different instruments – reach to deep levels of aesthetic sensibility and express many different aspects of the experience of the sacred. It is particularly powerful when words are wedded to music in sacred chants, mantras, hymns, and the like. The art of music, whether a solitary flute or the ringing 'Hallelujah Chorus' of Handel's *Messiah*, gathers and directs spiritual emotions and evokes the sacred presence as no other art does.
>
> Ludwig 2005: 19

The Kakais also belong to this tradition. The story recounted above from the Saranjam very closely resembles another story handed down by Quintilianus in his, *De Musica*, where he presents Pythagoras as the first philosopher to attribute to music a healing power connecting it with the idea of a musical ethos, in short, the power of music behaviour. The anecdote is the following:

> Thus Pythagoras, when he once observed how youths who had been filled with Bacchic frenzy by alcoholic drink differed not at all from madmen, exhorted the flute player, who was joining them in the carousal, to play his *aulos* for them in the spondaic *melos*. When he thus did what was ordered, they suddenly changed and became as temperate as if they had been sober even at the beginning.
>
> Sextus Empiricus n.d., quoted in Zhmud 2019: 124

Pythagoras' stance on the healing effect of music was never completely accepted by philosophers after him. However, it is interesting to see how some of them have been intrigued by this possibility and how many of them have actually developed this idea into more sophisticated stances. Plato, for example, in one of his most famous dialogues, *Timaeus*, assigns to music the same function. The link with Plato is very pertinent to talk about in the case of the Kakais because, among others, he is one of the philosophers they consider to be reincarnated souls of angels, and therefore worthy of respect as thinkers. In the *Timaeus*, a philosopher from Locri in Italy offers an account of the origin of Athens from the origin of the universe to the creation of man. Timaeus says that the universe was created according to an archetype which cannot be understood by men and that always existed. He says that all creation is based on the interaction of four basic elements: water, air, fire and earth. He also gives precise measurements of the geometrical solids that formed them. Plato, through *Timaeus*, also hypotheses that: 'Transmutation of the elements can occur, but only amongst fire, air and water, whose particles are made up of scalene right triangles. There is also a fifth element called quintessence. Particles of quintessence are dodecahedrons, and God used them as a model for the twelve-fold division of the zodiac' (Burton 2009). Many of the studies of the *Timaeus* consider Plato's vision of the role of music as some kind of an accessory necessary to understand his most elaborated vision of the formation of a political philosophy. The preference for a rational Plato, precursor of current political theory, had the effect of obscuring at least in part his preoccupation with the role of music in the process of creation. In *Timaeus*, it is evident how creation, soul and body are tied together by music because:

> Platonic investigation of the phenomenon of music would seem to offer an ideal situation – what we might call *laboratory conditions* – in which to study the structure of the soul and the relationship that it maintains with the body.[18]

In the *Timaeus* establishing a link between music and the harmony of the universe, Plato says:

> Concerning sound also and hearing, once more we make the same declaration, that they were bestowed by the Gods with the same object and for the same reasons; for it was for these same purposes that speech was ordained, and it makes the greatest contribution thereto; music too, in so far as it uses audible sound, was bestowed for the sake of harmony. And harmony, which has motions akin to the revolutions of the Soul within us, was given by the Muses to him who makes intelligent use of the Muses, not as an aid to irrational pleasure, as is now supposed, but as an auxiliary to the inner revolution of the Soul, when it has lost its harmony, to assist in restoring it to order and concord with itself.
>
> Plato, *Timaeus*, 47c–d

In Plato's vision, music has the purpose of overcoming the disturbances which overwhelmed the soul and to bring peace and harmony in it. Music works on men's life to solve the inevitable inconsistencies born from the meeting between body and soul.[19]

Also, for the Kakais:

When we face threats and ignorance we close our doors and listen to the harmony of the tambur. The rhythm of the music corresponds to a need proper to the human mind. As for ancestral music and to think that the rhythm comes from the beating of our heart. From an alternation of dark and light that is also transmitted to the events we experience as individuals and as a community. Eventually with the eternal alternation of natural events that give the rhythm to our life. Of the time that passes inexorably. The music, the rhythm, have the power to silence the anxiety that as human beings we feel in the face of the unfathomable of the infinite and of God. Music produces an identification between musicians and audience.[20]

In the case of the Kakais, music unites humanity with God, the immanent with the eternal in a common, endless beat that does not stop even when the music fades away. It is through the singing and playing that Kakais were able to pass from one generation to another their cultural identity otherwise denied by history. Music provides a bridge to the eternal survival of the human spirit. One of the Kalams quotes: *Yar didakani, Benyamin saza, Pir Mosi sima, Davood avaza*; which means, *Hey, companion of my eye and soul, Benjamin Holiness is sculpture himself, Master Moses is string of this instrument and David is a vocal that comes from that side*. These verses mention three of the four angels who assisted God in the creation of the universe. Both Benyamin and Dawūd shared God's secret. Benyamin is in charge of receiving the prayers of people, for this reason he is *sculpture himself*, which is probably a reference to his being the receptacle of people's desires and wishes. Dawūd is in charge of helping not only people who are in grave need but also *a vocal that comes from that side*, meaning from God. Pīr Mousa is in charge of guiding humanity through the good and evil deeds which appear in its path on a daily basis. For this reason, he is *string of this instrument* (tambur), because through it he is able to talk the word of God and to make humanity choose between good and evil. Only Pīr Ewan, the fourth angel, is not present in these specific verses, but the Saranjam says that his role is to keep faith alive in people's hearts.

As for the other verses mentioned earlier, they constitute an inevitable link between music and mysticism written between 1299 and 1397 CE, exactly in the time in which history places the deeds of Sultan Sahaq and his efforts to organize the religion. However, the inclusion of music in Kakai liturgy along with the tambur date back to 2000–1500 BCE, as attested by sculptures in museums. One of them representing a young woman playing the tambur, has been found in Hawar and is now in a museum in Iran. It testifies that this particular area has been a sacred place to the Kakai people for a long time, well before Islam and Christianity.

That night in Sulaymaniyah, the miracle of *maqamas* was repeated again, together with the renewal of an indestructible link between an ancient past and the present. *Maqamas* are the Kakais' identity, their history and memory. A cultural heritage still unfolding in the present, because the original seventy-two *maqams* constitute the basis on which the Kakais compose others, whose content describes the most recent events. Different groups played that night, including a group of young performers accompanied by their teacher. One of the players was a 13-year-old girl. When we interviewed her, she talked to us about her joy and enchantment for the tambur and the music. She said that some of her Muslim girlfriends in school are not allowed to play or to listen to music because it is *haram*, prohibited. Nevertheless, she will go on doing this despite it being unusual among young women. However, here the situation is different from that in Kirkuk or Khanaqin, because in Sulamanyiah, they can play in the houses without the pressure of being reported to the police for meeting illegally. In the other areas, under the control of the Iraqi government, Kakais do not have any other choice than to meet in hiding in order to sing their prayers. People in Kirkuk and Khanaqin close their doors and play in the basement so nobody can hear them. It is very sad on a special night like this to know that Lela, the young musician, would not be free to be seen carrying her precious instrument in other parts of the country without running the risk of being kidnapped or even killed.

Old stories, new stories, old fears, new fears: We are not Muslims!

The tensions Mir-Hosseini[21] noticed as early as 1992 in the Yarsan community of Sahne in Iran between those who adhered and those who refused the 'Jeyhunābādī' school that claims the Islamic roots of Yarsans, affected also the Kakai community in Iraq. Despite the Kakai religion being recognized by the Kurdish Regional Government (KRG) in 2015,[22] the lack of recognition on the Iraqi government side still has a detrimental effect on their present state. Persecution, discrimination and killings are still very much part of daily life for the Kakais. Despite having started to participate in the political life of the country, Kakais in Iraq feel very unsafe, to the point that many of them hold *jams* or *Jamkhānes* in private houses, mainly in villages where they can be performed without the threat posed by Muslims.[23]

The Saranjam, also tells stories whose content can be interpreted in different ways. Recently, the discussion about the origin of the Kakais had revolved around whether or not they belong to the Shi'as, an allegation that a part of the community rejects and which depends on a double interpretation of a specific story included in the Saranjam itself. The sacred book tells the story of Sha Koshin, who lived during the years when Alexander the Great set out to conquer these lands. The story says that when Sha Koshin was a child, he performed many miracles. During an attack by the Macedonians, Sha Koshin was holding a sword, the very same sword that Ali, Mohammed's cousin, would use in Karbala centuries later. Thanks to his holiness, he managed to save his village from the attack. The story continues revealing Sha Koshin's power of divination: 'I will be in Karbala and fight against the enemies and lose my sons.' While a part of the Yarsan community, especially in Iran, read this story as a confirmation of their belonging to the Shi'as, the Kakais in Iraq, on the contrary, think that the fact that they respect and praise Ali as the reincarnation of a divine man, as well as they do Jesus and other religious figures, does not make them more Muslim than their reverence for Christ makes them Christians. This is not just a philosophical or historical exercise, as this discussion about the Kakais' eventual belonging to Islam is causing a lot of pain and their persecution and threatens to split the community. But, most importantly, it threatens to silence the stories. For all religions, but especially for the Kakais, story is dream, and dream is story, because 'the future belongs to those who dare to dream and strive to convert their dreams to stories'.[24]

The Kakais' stories are stories not only of suffering and struggle but also of hope, faith and compassion. That is why it was important to collect as many stories as possible, because people without stories are destined to disappear. But telling stories is also dictated by the need to be closer to God: 'in the beginning was the Story, and the Story was with God, and the Story was God'.[25] Simply replacing 'word' with 'story' offers the key to understanding why these people felt the urgent need to tell their stories. There is no teleological spirit, it is because only through sharing with others what they experienced and suffered can they feel a direct connection with God. Concepts, ideas, dogmas, all these abstracts do not have any meaning for them. We are simply what we live, we are the stories we tell which make us what we are as individuals and as a group. When we are confronted with an inexplicable pain, the only thing we have left is a story. That is why whoever tries to oppress or conquer the other in the name of an absolute, indisputable truth, from the conquerors of the New World, the godless religion of European ideologies of the twentieth century to ISIS, all of them felt the impelling need to destroy every trace of the past in order to impose a unilateral idea of what the future has to be. By so doing, they created an artificial Hell, where it is not possible or recommendable to dream any more. And without dreams, there is not Story and without Story, individuals and groups lose their identity until they disappear into oblivion.[26]

When Jawaher and her son travelled kilometres from Khanaqin to the relatively safer area of Kalar in December 2018 and to Sulaymaniyah a few months later in April 2019 to tell us their story, they were also following God's will to talk because being silent is in some way to deny God's will to talk, to make a story their/our story. No ideology or abstract concepts were directing their actions. Only the ancient call to give a sign of life in a place and time which has transformed their lives into a living hell. They are scared and the only thing they can do is to tell their story, which is the only way to rebel against the forces of evil.

On both occasions, our expectations and theirs were completely different. We were trying to comply with an academic aim or to record a radio programme for the BBC World Service, while they were complying with their inner conviction that telling their story would reaffirm their identity and their right to be alive. For them, tragedies do not obey our cruel passing of time. Endless wars and deaths confuse chronology in an indefinite time in which it is not possible to process the pain. Eight or ten years later, Jawaher's story is still very current because fear and terror for them are still very much a reality.

Kalar is an area very close to Khanaqin but still under the military control of the Kurdish Regional Government. Since it was very dangerous for us to cross that unpredictable and precarious border, Safa Abdullah Ali al-Kake, a member of the community, who was later killed in a gunfight with Iranian-backed militias in this very area in 2020, offered to organize our meeting in a safe area. On the road to Kalar damages to the buildings caused by the last earthquake of 12 November 2017 were still visible. Kalar is the last outpost of the KRG before entering the district of Diyala where Khanaqin is. Khanaqin is an old city, 8 kilometres from the Iranian border, on the banks of the River Diyala. Because of its strategic position on the road to Baghdad, together with Kirkuk and Sinjar, it constitutes one of the most disputed areas between the KRG and the central government. Its ethnic complexity makes it very vulnerable to attacks between different militias.

We met Jawaher and her son just a few months after the referendum on Kurdish independence, held in the region on 25 September 2017. As retaliation for the result of the referendum which saw overwhelming support for independence, the Iraqi military expelled the Peshmerga from the area, thereby compromising the security of its population. Suddenly, Khanaqin became a no-go area in which civilian members of minorities were particularly targeted. This is the reason why, in order to meet us, Jawaher and her son had to travel to the safety of the KRG. The meeting was going to take place in the house of two university professors, a couple with a 6-year-old child. During our trip, my guide told me that Jawaher's story was worth telling. Jawaher lost one son in the Iran–Iraq War and three sons at the hands of Al-Qaida in 2009. She had only one son left. They were running late, and this gave us the opportunity to familiarize ourselves with our guests. From the sitting room where we were, it was possible to see inside another small room. A piano occupied it almost entirely. On it, a sheet of Mozart's music was waiting to be played. I was very surprised to see that in this highly insecure outpost, a child can still have the opportunity to study music, even in the company of the two Kalashnikovs ready to be used.

Jawaher and her son finally arrived. She wore a black dress which covered all her body, and was veiled. It was very difficult for me to determine her age. Men and women alike age very quickly in this part of the world. Jawaher sat at the centre of the room, her only surviving son sat close to her, ready to add new details to her story. Jawaher started saying that they did not feel safe in their homes. Every day they are afraid that ISIS or the Iraqi military would come to take them away for any excuse. It would not be the first time. Her son told us that each time they leave the house, they say goodbye to their wives and children as if they are not going to return. Death, sorrow and fear is what define their daily lives. This is why they accepted to talk to us on two different occasions. For them, for their culture and their faith, telling a story is not a waste of time. On the contrary, they are still alive exactly because they are still able to tell their story and they will repeat it until the end of their days.

After talking briefly about the present, Jawaher started telling us what she remembered about that day. She talked very quickly, hardly breathing, as if haunted by those memories. It happened in 2009, at the height of the Sunni–Shi'a War, in which all the other minorities were caught up, unable to defend themselves in what was basically a showdown between the two main branches of Islam. Two army vehicles stopped the car in which she was travelling with three of her sons and one of her nephews. They ordered the men to get out of the car and to follow them. When they asked the soldiers why they were being arrested, the military answered that they were *kafir*, infidels, and for this reason they were spies on the American payroll. Despite this explanation, Jawaher kept repeating the same question: Why? Why, did they attack them? They were unarmed. They were not doing anything wrong. 'Why? If before we were Kakais and Kurds, now we were the enemies?' Jawaher recalled that the soldiers told them immediately that they would be 'skinned alive'. Without stopping crying, she remembered that she begged them to spare her youngest son. They laughed at her.

We were in Sulaymaniyah for our second meeting with Jawaher and her son. During the interview, Jawaher's son interrupted her to tell his part of the story. It was only by chance that he was not with them that fatal day. When he found out about what happened a few days later, he went personally to the police station in Diyala to have information about his brothers. He knew he was putting his life at risk, but he felt he had no choice. It is only during this second meeting that he has the courage to reveal to his mother and to us that on that occasion they showed him his brothers' corpses. They were all black from beatings and they showed signs of torture. Their executioners even used drills to abuse them.

At this point we had to stop the interview. When I restarted it, I decided it would be better to step back from that day and from the pain that these memories had triggered. I decided to ask how their life was before, where 'before' meant both before 2003 and 2014. Jawaher and her son said that their lives were good before 2003. They still did not have any rights and their religion was not recognized, but at least they felt safe. Now they wanted to make their voices heard and to have their rights respected. Muslim people deny that the Kakais have a God and some Kakai people wonder if their ancestors were right in keeping their religion secret. Jawaher's son says that if you wear the moustache distinctive of the Kakai, you become a very likely target. However, even without, it he was the target of verbal and potentially physical attacks. 'When I am in the market, people insult me, calling me evil or dirty. I cannot do anything about it because I do not have any rights.' He knew that the law does not protect him. Those responsible for this crime are in jail and that they confessed to their crimes. However, none of his family were allowed to attend the trial and make their voices heard in a court of justice. While he was saying this, Jawaher showed us her children's photographs. They paid US$2,000 for them and another US$1,000 to have a copy of the perpetrators' signed confession.

Jawaher's son always dreams of his brothers. He knows that their souls will be reincarnated and that they will have another chance on this earth. He seemed to think that our hosts' 6-year-old son who was with us today was the reincarnation of his younger brother. I could not but wonder if this 6-year-old boy should be listening to this story, but I immediately realized that this was a very Western concern. What did he have to be protected from? This was his story, 'his way out of hell', his identity. Without these stories, this young child would never know about his father's dreams, he would not be able to understand his grandmother's tears. Nor would he understand why his aunt, once she learnt about the death of her husband, chose to leave her adoptive family, abandoning her 3-year-old daughter. He could not understand his father's concern for him and his brothers and sisters because of the persistent presence of ISIS in their area. These peaceful people just wanted to live in peace and have their rights recognized, not only in Khanaqin but also all over Iraq because, 'If before we had to keep our religion in secret, now we are scared to leave our houses. We feel foreigners in our own country.'[27]

Some Kakai villages lay on the Zab River, connected to Erbil by a very busy stretch of road. These villages between Erbil and Mosul have been attacked repeatedly during the past twenty years. Before 2001, the villages were destroyed by the Iraqi Army, in 2009 by Al-Qaida and in 2014 by ISIS. The community suffered different waves of military incursions that compromised their already fragile infrastructure. The Kakai Peshmerga built an improvised outpost at the entrance to the area. The men could be recognized by their big moustaches. One of them was praying, raising his hands to invoke God's protection on his comrades so nothing can happen to them. The oration was also intended to protect visitors from evil

Behind the improvised shelter were kept caskets of weapons that ISIS used against them. Mortars mainly. We proceeded with their guidance to the closest and safest point on the margin of the fields which surrounded the outpost. They explained to us that the red metal bars visible through the fields were the sign that an unexploded mine was there and they were waiting for someone to defuse it. Unfortunately, despite the presence in Iraq of NGOs specialized in this kind of work, they were not enough of them to demine all the areas affected, which prevented the Kakai villagers from returning to their lives when they could live mainly on the production of wheat and barley. Sheep-farming was also a good source of income. Today, some of the agriculture still survives, however, the mines left by ISIS make it difficult for the families to return to the previous levels of production. There have been many accidents in which people have suffered serious injuries when daring to enter the fields. Unfortunately, sheep-farming as well as other kinds of livestock-farming, like cows, for example, diminished dramatically with the intervention of ISIS. Most of the livestock were stolen by the invading forces or killed as part of the plans to clear the area of its inhabitants.

With destruction comes displacement and many families fled the area for nearby Erbil. The community is in danger because the violence destroyed all the infrastructure. The same one we came from, which was not a very easy one. This means that for any activity, transportation is difficult, thereby contributing to their isolation. Although the villages are very close to one another, the lack of bridges on the river makes the journey between the villages very difficult. Away from the ghost villages, we stopped to pay a visit to one of the leaders of the community. I asked him if people were coming back and, in reply, he showed me a few sheets of paper where he had been recording by hand the names of the families who decided to return to the villages. It is difficult to understand how these communities can cope without an organized system to collect the information, as anyone outside of this isolated area would never know what has been happening here, to these people. The headlines always talk about international relations. What is really happening is rarely told. I asked this old man in the small room, heated just for us with a humble electric heater, if he had hope that life would return here. He said yes. We were not done with the visits. A family had invited us for lunch. When we arrived at their house, lunch was already served in one of the rooms. Meat, rice and a lot of vegetables were displayed with the unpretentious abundance I got used from that day. The man of the house showed me that he could count only on the IQD10,000 (Iraqi dinars, IQD), less than US$10, he carried in his pockets.

A couple with their three children talked about their difficulties in remaining in the village. Not least because this area between Erbil and Mosul is part of the disputed territories between the Iraqi government and the Kurdish Regional Government. This means that administratively it does not belong to Iraq, but that also it does not belong to the KRG. Given the understandable mistrust these populations have toward the Iraqi government, they are more prone to trust the KRG since it supported them militarily during the war against ISIS, allowing the formation of community military defence units. However, due to the current economic crisis, they are not receiving any aid from any government or agency. They are left alone, struggling between resuming the life they once had and facing an uncertain future. The geographical areas where these communities live are very fertile since they are on the banks of two rivers. For this reason, agriculture is one of the economic sectors that should be developed. In addition to the fertility of the soil, the local agricultural knowledge of the community would constitute a strong asset for any development programme.

The villages have very strong links between one another. Each of them has a head responsible for various families. The young age of the population is a strong point. Most of the people are in working-age and willing to improve their current status. This includes both men and women. This is because the Kakai culture does not prevent women from actively participating in the running of all aspects of daily life or from having a profession. The destruction of the infrastructure and the consequent diaspora did not only mean the loss of the traditional economy based on agriculture. It also meant that the community suffered from the real danger of being disbanded or totally absorbed by the Arab population spared by the wrath of ISIS together with their mosques. In addition, the depopulation of the area contributed to the weakening of the Kakai culture. The couple told me that there was only one school for all the villages. This meant that the children from the different villages had to walk long distances before reaching it, which undermined their chances of receiving an education. Furthermore, due to their isolation, the teachers who taught in the school were not prepared and the level of education was very low and the language of instruction was not Kurdish but Arabic. This undermined the very sense of identity of the children, who did not necessarily identify themselves with the Arab community.

One of the deterring factors in the development of agriculture was not only the presence of mines in the fields, but also the impossibility to introduce the community to an alternative, more efficient form of agriculture, enriching their current knowledge. This, together with the provision of clean water and electricity, could provide both men and women the possibility to develop the production of arts and crafts to increase their income. Women, in particular, in addition to collaborating in agriculture, could produce textiles such as traditional carpets, bags and other products for local and international consumption. However, until that point in time, no international organization went to the area to assess the status of these villages because they were very concerned about helping non-Muslim communities. As the Kakais were not a recognized religion, they were very unlikely to be included in reconstruction and reconciliation projects and so these communities were left alone to cope with an uncertain future. One of the consequences was that, due to the lengthy duration of the conflicts, the Kakais living in this area developed a natural mistrust of the Arab population, whose villages were spared from the targeted devastation by ISIS, which left all their mosques and their houses intact. Both communities could only benefit from projects on coexistence and peace-building. A strong commitment is necessary to advocate for the economic and social recovery of these areas. A task that very few are willing to undertake.

One of the Kakais' temples in the area was on a small hill and was visible from a distance. Today, it is just a heap of rubble. The foundation was crushed under the weight of the collapsed roof. One of the religious men showed us the damage.

We walked through the debris, trying to understand what had happened and wondering how and when music will be played here once again. The current deep economic crisis affecting the region does not leave place for hope of a quick reconstruction. However, because of the destruction, the situation of the Kakais has been made public in the press and has entered in the internal and international debate on the fate of minority groups in Iraq.

Despite this, the Kakais living in different parts of the country have different experiences. Usually, it is in the territories more disputed between Erbil and Baghdad that the disintegration of the community is more evident. Some Kakai interviewees said that, in the past, in the Doquq area, different religions coexisted without any problems. Instead:

> In 2020 about 11 to 15 families converted to Islam in Kirkuk and Doqoq area because they do not have anything. One of them is my nephew. Now he is Shia, a mullah, he is reading Qur'an. This happens because the KRG does not support us. Nobody is listening not even from the European countries. Maybe I will be forced to convert, or I will be killed. It is a very difficult situation. Some of our religious men have been corrupted by Shia and they gave our holy books to them. They even changed their names by adding Ali and Hussein. We are facing pressions from Shia, ISIS, and also from inside our community because part of them joined the Shia and they threaten us. We are threatened by the KRG because each time we meet someone who we think can help us he is Muslim. I met the then minister of religious issues. I told him our story and you know our holy books. He said that if there are 200,000 members of your community and they consider themselves Muslims, there is no reason to change their identity. This is ISIS's talking after 2014. Many of our young men have to shave their moustache to hide their identity.[28]

In May 2020, local activists and NGOs warned the representatives of both the Iraqi and the Kurdish Regional Government that the Kakai community living in the area of Khanaqin was subject to continuous deadly attacks perpetrated by ISIS with the logistical support of Hashd al-Shaabi. According to Farhad asl-Kake, a religious man and Director of the Chraw Organization for Documentation, attacks of this kind on the Kakai community are not isolated and have been carried out since 2003. However, over the past few months of 2020, they had escalated.[29]

On 10 May 2020, ISIS killed Burhan Hatam Muhammed and Nabard Naser Fatehulla, two farmers. On 21 May 2020, *Shafaq News* published an interview with the leader of the 'Karmsir' axis of the Peshmerga forces, Mahmoud Sankawi, who was confirmed 'to be in possession of "solid evidence" of the involvement of hundreds of former ISIS militants in the Iraqi factions responsible for coordinated attacks against Kurdish peasants, with the aim of emptying their villages in the Khanaqin district of the governorate of Diyala'.[30] Then, on 13 June 2020, less than a month later, a new attack was perpetrated (according to witnesses) by members of Hashd al-Shaabi, leaving six members of the Kakais dead (Safa Abdulla Ali, Shahab Bashir, Khasan Aziz, Tariq Aziz, Eazan Jamal and Hussein Aasim) and three others injured (Muaid Khalil, Ali Shahab and Muhammad Shahab).

According to testimonies, the attack happened at 11 at night, in a house on the outskirts of Khanaqin in the Diyala Province, where a considerable number of Kakais live. Members of the community living in Erbil were notified and arrived at the scene at about 7 in the morning, on 14 June, only to find caskets on the ground. By then, local community members had already removed the bodies and begun to organize the funerals. The Iraqi police in charge of security in the area arrived fourteen hours after the events.[31]

Law 140 of the 2005 Iraqi Constitution provided for the restitution to the Kurdish Region of some territories forcibly 'Arabized' by Saddam Hussein and the Ba'ath Party. The law also provided for a referendum in the interested areas to determine whether their inhabitants wanted to be part of Kurdistan or Iraq. The referendum was supposed to take place in 2007, but it was actually never carried out due to the difficult relationship between Erbil and Baghdad. The result was that, after thirteen years, the disputed territories remain a point of contention, further exacerbated by the war with ISIS, during which the Kurdish Regional Government annexed most of the previously disputed territories. Law 140 also provided for compensation in money and lands to those who willingly decided to go back to the lands they occupied before the Arabization process. In the specific case of the Kakais, the Arab Kirwi clan which occupied Kakai lands received land plus IQD20 million in compensation for returning the lands to the previous owners, while Muslim Kurds received lands together with IQD10 million for the same purpose. Despite the compensation paid to them, the Arab Kirwi never actually left the area. Instead, many of them support militias and have created a security threat to the Kakais.[32]

The ethnic complexity of the region makes it very vulnerable to attacks from the various militias. In this context, it is not surprising that Hashd al-Shaabi – the Iranian-backed militia composed of members belonging to ISIS – has an interest in attacking Kakai villages which have strong, often familiar links with the Yarsans on the Iranian side of the frontier. The motivation is religious as well as political since the Yarsans in Iran are also a religious minority targeted by the Iranian authorities. Hashd al-Shaabi's goal is to gradually erase the presence of any non-Islamic groups and to complete the Arabization process started by Saddam Hussein during the previous regime.

Since 2016, the Kakais have been pressured into choosing between leaving their ancestral lands and becoming Shi'as. Witnesses report that Zayed Dalib, the leader of Hashd al-Shaabi in Dayala, showed up at the funeral of the victims, saying that 'it was their own call' to leave or to convert. At the same time, Ryan al-Kildani, one of the leaders of the Babylon Brigades[33] offered protection against Hashd al-Shaabi attacks.[34]

The situation of the Kakai of Iraq is a demonstration of the fact that the defence of their fundamental rights carries a high individual and group risk, and that guaranteeing protection to those who dare to oppose the single thought imposed by any religious or political belief is a difficult and dangerous task. The Muslim way of conceiving life, religion and faith is opposite to that of the Kakais, who believe in an inherent equality of all living beings and, therefore, in tolerance and freedom.

2

Hope and resilience

Christians in Iraq

Ce paysage est le grand jardin de la Bible, le paradis terrestre d'Adam et Ève. Au loin, j'apercivais Noé, Abraham, Jonas, Alexandre le Grand, saint Thomas et Marco Polo cheminant sur la route de Mossoul.[1]

Father Michaeel Najeeb (2017)

Christian presence in Iraq constitutes one of the oldest continuous traditions in the country. The city of Erbil, or Arbela as it was called in the past, between the fifth and fifteenth centuries, was part of the old province of Adiabene, which included a vast region of Upper Mesopotamia. The region included Mosul, Nineveh, Karkā d-Beth Slōkh (ancient Arrapha and today's Kirkuk), Beth Nuhadra (today's Duhok) and beyond, but as part of the central authority of the so-called Nestorian Church or Assyrian Church of the East. Today, Christians in Iraq are quite unknown, even by Christians in the West. The remnants of this ancient culture and its history are usually lost in the past. They are known, depending on the area and its affiliation as the Chaldean Catholic Church, the Assyrian Church of the East, the Syrian Orthodox Church and the Syrian Catholic Church. At different times, they have been labelled as Iraqi Christians, Kurdish Christians, Arab Christians, Nestorians, Chaldeans,[2] Persian Christians, Semitic Turks, Turkish Christians and an almost infinite number of other appellations. This myriad of definitions poses a problem to whoever tries to make sense of their difference. The simple use of 'Iraqi Christians' can sound too superficial and risks excluding other groups, thereby favouring a trend imposed by the dominant power which wants to favour their divisions.

In April 2019, with the producer Eve Streeter, we travelled to Iraq to record a series of programmes for the BBC World Service. The series, entitled, *Religious Minorities in Iraq: Exodus or Extinction*, was to be broadcast the following month, in May. For security reasons, the crew was not allowed to leave the borders of the Kurdish Region. In addition, leaving Kurdish territory meant the issue of visas from the central government in Baghdad against the one-month visas released to any visitors to the region from European countries and from the US. After many phone calls to decide which one of the Christian villages we should visit, we chose Alqosh, a village located 45 kilometres north of Mosul, the ancient Nineveh. It lies at the foot of the Alqosh Mountain or the Beth 'Aidhre or Ba'aidhre Mountain. We planned our visit for Palm Sunday, and decided to avoid being accompanied by any of the members of political parties. We planned to interview Father Ghazwan, the parish priest of the village, together with some of the refugees from the surrounding villages destroyed by ISIS.

We left Erbil at 7 a.m. Father Ghazwan told us that the Palm Sunday celebration would start at around 9 a.m. When we arrived, we learned that the new church was already full of students, teachers, believers and pilgrims. The congregation was singing and dancing. The atmosphere was overwhelming and different from any Palm Sunday celebration in which I had participated in the past. Gently, we were pushed back from the first rows we occupied in an optimistic first momentum of enthusiasm. I have never seen such a presence in a Christian church and my thoughts went to the almost empty monasteries and churches here in the West. Theirs is a faith full of joy, where the smell of incense does not inspire thoughts of guilt and punishment. Theirs is the joy of the faith fuelled by their determination to live and survive despite everything. It comes to my mind that we titled the programme on the Christians, *The Last Christians in Iraq?*, a title that despite the question mark, sounded like a sentence without appeal, as many of our interviewees would comment.

After the celebration, the congregants went on a procession from the newly built church to the old one. The people were walking and singing. To our surprise, we met some Iraqi Americans who came from the United States in support of the village of their parents and grandparents. They represent a diaspora started a long time ago, before ISIS, before the bloody war ignited by the American invasion of Iraq in 2003. I wonder what is left in them of the history of this place, apart from a vague sense of belonging through their faith. One of the bakeries of the village was open and selling bread to the pilgrims. It was a long procession and to rest also from an early April sun, we had the opportunity to talk to other members of the community. For the day, they opened their houses, to which they return every now and then or to attend a big celebration like Palm Sunday. We took the opportunity to interview some of them. They talked about their families, who spread out all over the globe in different waves of emigration. They talked about how their belonging to this land was inevitably intertwined with their families, who have been there for centuries, even for thousands of years, because they were the first Assyrians to be converted to Christianity. Saint Thomas is said to have arrived in this land on his way to India long before Saint Peter is believed to have reached Rome. Their pride for their ancient origins blends with their awareness of being the very first Christians to inhabit this land.

The etymology of Alqosh confirmed this version. The name Alqosh (or Elqosh) apparently originates from the combination of the Assyrian Akkadian name, Eil-Kushtu, where 'Eil' means God and 'Kushtu' means 'righteousness' or 'power'. Therefore, Elqosh, or as casually pronounced Alqosh, means 'The God of Righteousness' or 'The God of Power'. According to another interpretation, the name, Alqosh, could also originate from the Aramaic, Eil Qushti, which means, 'The God of the Bow'. It is here that it is possible to establish a direct connection with the Assyrian past of this town because in Assyrian symbolism it can be found as a winged disk symbol of God Ashur holding a bow. Its name could also draw its origin from Aramaic where the rainbow was called 'Qeshta d'Maran', the 'Bow of Our Lord'. Alqosh, now Chaldean, is also known as Yimma d'Athor (Mother of Assyria) or Yimma d'Mathwatha (Mother of all Villages). In 2019, the population was around 5,000 from the estimated 6,000 in 2004.

The history of this small town is fascinating, starting with the fact that a city with the same name can be found in Israel, and its links with the Jewish faith and tradition has been recorded since the eighth and ninth centuries BCE, when Assyrian and Jewish prisoners found themselves sharing land and places of worship. Alqosh hosts the resting place of the biblical prophet, Nahum, and a monument survived dedicated to the persecution and diaspora suffered by Iraqi Jews after the Second World War, when 121,633 Jews left Iraq between 1948 and 1951. This 800-year-old tomb was incorporated into a synagogue, which since then has been protected by the local Christian community.

According to local families, Nahum was venerated by the Jews, Christians and Muslims, and preserving this monument has become even more important after 2014, in particular due to the massive destruction of ancient tombs such as that of Jonas in Mosul, perpetrated by ISIS. People in Alqosh are sure that if ISIS had entered their village, this place of worship would have been lost as well. Before going to the monument, we were warned that it would not be possible to visit the interior. In front of the building is a note telling visitors that a restoration project is being carried out, thanks to the financial contribution of the Kurdish Regional Government, the Government of the United States and private donors. It was completed in May 2020.

Nahum, an obscure prophet from the Old Testament, was highly venerated in this area. Nahum is an abbreviation of Nahumja, meaning, 'The Lord has comforted'. He was originally from a small village called Elcos, which some locate in Judea and others in Galilee. Nahum lived in the seventh century BCE, which saw the dramatic fall of Thebes by the Assyrians in 663 BCE and of Nineveh in 612. The Book of Nahum consists of an alphabetical (1.2–14) psalm, followed by the description of the fall of Nineveh and Thebes (2.1–3.19). Nahum does not address the Chosen People directly: his prophetic work is aimed at Nineveh, the capital of the Assyrian Empire, with all that it represented for Israel and antiquity: invasion, destruction and deportation. Nineveh will be destroyed and will never rise again, but the Lord will restore Judah and Israel (2.1–3; Aprim 2004).

The prophet lingers on the sins committed by Nineveh, who used violence to oppress other peoples. But his prophecy was also to be a warning to whoever bases their power on violence. Both Thebes and Nineveh have ruled entire populations with the sword and both of them suffer the same tragic end. In 2.11–13, Nahum talks about Nineveh's desolation in contrast to her former glory. Nahum's last words seem to refer directly to ISIS and the destruction, deportation and death they brought to this area. Nahum warns whoever looks for power through violence that they will pay the price because, 'The Lord will not leave the guilty unpunished' (1.7). It is a message of hope, especially in this moment of uncertainty about the future of Christians in the country.

The relationship between the Jewish and Christian communities in Alqosh has not always been devoid of tensions. In 1891, Vital Cuinet reported that a few years earlier, in 1883, Prophet Nahum's remains 'were secretly removed overnight, and placed in a Christian church, without the Israelites knowing, so that they go on venerating an empty tomb'.[3] This event has also been confirmed by one of the inhabitants of Alqosh, Louis Djeuma, who, in 2017, reported that when he was a child back in 1976, he saw how 'Nahum's remains were taken out of the pillar, then placed in a bottle, then put back again in the pillar and embedded in the royal gate's pillar, at the very same place it used to be before.'[4] Besides being an interesting story, this fact shows how, even after the virtual disappearance of the Jewish community from Alqosh, the population still venerated Nahum, whose remains are embedded into the pillar of the royal arch just in front of Mar Mikha's ones.

On that Palm Sunday, we were invited for lunch with Father Ghazwan by a family whose little courtyard looks at the square and at the old church. Before entering the house, one member of the BBC crew found some respite from the heat by sitting in the shadow of one of the houses surrounding the square, when I noticed a young boy running towards him with a bottle of water. The boy gave him the bottle without a word and immediately left without waiting for a thank you. A rare act of generosity towards a foreigner in a country destroyed by internal wars.

The table was ready in the courtyard in the shadow of an old fig tree. Kubba, soup, bread and vegetables, the simple tasty Iraqi traditional food. Kubba is a Babylonian dish that has been prepared through the centuries. At the table, Father Ghazwan talks about Alqosh. Some of the families of this village have been there for 2,000 years, since the beginning of Christianity. His own family has been in Alqosh for 500 years. Father Ghazwan also told us that Alqosh became Chaldean Christian in the first century CE. 'The Koja and Shiquana, are originally from here. We speak Aramaic which is the same language of Jesus. We speak a dialect of Aramaic or Sureth.' Later, after reciting 'Our Lord', he said in Aramaic: 'This is how Jesus would have said it.'[5]

When part of the ancient province of Adiabene, which included Arbil, Kirkuk, Mosul and in different historical moments also Edessa, Alqosh became one of the main Christian strongholds in the region. Already in the fifth century of the Christian era, it is possible to find references to the village. In 441 CE, Mar Mikha from Nohadra, the modern Duhok, talks about his visiting a church which was built on the ruins of an old Assyrian temple. This proves that Christianity was already present before his arrival and that churches existed. However, archaeology shows that Alqosh was a very important destination for religious pilgrimage before the Assyrian Empire gained control of the area. An inscription found on a mural inside King Sennacherib's palace states that: 'this rock was brought from Alqosh's Mountain'. The name Alqosh is also believed to derive from the name of a very ancient people and local deity called El-Qustu. It is also believed that people living in the Nineveh Plain gathered every new year, Akitu, in Alqosh in order to re-enact the Enuma Elish, the Akkadian epic of creation which would be incorporated into both Assyrian and Babylonian cosmology. Archaeological documents also show that people gathered in Alqosh on the occasion of a religious ceremony in honour of Sin, the moon, when an image of the God would have been carried in procession.

Wandering through the narrow alleyways of Alqosh, it is possible to visit what is believed to be one of the oldest churches of the village. In the fifth century CE, when Mar Mikha reached Alqosh, all the inhabitants had already converted to Christianity. It was Mar Mikha who was to strengthen the Christian faith in the region. The oldest church in Alqosh was built to be his resting place. From the bare simplicity of the church, it is possible to distinguish the most ancient elements of the construction. The only access to the church is a marble door, with a lintel ornamented with carved crosses. Probably very little has survived of the ancient church, which was last time restored in the nineteenth century. The church was at first under the authority of the Church of the East, but then passed to the Chaldean Church, like all other churches in Alqosh during the centuries immediately after the creation of the Chaldean Church in 1553. Rebuilt between 1578 and 1581, construction on the modern building began in 1876.

Jean-Maurice Fiey, in his *Assyrie chrétienne*,[6] describes the original church with three naves. Now it is a single-nave church. At the eastern end of the church, it is possible to see a large royal gate made out of Mosul marble. There are two important plaques in the building-work of both pillars of this arch. An ancient plaque at the bottom of the left-hand pillar looking towards the altar indicates the place where Mar Mikha's remains are placed. This plaque says in Syriac that the remains are in a 'jar embedded in the building work'. On the right-hand side, at the bottom of the right-hand pillar, another inscription indicates the place of the remains of the prophet, Nahum. A small, unpretentious door leads to the resting place of the priests and monks of the church. According to an inscription in Syriac placed above a painted map of Iraq, the school whose walls surrounded the courtyard, in 1923 Mar Mikha school was built, sponsored by the Bishop of Alqosh. This happened under the pontificate of Pope Pius XI and the patriarchate of Emmanuel II, the Catholic Chaldean patriarch of Babylon.[7]

Together with the inscriptions written in Syriac, Arabic and English in the Mar Georgis Church on the tombs of priests and patriarchs who lived in Alqosh, the establishment of this school shows the relevance of Alqosh in the history of the Church of the East. It was two centuries later, in 640 CE, that the special place of Alqosh was confirmed after the arrival of Monk Hômîzd who built the monastery that took his name.

According to recorded history, Mar Mikha came from the Monastery of Tur Abdin, the original place of the Syriac Orthodox Church, founded in the fourth century CE by two monks. The name means 'The Mountain of God's Servants'. At the time of Mar Mikha,[8] this monastery already counted 1,000 monks. The tradition is that he was following the tradition of Mar Awgin, the emblematic figure who was the initiator of Eastern monasticism in Syria and Mesopotamia two centuries earlier. The monastery was founded in the early seventh century, and was named after its founder, Hômîzd, a native of Persia and an important monastic figure in Syriac Christianity.

It was in 1892 that Deacon Îsâ bar-Isha'ya' reproduced for Ernest Alfred Wallis Badge, an expert in Assyrian studies and languages at the British Museum, a manuscript that was highly praised by the monks of Alqosh. As the British scholar remembers in the preface to its publication in English, 'the composition contains 3,496 lines, and is divided into twenty-two "gates" or sections, each of which is named after a letter of the Syriac Alphabet; the longest "gate" contains 1,098 lines and the shortest 50 lines, and the last letter of the last word of each line ends with the letter after which the "gate" is named'.[9]

It was not easy, not even for an experienced scholar such as Budge Wallis, to establish the exact date of the composition of this manuscript. However, through an analysis of the Syriac language and its content, he was able to establish from the copy they provided that the manuscript in praise of the Life of Rabban Hôrmîzd, without a date or colophon, appears to have been written in the nineteenth century. Wallis Budge's curiosity could not stop there and, after further enquiries, he was able to establish that the text was copied from a manuscript of the twelfth or thirteenth century and that:

> It had been in the possession of a native gentleman of great age, but which at his death had disappeared and could not be traced. The manuscript of the metrical Life of Rabban Hôrmîzd from which my copy was taken was declared to have been written in the 17th century, and this manuscript was, in turn, said to have been copied from one belonging to an older period; further information on the subject I was unable to obtain.[10]

What was certain for the eminent scholar, and to us, is that the life of the founder of one of the most important monasteries in the Nineveh Plain, just a few kilometres north of Mosul, was the result of the ongoing confrontation between Nestorians and Jacobites for control of the area. According to the Babylonian priest, Berossus (fourth century BCE), the Monastery of Rabban Hôrmîzd is located, like an eagle's nest, on the mountain of Alqosh, about 42 kilometres north of Mosul in Iraq. It was Mar Mikha who prophetized that an eagle would nest on the same mountain where the monastery would be founded. In a manuscript written in the seventh century BCE he says: 'He (Rabban Hôrmîzd) will come as an eagle and he will nest in Alqosh Mountain and he will generate spiritual sons.' This mountain is part of a chain of mountains called Qardû, famous for no other reason than welcoming the Noah's Ark or his Mesopotamian counterpart after the Flood.[11] What is sure about the founder of the monastery is that he came after spending thirty-nine years in the Monastery of Bar-'îdta and a few more years in the Monastery of Abba Abraham of Rîsha. When he reached Alqosh, he was already well known for performing miracles.

It was because of his reputation that:

> the people in the neighbourhood offered to build him a monastery, and Khôdhâhwî, the son of Shûbhhi, having contributed seven talents of silver, and 'Ukbê, the governor of Môsul, three more, the work was taken in hand straightaway, and the building was finished in twenty months; the consecration ceremony was performed by Jomarsâ II, the Catholicus, who signed a deed declaring that the monastery was to be under the direct jurisdiction of the Nestorian Patriarch, and that no Metropolitan or Bishop should have any authority to interfere in any way with Rabban Hôrmîzd's administration of it'.[12]

This was easier said than done, because, on reading the manuscript, we see that the confrontation between the Nestorians and Jacobites was fierce, to the point that Rabban Hôrmîzd himself was attacked and almost killed by monks from the monasteries of Bezkîn and Mar Mattai. The manuscript talks about this rivalry and the strenuous fight against the Jacobites, who were labelled idol worshippers and accused of being dedicated to sorcery. Rabban Hôrmîzd performs different miracles, including resuscitating the dead, transforming water into oil, healings and exorcisms. In one of the episodes, he was able to reach the Monastery of Mar Mattai with the purpose of stealing the idol that Satan had hidden in the shrine. On another occasion, an angel assisted him in the destruction of the books of the heretics by introducing him and then transporting him out of the monastery of the 'deceivers'.

All these stories have the purpose of reminding the readers about the acts of this Nestorian priest who fought against the enemies of the Church who were guilty of perpetuating the wrong message by subverting the real faith. Rabban Hôrmîzd's enemies in Bezkîn Monastery are depicted as wicked and devoted to evil. These monks:

> who performed the works of whoredome in a shameful way and after the manner of dogs, and moreover, without modesty, and improperly, and contrary to nature, they behaved with lasciviousness in the manner of the men of Sodom like unto mad dogs, and they worked their deeds of wantonnes and lust upon that woman, and upon others who were unto her,

were able to double

> their [evil] business in a manger which was more wicked than that which they had done at the first.[13]

They murdered the woman and her newborn baby and left their corpses in front of Rabban Hôrmîzd's cave. There was only one way to ease the wrath of the governor of Mosul, called in to have justice. To make the dead woman speak. With grace and humility, Rabban prayed and then asked the murdered woman who killed her and who was the father of her child. The miracle was performed. With 'a miraculous manner', the woman began to speak, accusing five monks from the Monastery of Bezkîn and acquitting Rabban Hôrmîzd. The inhabitants of Alqosh were affected by this and went in a procession and buried her in a grave at the foot of the mountain. Rabban Hôrmîzd also managed to make the newborn baby speak and tell everybody who his father was. After that, he was adopted and 'at the age of twenty years, he became a monk in the Monastery of Rabban; and he excelled greatly in the glorious deeds of asceticism and went out of this world with merit unspeakable'.[14] Rabban Hôrmîzd appears to have many enemies besides the Jacobites. At that time, sorcery was still very frequent in the region, probably inherited from ancient Babylonian times. Chapter XVII of the manuscript talks about how the worship of idols grew at the time in the whole of Mesopotamia thanks to the teachings of an Egyptian sorceress. Exorcism was necessary in order to defeat the evil.

The reading of this manuscript is wide-ranging, as well as being interesting from an historical point of view, with accounts of murders, kidnappings, magic, resurrections, conversions, betrayals, divine interventions. Jorge Luis Borges used to say that sacred texts belong to the category of fantastic literature, and this text seems to agree with him. The characters of these tales come to us stiffened by their function. They are fascinating symbols surrounded by a fantastic halo. For those who have read and spread these stories orally, the only certainty was their survival in the collective imagination, while their uncertain historical truth does not really add too much to the influence they had on the Christian communities in the area. In Alqosh, we can see a thread which reaches from the Babylonians and comes directly to the Christian world via the Jewish world.

Confronting this text with the Syriac literary tradition, the figure of Rabban Hôrmîzd and his relationship with the inhabitants of Alqosh refers to the importance that a village-level holy man acquired, in particular after the schism between the Nestorians and Jacobites, which had as a first consequence the intensification of the isolation of the Church of the East, already begun in the second century. The patron, the holy man originated in Syria, was the figure who acted as a bridge between the village and an outside world that seemed more and more threatening now, when Byzantium is very far away and when Mesopotamia found itself in the middle of a geopolitical war between the Sacred Roman

Empire, the Persian Empire, the threat from the Mongols and the already looming expansion of Islam. In this exasperated vacuum of power, it is understandable that the presence and actions of a holy man such as the protagonist of this fascinating manuscript which narrates the foundation of a Nestorian village, constitute an act of faith in a single individual that could surprise a Western observer. A Christian from the West would worry that its members would follow the rigid hierarchy of the central Church.

On the contrary, in the East, the devotion of the faithful depended on the personal trust that the holy men gained with their pure actions. At the end of the day, there was no need for a priest because a person who was for forty years on a pillar could be trusted as a confessor (Brown 1971). However, Rabban Hôrmîzd is much more than that, because with its miracles, he actually reminds us of the very origins of the sacred scriptures in which the Christian communities fear for their survival. In particular, we are dealing with communities that have to be forged in their faith through the creation of a common religious memory and 'lineage of orthodoxy and distinction' (Mellon Saint-Laurent 2015). Our holy man from Alqosh is the one who has the onerous task of encouraging and giving a sense of identity to a village, a small community which otherwise would be completely lost in a game of power which it does not understand but of whose massacres it keeps a sad memory. They are exercises of self-assertion against whoever from the Roman or Sassanian empires or, as in this case, from within the same Syriac Church that constantly tries to destroy their beliefs and with them their community. In order to achieve this goal, the authors of these stories have forcibly to refer to models not necessarily drawn from the sacred canonical scriptures. In this effort, it is easy to find representatives of both the Miaphysite Syrian Orthodox (Jacobite) or the Dyophysite Church of the East (Nestorian) who compete in creating a narrative in support of their own communities. The result of this combined effort to find a place or a sense of belonging in the turmoil of history is a narrative that united Christians despite their fierce theological disputes.

The creation of the hagiographic tradition, of which the Miaphysite John of Ephesus is probably the most known but not the only example, had the purpose of instilling and strengthening in these communities the cult for the saints and martyrs. John the Ephesus, who was born around 507 near the Christian city of Amida in Mesopotamia, answers to the need of rewriting a history of a church which rivals in parallel that written in the West. He writes the *Acts of Thomas*, *The Teaching of Addai* and the *Acts of Mari*, providing an apostolic foundation for the Church of the East (Mellon Saint-Laurent 2015). St Thomas was the apostle who, as well as Peter and John, received directly from Jesus the commission to travel to the East and convert, travelling as a slave on the trade route to India. In these stories, circulating both in Syriac and in Greek, the reader can find the same topics of the *Acts of the Apostles*, where the Apostles, and Peter in particular, have to perform miracles to convert individuals and groups of people, mirroring the acts performed by Jesus. What is evident from reading St Thomas' adventures is that 'the creation of a new Christian society is accompanied by chaos and miracles, turmoil and rebirth' (Mellon Saint-Laurent 2015: 22), in a crescendo which at the end aimed at establishing figures who can lead the Church and its faithful through an increasingly complicated sociopolitical environment. The continuous persecutions can be overcome only through the incessant work of itinerant Christian preachers on the model of the first apostles as an answer to the waves of destruction of Syriac monasteries and villages by whoever detained the power in a specific historical moment. In the second act alone, of the thirteen in which the book is divided, St Thomas converts King Gundaphorus after using the money with which he entrusted him to build a new palace to preach Christian values to his subjects. After this, he can continue his journey.

The Histories of Rabban Hôrmîzd, in the Persian found and translated into English by Wallis Budge, were probably written after the lives of those mentioned in them by the Jacobite John of Ephesus. The author, in his zeal to present his fellow Christians as non-believers, uses the same topics and symbology as those used by the Jacobites. Rabban Hôrmîzd's miracles and conversions established Alqosh as one of the firmer Nestorian strongholds. The monastery along the years would host one of the main centres of production of Syriac literature and a library that, even after many military incursions and tragic natural disasters, offered invaluable material to forge the history of the Church of the East and its development. The theological dispute between the Jacobites and Nestorians resulted in the production of sacred texts which competed in the effort to reforge Christian history in the area. This resulted in the composition of texts which aimed at retelling and reinterpreting the sacred texts. It is again Wallis Budge's tireless effort to recover old Syriac manuscripts that lead us to the discovery of text written 'in a fine Nestorian hand' (2018: 7). Writing about the *Cave of the Treasures* and his visit to Alqosh between 1891 and 1892, Wallis Budge remembers the circumstances of the findings of this precious manuscript:

> This manuscript contains twelve complete works, all of which were written, in a fine Nestorian hand, by the priest Hômo, the son of the priest Daniel, a native of

> Al-Kôsh [...] While I was in Al-Kôsh in 1890-91 collecting manuscripts for the British Museum, I found there some Hômo descendants, and of these one or two were professional scribes. They possessed a few ancient Syrian manuscripts, and from one of them I had copies made of the *Cave of Treasures* and the *Book of the Bee.*
>
> 2018: 7

Both of these texts belong to the Syriac traditions and are particularly interesting because they offer a different version of the sacred texts suggesting the existence of biblical accounts different from the ones that would become canonical. Written with all probability in the fourth century CE since, as the translator states, the proud use of Assyrian language is ever-present. Wallis Budge is also very good at describing this text both as part of a series of 'wonder-books intended by the their authors and editors to amuse as well as instruct', and also as a series of 'vain stories' and 'legends' which had a deep influence on Christian communities in Mesopotamia, Palestine, Egypt, Nubia and Abyssinia for centuries (ibid.).

All the apocryphal texts written in early Christianity had the purpose of educating a group of faithful who were mostly illiterate and therefore could not understand the sacred texts. For this reason, the creation of stories and fables had necessarily to draw on the patrimony of legends and folk tales of Assyro-Babylonian origin. *The Book of Treasures* (Anonymous n.d.) fulfills two specific purposes: the first is the establishment of a chronological sequence of events from the creation to the birth of Christ. The second is that it provided the new established church with the right credentials and with a much needed sense of belonging to an already established religious as well as historical tradition. The book proposes a division into five millenniums plus 500 years which starts from the second year of Cyrus (c. 541–539 BCE) to the birth of Christ.

Archaeological excavations proved that *The Book of Treasures* contains stories belonging to the Assyro-Babylonian world and not that they have never been included in the Bible. The legend of a wind-flood ordered by God to put an end to the terrible tradition of children sacrifice was historically placed at about 2000 BCE. At that moment in time, God realized that human blood was not acceptable to Him and for this reason He sent a wind-flood over the earth and put an end to idolatry, confirming His uniqueness as the only God worth worshipping as well as the abandonment of old rituals. There is no trace of this story in the Bible; however, it can be found in subsequent apocryphal Syriac books such as *The Book of the Bee*, written in 1222 by Solomon Bishop of Perâth Maishân (Al-

Basrah) and *The Book of Adam and Eve*. The introduction of apocryphal stories or legends that for sure circulated at the time of his composition is also confirmed by the insertion of elements that did not find any space, neither in the original Jewish nor in the Christian ones, but that appear in other religious traditions contemporary or in existence prior to its composition, or others which were adopted by Islam, for example. In *The Book of Treasures*, on the first day:

> God created the heavens, and the earth, and the waters, and the air, and the fire, and the hosts which are invisible (that is to say, the Angels, Archangels, Thrones, Lords, Principalities, Powers, Cherubim and Seraphim), and all the ranks and companies of spiritual beings, and the Light, and the Night and the Day-time, and the gentle winds and the strong winds (i.e. storms).

The reference to the four elements of air, fire, earth and water present in pre-monotheistic religions and also in pre-Socratic philosophy is even more present on the Eve of the Sabbath, when God called all the angels and hosts of Heaven to assist in the creation of Adam:

> And they saw the right hand of God opened out flat and stretched out over the whole world; and all creatures were collected in the palm of His right hand. And they saw that he took from the whole mass of the earth one grain of dust, and from the whole nature of water a drop of water, and from all the air which is above one puff of wind, and from the whole nature of fire a little of its heat and warmth.
>
> Wallis Budge 2018: 33

When the angels saw this, they interpreted it as if God had decided that all creation on earth should be subordinated to Adam. This is why:

> He took a grain from the earth in order that everything in nature which is formed of earth should be subject unto him; a drop of water in order that everything which is in the seas and rivers should be his; and a puff of air so that all kinds [of creatures] which fly in the air might be given unto him; and the heat of fire so that all the beings that are fiery in nature, and the celestial hosts, might be his helpers.
>
> Ibid.

In this version of the creation, Adam immediately appears as a supernatural being endowed with great beauty and is extremely powerful:

> For they saw the image of his face burning with glorious splendor like the orb of the sun, and the light of his eyes was like the light of the sun, and the image of his body was like unto the sparkling of a crystal. And when he rose at full length

and stood upright at the center of the earth, he planted his two feet on that spot whereon was set up the cross of our Redeemer; for Adam was created in Jerusalem.

Anonymous, *The Book of Treasures* n.d.

The account of the second millennium which goes from Yârêd to the Flood, begins with the condemnation of music and musical instruments. At end of the first millennium, the fall of the House of Seth by the evil Satan had already started and the book warns against music and instruments as tools of sin and eternal perdition. *The Book of Treasures* tells that:

> Yôbâl (Jubal) and Tôlbakîn (Tubal-Cain), the two brethren, the sons of Lamech, the blind man, who killed Cain, invented and made all kind of instruments of music: 'Jôbâl made reed instruments, and harps, and flutes, and whistles, and the devils went and dwelt inside them, and sent out sounds from inside them. Tôlbakîn made [Fol. 12a, col. 2] cymbals, and sistra, and tambourines (or drums)'.

This was a scandalous noise that with the laughter of the sinners inevitably reached the holy mountain. This condemnation of music would later be included in the Quran.

Hôrmîzd's work in Alqosh was also part of a tradition that between the fourth and seventh century saw the expansion of monastic life and institutions from Syria to the Nineveh Plain. Founded in the late sixth or perhaps early seventh century, the Upper Monastery in Alqosh in a few years became very famous for its library and was an important place of learning until probably the tenth century. All this tradition of monasteries with annexed schools had its beginning in the fourth century, with the expulsion of the Nestorian Persian Christians from Edessa in 489 and the foundation of the school of Nisibis, an institution which played a pivotal role in the intellectual life of the Church of the East.[15] Thanks to the school curriculums that have survived the centuries, it is possible to reconstruct the life in the schools which had the purpose of forming monks with the literacy and knowledge to transcribe old manuscripts for the diffusion and preservation of Christian culture. Rabban Hôrmîdz Monastery belonged to this tradition.

At the time of Rabban Hôrmîzd arrival in Alqosh, the contraposition between Christianity and Islam is not yet a real concern.[16] It is only very recently that historiography has given attention to Syriac sources regarding the sixth century to find out that none of them written before Mohammed's death in 632 CE speak of Islam as a definite religion. Until this moment, Syriac literature focuses on the creation of heroes who can face the dangers coming from contrasts within their own schismatic groups or from the threatening expansionist aims of both the Sassanid and Roman empires.

The presence of Christian bishops at the court of subsequent Sassanid rulers is very well documented as well as the rise of a Christian aristocracy which worked alongside the King of Kings since the beginning of the fifth century, in particular since the 410 CE synod, after which the Church of the East started its institutional development in Mesopotamia. Due to the isolation of the region from the centres of Christianity, this could never have happened without the support of the non-Christian economic, culture and political system of the Sassanid Empire (Payne 2015). The creation of a Christian aristocracy and the institution of bishoprics with the support of the Sassanids, in particular in main cities such as Arbela (Erbil) and Karka d-Beit Slok (Kirkuk), show how the development of the Church of the East was intertwined with the religious and social institutions of the Zoroastrians. This could sound paradoxical, but it actually shows that the persecution and punishment of Christians happened only when Christian elites, in competition for power, started to undermine the institutions of the state and the position of Good Religion in the empire. Attacks against sacred fire temples did not only have a religious component, but had an institutional one as well that the Sassanid authorities could not ignore. From the Sassanid point of view, the Christian elite were part of the establishment and as such they owed obedience to the state. Their disobedience had to be punished to put them in line with the rules of the administration of the empire and, in this sense, it is fair to say that the famous case of Shapur II, 'The Great Persecution', was thus a myth because: 'Christians were not systematically persecuted as a recognizable group on account of their religious identity, but rather ecclesiastical leaders were executed for disobedience in their capacity as potential intermediaries of particular provincial populations vis-à-vis the court' (Payne 2015: 43).

The Syriac Christian legends written in the seventh century such as *Mar Qardagh* and *History of Karka*, exorcise the already vanishing power of the Sassanid Empire which spanned 224–642 CE, when this text was composed. It looks as though its anonymous author lived during the reign of the Sassanid ruler, Khusro II in 590–628 (Walker 2006). The historical context is important because it is exactly in 628 that the most sacred shrine of the Zoroastrian, the fire of Adur Gushnasp at Takht-e-Suleyman, was destroyed by the Roman troops led by Roman emperor Heraclius, who, interpreting the hagiographical tradition of the Church of the East, transformed his soldiers into martyrs of the faith, advocating for the sanctity of the final sacrifice to God 'for the salvation of our brothers. May we sin the crown of martyrdom so that we may be praised in the future and receive our recompense from God.'[17]

Both the *History of Karka* and the *Mar Qardagh* provide answers and viable alternatives to a Christian community in search of a distinctiveness in a world on the edge between different great powers. The *History of Karka* is a text which recounts the history of the city and its connection with an ancient past before the Sassanid Empire. The insistence on the city's long history and its legacy is pivotal to understanding the effort made by the Christian community to build a sacred landscape to which to belong. The physical construction of Christian places of worship in Karka shows a continuity which goes beyond the vanishing Sassanid Empire. Contrary to what happened with the sacred texts of the Zoroastrians, all Christian hagiographies were recited loudly during major gatherings. This had the purpose and effect not only of strengthening the identity of the group but also of bolstering a sense of belonging to the land they were living in. The *History of Karka* is a very good example of this. Its beginning recites: 'The foundations of this stronghold were laid by a king of Assyria whose Syriac name was Sar-danā' (Mellon Saint-Laurent, Michelson, Zanetti and Detienne 2016: 22). These incipit must have immediately called the attention of the auditors to an ancient past, where Sardana of the Hellenistic tradition, Sargon of the Hebrew Bible and the Assyrian king Esarhaddon belong to the same hybrid historical tradition (Payne 2015). King Esarhaddon/Sargon was the King of Nineveh who saved his city following the preaching of the biblical Jonas and, for this reason, is considered pious in the eyes of both Jews and Christians.

We have to imagine that the Christians gathering in this same square would feel that sense of belonging which connected them, not necessarily with the history of the Sassanid Empire, which in the middle of the seventh century was on the verge of collapsing, but to a much longer history which went back to the Assyrians, Achaemenian and Seleucids, whose construction surrounded them. Most of the auditors were Christian aristocrats who saw that by belonging to the history of an ancient city such as Karka, the legitimacy of acting in the land put them at the same level as the Zoroastrian ones. In this search for legitimation, they inaugurated a new, symbiotic relationship with the cities which would contribute to the flourishing and survival of Christians in Mesopotamia, also after the advent of Islam. The *Book of Karka* narrates the history of Persian martyrs in the town and relates how Christians gathered in the city to worship them (Brock and Ashbrook Harvey 2008). The 'conquest' of an urban space in contrast with the building of churches and monasteries in cities was favoured by the Zoroastrian authorities after the Synod of Joseph in 554. Starting from this moment, the shrines belonging to both religions were present in cities and overlapping each other. Most of them became a destination for pilgrimages for both religions, sealing a symbiotic coexistence that only very rarely resulted in open conflict.

Another example of how this coexistence worked is the *History of Mar Qardagh*. This text has little religious content in it; however, it is very important because it offers a unique insight into the reality of Christian communities in northern Iraq at the time of its composition around the sixth century. The protagonist, Mar 'Saint' 'hunts like a Persian king, argues like a Greek philosopher, and renounces his Zoroastrian family to live with monks high in the mountains west of Lake Urmiye' (Walker 2006). He is the quintessential hero of the Syriac Christian community, the man who with his strength and humanity can fight and win thanks to his new faith in the real religion, Christianity. A very important detail to note here is that he is executed in Arbela (Erbil), the city that together with Karka in the sixth century became the centre of the cult of Christian martyrs. Far from being a contradiction, this book, recited during the annual feasts on the tells of Beit Teta in Karka and of the still unidentified tell of Melqi in Arbela, left its auditors with the conviction that their claim of belonging to this land was carved in its more ancient stones because:

> Now holy Mar Qardagh was from a great people (*gensā*) from the stock of the kingdom of the Assyrians (*'ātōrāyē*). His father was descended from the renowned lineage of the house of Nimrod, and his mother from the renowned lineage of the house of Sennacherib. And he was born of pagan parents lost in the error of Magianism, for his father, whose name was Gušnōy, was a prominent man in the kingdom and distinguished among the *magi*,[18]

thereby levelling Christian aristocratic elite with its Persian counterpart.[19] After abandoning his position in the army, Mar Qardagh, already converted to Christianity, resumed the command and, thanks to his faith, saved the Iranian Empire from Roman and Arab attacks. To the amazement of the auditors of the sixth century, Mar Qardagh faces his enemies, before the battles, he sprinkles *hnana* on his horse and his soldiers, a sort of dust believed to have magic powers after coming into contact with saintly remains and goes into war wearing a cross 'which was fastened the Holy Wood of the Crucifixion of our Savior'.[20] The Christian cross will triumph, definitively sanctioning the Christian presence in the territory.

The *History of Karka* and the *History of Mar Qardagh* are the literary answer to the 'Great Massacre' that took place during the reign of Shapur II (309–79), followed by other outbreaks of persecution under Barham V (420–38), Yazdegird II (438–57), Khusro I (531–79) and even under Khusro II (590–628). The protagonist is a new aristocracy and a new lineage that, with a remarkable creative leap thanks to a mixture of literary and cultural traditions present in the area, managed to create a link with the ancient past which did not exist before and which weakened that already officially accepted in the 605 Synod of Mar Gregory and supported by many Christians and East Syrian bishops, to ally with the Sassanid Empire and King Khusro. The Sassanid Empire ended in 642 CE, giving way to the advance of Islam. Christianity in Iraq will still need martyrs and saints, and hagiography as such will continue to be an important part of its literature. For the time being, Syriac churches and monasteries will have to deal with another strong opponent who will completely change the history of Iraq and the whole of the Middle East: Islam.

At this moment in time, Alqosh, the city of God, became an important point of reference for all Nestorians. Only now do some Syriac authors starts to record their lives under Islam. These are very valuable documents, and we can imagine that Rabban Hôrmîzd must have been aware of their existence. The earliest surviving Syriac reference to Islam, the *Account ad 637*, was most likely written as the Islamic conquests were unfolding. The British Library holds a very interesting document, *Chronicle ad 640*. This chronicle of uncertain authorship is important for the reference to historical events which testify to the first clashes between Christian and Muslim communities. Even if at the time many probably did not see the advent of the Arabs as a threat to the Christian faith, we cannot exclude the possibility that monks in Alqosh as well as others felt the need to expand and preserve the message and culture of the Christians. Among the facts registered in *Chronicle ad 640* appear also attacks to monks and other symbols of Christianity. *Chronicle ad 640*, from only a few years later, also briefly speaks of the conquests and of the possible threat that this new force represents for other groups. Both these chronicles refer to Mohammed and show how quickly Syriac Christians were aware of the emergence of Islam. However, both chronicles refer to the new conquerors with the Syriac word. Neither source, though, attributes any particular religious beliefs attributing to them any particular creed.[21] It was only later, in 656, with the crisis of succession that started with the assassination of the caliph 'Uthmān and the first Arab civil war (*fitna*) in 661 and the foundation of the first Islamic dynasty with Mu'āwiya, that Islam began to be perceived as an imposing presence with a distinctive religious connotation. Mu'āwiya's family, the Umayyads, would retain control of most of the Islamic Empire until 750.[22]

Starting from the 650s, however, Syriac writings record through inscriptions and chronicles their history, which is inevitably entwined with that of Mesopotamia and, starting from the seventh century, with the advent of Islam as well as the not always amicable relations between the Church of the East and the West. Amir Harrak published the translation of Syriac and Garshuni inscriptions and among them the ones present in the old monastery.[23] What is remarkable about these sites are the nine patriarchal graves located near the grave of Rabban Hôrmîdz. The beauty of the inscriptions is undeniable and still remarkably alive. They are written in Estangela calligraphy,[24] a masterpiece in itself. These graves testify to a world in conflict with itself and with the world outside, a series of conflicts which were to last until the nineteenth century. But the important feature of these inscriptions is their literary and historical value. Harrak, comparing them with other Syriac inscriptions, notices that they are written in the first person, not a typical trend.[25] Moreover, it is a remarkable fact that the patriarchs transformed their epitaph into confessions of faith 'particularly the Christology of the Assyrian Church of the East'. All of them are very similar, a copy of each other despite the patriarchs having lived and died at different times. They can be divided into two sections, the first one being a profession of faith and the other details about the date in which they died. They testify to the continuity of the belief of the Church of the East and its faith in its version of the nature of Christ with the insistence on the inscriptions of the 'two natures, two *qnōmē* and one *parsōpā*', another reminder of the Nestorian nature of the monastery.

In 1551, Alqosh was at the centre of the contention between the old Nestorian Church and the new one that aimed at a reconciliation with Rome when the Nestorian Assyrian Youhanna Sulaqa, the head of the monks of the monastery, decided to join the Catholic Church in opposition to the hereditary process in selecting new patriarchs. However, it was only around 1762 that Deacon Shamasha Hadbesha, after his return from Diyar Bakir in Turkey, started to propagate Catholicism in Alqosh. It was only in 1830, that Patriarch Youhanna Hurmiz officially submitted to the Vatican and that the old denomination of Nestorians was substituted with Chaldean. Alqosh has been the birthplace of many relevant religious figures throughout the centuries: Youhanna Sulaqa, born in 1513, famous for having been imprisoned by the governor of Amadiya and suspected of having been killed during his detention on 12 January 1555; Patriarch Youhanna Hirmuz, born in 1760, who accepted Catholicism in 1826 and officially established the Chaldean Catholic Church in 1830; Patriarch Joseph VI, born in Alqosh in 1793, who was consecrated as the Patriarch of the

Chaldean Catholic Church on 11 September 1848; Patriarch Joseph Emmanuel II Toma, born in Alqosh in 1852, who was consecrated as the Patriarch of the Chaldean Catholic Church on 9 July 1900; Mar Toma Audo, born in 1853, who was murdered by Kurds and Turks during the Assyrian Genocide in 1917 while serving the Assyrians as an archbishop in the Urmia region, Iran; and Patriarch Paulos II Shiekho, born in Alqosh on 1 November 1906, who was consecrated as the Patriarch of the Chaldean Catholic Church on 16 January 1958.

A few kilometres separate Alqosh and Rabban Hôrmîzd Monastery (Figure 2.1). A winding road leads to the top of the mountain where the monks lived, studied and copied for centuries. At the base, cells carved into the rock of the mountains seems to warn potential intruders. Every year on 'Shara d'Rabban Hurmiz' or the 'Festival of the Monk Hurmiz', which occurs every third Monday following Easter Sunday, Alqosh and its ancient monastery come to life and renew their faith. On that day, it is as though all the history of the place and its prominent religious figures come to life again to renew Alqosh's special pact with God.

Inside the monastery, the small opening visible from the road turns out to be the windows of the cells from which only a fragment of the valley can be seen, as if the monks wanted to deny entry to the beauty of the landscape that surrounded

Figure 2.1 Rabban Hormizd Monastery. Source: Wikimedia Commons.

them and its temptations. The monks relied on the dim light of a single oil lamp placed inside one of the small niches carved into the wall of each cell. On the walls of the caves, several inscriptions speak to us from different centuries. Besides its famous library, the monastery hosted a large dining room, carved into the mountain stone, able to host more the 100 monks. The monastery also has a 'Beth Sahdeh' or 'House of Martyrs' and 'Beth U'matha' or 'House of Baptism'. The mountains surrounding the monastery deepen a sense of blessed isolation.

The history of Alqosh and its monastery is not devoid of violence despite its religious vocation. Mongols, Turkomans, Persians and Kurds have attacked, conquered or destroyed Alqosh, in particular in the sixteenth, eighteenth and nineteenth centuries. Patriarchs as well as monks have been imprisoned and murdered. Among them was one of the most venerated reformers of Rabban Hôrmîzd Monastery, Father Gabriel Dambo, killed in 1832 by the Kurdish Emir Mohammed Pasha of Rawanduz. It is an episode that still resonates in the prayers of the community of Alqosh.

It was in 1856 after, Alqosh became a Chaldean stronghold, that the building of the new Monastery of Our Lady of the Seeds was completed under the Chaldean patriarch, Joseph VI Audo, whose elaborate tomb can be seen in the interior of the church of the monastery. He was the first patriarch to be buried in this monastery. Until then, patriarchs were buried in the Rabban Hôrmîzd Monastery. The construction of a monastery on the plain was necessary because the old one on the mountains was not suitable for use by the monks. Its position made it almost inaccessible and prevented the establishment of a stronger link with the population of Alqosh and with all the Christians living in the Nineveh Plain. The new monastery, called Our Lady of the Seeds, confirmed more firmly the importance of Alqosh as a Christian, now a Catholic Chaldean town. Situated on a higher level, from its walls it is possible to see the old town as well as the old monastery. What attracts the attention of the European traveller is that the entrance is a syncretic architectonical work which, with its battlements, is a reminder of its Assyrian–Chaldean origins in its construction. Our Lady of the Seeds owns its name to the devotion to the Virgin Mary, protector of agriculture, who, with her open arms receives the visitors. It is the interior cloister just after the main door. With its well-kept gardens planted with different species of flowers and fruit trees, that, with the calming sounds of running water coming from the basin fountain, makes its visitors forget the tensions prevailing outside these walls. In the beautiful church, the tomb of the Chaldean patriarch, Joseph VI Audo, has the inscription: 'the Holy Church grieves for him, lamenting over and over this holy chief of our nation'.[26] He was the first patriarch not to be buried in the old Rabban Hôrmîdz Monastery and it constitutes the link between the old and the new. On one hand, it opens onto the refectory, the kitchen, the cellar, the chapter house and the monks' cells, on the other hand, it opens onto the southern porch of the abbey church.[27]

The history of Alqosh shows that the dramatic history of the area did not spare the city either. Besides wars, famines and plagues, with inevitable demographic fluctuations through the centuries, its population managed to survive and keep alive their faith, remaining a beacon of hope for all Christianity. Alqosh never stopped being the light in opposition to darkness, hope in opposition to desperation, not even when ISIS destroyed all the villages around it. Father Ghazwan, and with him others, believe that it was not by chance that Alqosh was spared the destruction suffered by other Christian villages. During the four years, the glowing cross of Alqosh and the sounds of the same bells which the sacristan rings every day, testify to the endurance and resilience of this remarkable town. ISIS fighters could not do anything against it because 'we are here to stay, and we will rise again like the phoenix'. There is no pretentiousness or naiveness in his words, only faith in the plans that God had and still has for Alqosh. While the West discuss the nature of the events unleashed by the cruel ideology of ISIS, in this part of the world. ISIS has been like a tsunami from whose destruction it is still possible to rise. There is no space for ineluctable facts of history. On Palm Sunday 2019, five years after the ISIS onslaught, Alqosh chants still resonate across the plain.

Father Ghazwan as well as other survivors from ISIS are convinced that they are not the last Christians in Iraq, but that they are here to stay and strongly believe that the catastrophic events unleashed by ISIS are only a minimal part of a story which originates in a distant and sacred past; that the world we live in is not finished but has just begun because, up there, time is measured in billions of centuries. This awareness of belonging to the creation is at the base of the humility and inner peace of Father Ghazwan and his parishioners. It really looks as though this town, founded around 15000 BCE, cannot be destroyed, really enjoys some secret pact with God.

Jonas the Prophet of Mosul

The name Mosul comes from al-Mawsil junction in Arabic. In the sixth century, at the dawn of the Islamic period, it was just a garrison whose inhabitants were mainly Christians. An essential passage 'junction' for merchants, preachers, soldiers and adventurers, Mosul soon became a city where everyone from the East and West collided and where the Christian aristocracy flourished in the same way in which it had developed its strength and influence in Karka (Kirkuk) and Arbela (Erbil). Starting from the seventh century, the Syrian Orthodox Church, as depicted in such a colourful way in the manuscript about the Rabban Hôrmîdz, managed to control many of the East Syrian monasteries. This eased the rivalries between the two churches and favoured the supremacy of the Syrian Orthodox Church that was also in the region of Mosul, in particular in Alqosh. By the twelfth century, Mosul was surrounded by a series of monasteries, which constituted a Christian belt around the city where Christians could speak their own language, Aramaic, and practise their unique culture, which they do to this day. However, it is in the city of Mosul that we can find the best example of Christian–Muslim symbiosis.

Looking at religious buildings and art, we discover that Christians and Muslims in Mosul have shared the vicissitudes of a city for its strategic geographical position, often contended among the subsequent invaders who have been trying to control it. The proof is that, during the period before the thirteenth century and the so-called Syrian Renaissance, Christian and Muslim rules have governed the city. Fakhr al-Din 'Abd al Masih, a Christian captive from Antioch, governed Mosul up to 1170. Less than a century later, in 1262, Shams al-Din al-Ba'shiqi was only one of the various Christian governors who ruled the city under the Mongols (Patton 1982). This should be no surprise because, only thirty years earlier, Badr al-Din Lu'lu' declared himself 'King of Mosul', and under his rule the city saw an increase of 'monumental churches, mosques, and civil buildings of beautiful architectural and iconographic designs that characterize his time. The building material consisted of local stone called *farsh*, used by the ancient Assyrians in the construction of their palaces and temples' (Harrak 2014).

All this contributed to a Syrian Renaissance which saw the development of Syrian literature, comprising hagiographies and commentaries on the Bible. From authors such as Bar Shakko who wrote *The Book of Treasures* in 1231 and Barhebraeus who, in his writings, recounts how the Syrian Church was able to undertake building construction campaigns which strengthened their presence in the area. Christian culture and influence developed under Islamic rule and it survives in the architecture and material art that shape Mesopotamian cities and villages, creating a fascinating cultural and artistic syncretism. Barhebraeus himself built the Monastery of Yuhanon Bar Nagarre, now lost in his native

Bartalla, just a few kilometres from Mosul and Alqosh. In his *Chronicles*, Barhebraeus refers to a building construction and decorative campaign which lasted three years, from 1283 to 1285. The details of the wall paintings suggest the presence of this kind of art in churches and monasteries of the area. The discovery in 2005 of what can be considered one of the few surviving examples of wall-paintings in the Church of Mar Giworgis in Qaraqosh, confirms this revival of Christian culture in the area.[28]

In 2019, Father Michaeel Najeeb became the new Archbishop of Mosul. In his memories, this is a city where all the cultural heritage of the area unite like rivers that flow into a single sea. Ancient Assyrian/Babylonians, Christians, Muslims, all of them have shared this land for centuries. It sounds like a common saying, but it contains a lot of truth, at least if seen from the point of view of a micro-history. It is not always easy to make a place talk about its past, and is less so when it is very ancient and when so many centuries have shaped its stones and monuments, when many languages, cults and religions have gone through it, leaving traces behind them.

But it is from architecture that we have the most convincing proof of the daily exchange between Christians and Muslims in the twelfth and thirteenth centuries, in particular from a stylistic analysis of the Royal Gate, a feature present in churches in the Mosul area. Bas Snelders describes it as 'an east wall separating the nave from the sanctuary. Often it was pierced by three entrances, of which the central one, the Royal Gate, is commonly the largest' (2010). Snelders analyses, in particular, the Royal Gate of the Church of Mar Ahudemmeh in Mosul and the whole style and iconography of that in the Church of Mart Shmuni in Qaraqosh. Remarkably, both Royal Gates betray their belonging to a local tradition that is distinguished by the lack of properly Christian elements. The 'mounted falconers and the enthroned figures holding a cup' (ibid.: 198) are of Islamic origin and are more reminiscent of life at the Islamic court to the detriment of a clear Christian message. This shows the presence of religiously mixed workshops which produced architectural features for both Christian and Muslim clients. Other sources can testify to this undeniable symbiosis between the two religions. In 1169, both Christians and Muslims in search of healing went on a pilgrimage to the Monastery of Deir Mar Barsauma to ask for the intercession of the saint. It must be for this reason that, as Patriarch Michael the Syrian tells in his *Chronicle*, Christian and Muslim workers participated in the restoration work of the monastery (Syrian 1899–1924).

Christians and Muslims were not only sharing workshops and market places. By that time, the Muslim tradition of *ziyara* was well established and included visitation to the tomb of holy figures (Rahimi and Eshaghi 2019). It was very common to share worship places, saints and holy figures which had the power of healing and making miracles for the faithful. In addition, Islam taught its followers to respect all Jewish and Christian prophets and patriarchs. It was not uncommon to share spaces dedicated to prayers, as well as symbols and saints. This belonged to a very widespread tradition which saw the three Abrahamic religions praying in the same space also in Syria, Palestine and Egypt. In Damascus, for example, the Great Mosque containing the shrine dedicated to Yahiya ibn Zakkarya, St John the Baptist, was the destination of pilgrims belonging to the three religions. In Teleskof as well as in almost every Christian church in the Nineveh Plain, it is possible to find a representation of St George slaying the dragon carved in stone. A veneration that Christians shared with Islam because, in Muslim popular culture, St George and Moses' anonymous servant are identified with al-Khidr. According to the Muslim tradition, Mosul was the site where St George suffered his martyrdom and in this city a shrine called Mashad al-Nabi Jirjis containing St George's tomb occupied a special place in one of the city's most important mosques. This same site was destroyed by ISIS in July 2014 (*The Guardian* 2014). It was not the only one. A few days earlier, ISIS had destroyed the most iconic shrine in Mosul, the tomb of the prophet Jonah, sacred to Jews, Christians and Muslims alike, this building was an ancient Assyrian temple and palace, a Jewish shrine and a Christian church, transformed in the twelfth century into a mosque.

It is again Ernest Alfred Wallis Budge who, remembering the archaeological discoveries made by Layard, Rassam and Smith in Nineveh, dispels all doubts about the original scene of the biblical account of the book of Jonah, asserting that:

> Thanks, however, to Christian, Roman and Muhammadan tradition, there is no room for doubt about it, and the site of Nineveh has always been known. The fortress which the Arabs built there in the seventh century was known as 'Kal'at-Ninawî,' i.e., 'Nineveh Castle,' for many centuries, and all the Arab geographers agree in saying that tile mounds opposite Môsul contain the ruins of the palaces and walls of Nineveh. A few of them fail to mention that close by them is 'Tal Nabi Yûnis,' i.e., the Hill from which the prophet Jonah preached repentance to the inhabitants of Nineveh, that 'exceeding great city of three days' journey' (Jonah, iii, 3). Local tradition also declares that the prophet was buried on the Hill, and his supposed tomb is shown there to this day.
>
> Wallis Budge 2020: 6

Jonah is not like other prophets; his story of conversion and forgiveness represents a passage from a vindictive God to a God who can show His great love for mankind. Taking fate into their own hands, the king and the inhabitants of Nineveh believed in Jonah's apocalyptic words, and decide to strip off their rich robes to put on humble sheepskin tunics, showing for the first time that men are the real masters of their own destiny. Men can choose their way and by doing so they can make God change His mind. It is God Himself who explains to a disappointed Jonah the reason for his unusual behaviour: 'And should not I care about Nineveh, that great city, in which there are more than a hundred and twenty thousand persons who do not yet know their right hand from their left, and many beasts as well!'[29]

For the inhabitants of Mosul, Christians or Muslims, Jonah was the protector of the city, the prophet more quoted in the Quran as Nabi Younis is mentioned forty-three times and there is a complete *surah* dedicated to him as 'the one chosen by God'. His tomb was so sacred to Muslims that 'sept visites à la mosquée de Nabi Younis équivalent à un pèlerinage à la Mecque' (Najeeb 2017).[30] Abu Bakr al-Baghdadi, the head of ISIS, wanted to destroy the image of that merciful God that belongs to all believers. He wanted to obliterate the mosque, the Christian church, the synagogue and the Assyrian palace from the face of the earth, the remains of which were still visible. Mosul/Nineveh was not spared this time. The wrath of ISIS led to the destruction not only of a building, but of the intimate relationship of the city with its remote past. Father Michaeel Najeeb devoted his life to the preservation of the Christian and non-Christian heritage in the area. A native of Mosul, in his book, recalls the legends surrounding Jonah:

> Tous les habitants de la ville connaisent l'histoire de ce prophète. À Mossoul, les parents font croire à leur progéniture qu'à condition d'être bien sage, elle pourra apercevoir la baleine se baigner dans les aux du Tigre. Et quand un enfant un peu moins crédule que les autres émet des doutes, les adultes lui expliquent que la meilleure preuve que la baleine nage encore dans le fleuve, c'est que personne n'a jamais retrouvé son tombeau. Enfant, moi aussi j'ai été bouleversé par cette histoire.[31]
>
> Najeeb 2017

Now, everything seems lost, the memories and the shared culture which made the spirit of these lands for centuries. Christians still living in the area sound even stronger in their faith. 'Christ is in our heart. There is nothing that cannot be rebuilt again. Building as well as tradition stay with us and our faith.'[32] This is what one of the survivors in the now almost completely destroyed village of Batnaya said in April 2018 in Alqosh, where he sought refuge with his wife and his younger son. He added: 'Hope keeps me going. Without it I would die. We pray God to sort this out for everybody.'[33] Out of the penumbra of the small house facing the main square of Alqosh, the cheerful music and chants of the celebration of Palm Sunday seem to agree with him. His words suggest that ISIS and its intolerance did not win and that what happened in 2014 was only a bump in the road of Christian history. He strongly believes that the haemorrhage of Christians leaving the country will slow down, and that he will be able to go back to a rebuilt Batnaya and that his 10-year-old son could have the future his father wishes for him, to become an engineer and serve his country.

From Baghdad to the Nineveh Plain and back

In 1978, Saddam Hussein changed the constitution and declared that in Iraq there were only two ethnic groups: Arabs and Kurds. Christians as well as other minorities were left to choose where they belonged. In addition, as part of his policy of forced Arabization, he decided to move Christians from their traditional villages in the Nineveh Plain to the south of the country. In his plans, Christian houses and properties were assigned as a reward to members of the Iraqi Army. This wave of forced displacement of the Christian population gave rise to the creation of Christian communities in Baghdad and other cities. After almost thirty years, in 2003, due to the recrudescence of the war between Sunnis and Shi'as, Christians had to flee again and return to their original villages. Some of them still remember their previous life in Baghdad with a hint of nostalgia. Life as they remember it ended with the surge in violence as early as 2004, when the US took control of Baghdad causing the fragmentation of the city into Sunni and Shi'ite enclaves protected by local militias. In this explosive environment, the Christians and other minorities got caught up in the middle of a war they did not start.

Attacks against the Christian community in both Baghdad and Mosul have been denounced. In June 2004, these two main cities were heavily targeted with a series of attacks starting on 1 August when a bomb was thrown at the Holy Spirit Church in Mosul, followed on 4 August by a twin attack on four churches in Baghdad and another in Mosul. Daniel Williams defines as 'ecumenical' the way in which the attackers chose their targets since the first bomb hit Our Lady of the Flowers Armenian Catholic Church; the second hit Our Lady of Salvation Assyrian Catholic Church; and, later on, Santa Peter and Paul Chaldean

Catholic Seminary and Saint Elia Chaldean Catholic Church in Baghdad, and finally St Paul's Chaldean Church in Mosul. These attacks were probably never considered as anti-Christian but as a consequence of the ongoing confrontation between Shi'as and Sunnis. The situation worsened with attacks on Christian neighbourhoods followed by the kidnapping and killing of Christians who were left without any protection.

Testimonies reported by Daniel Williams talk about payments being made in exchange for protection, attacks on properties and individuals being threatened, in some cases, with death if they did not convert. The neighbourhood of Dora in Baghdad is an example of how the Christian community suffered in those years. In 2007, its church, St Jacob, was attacked and transformed into a mosque. Its population of 10,000 people halved. In 2014, just before the advent of ISIS, only 1,500 Christians remained (Williams 2016). The sensibility of a child can offer an idea of the living conditions for a Christian in Baghdad before and after 2003. R., a witness who wanted to stay anonymous, remembered that before the US invasion, not everything was available because of the economic embargo:

> When still children we were advised not to discuss politics in schools. We used to have math, and Arabic language part of the Arabization process. Many teachers had a Baath affiliation and were controlling the kids. We used to march militarily. I particularly remember how tough was one of the teachers and the power she had even on the manager of the school. We were allowed to talk about our religion but not about our ethnicity because we all had to be Arabs. I experienced violence against religious and ethnicity. Many Sunnis provoked Shias publicity. And the Shias did not react because the others were members of the party. When I was in school children used to insult each other with the words 'zionist', 'jew', 'traitor', 'imperialist'. This was pre-2003. Only when I grew up I realized that those kids had to hear those insults from their families, and I started to think what sectarianism meant. In those years no history book mentioned Christians and I started to wonder where I fitted in Iraqi history. Then when I was in fifth grade, they began to talk about how Jews did not have right to their own states. At that point my parents started to tell me that even the walls have ears.

It was in 2003 with the US intervention, that R.,[34] who was 10 years old at the time, tried to make sense of what was happening around him:

> I started to think I was different. My celebrations, clothes, food was not like theirs. I started to create symbols. I stopped when in 2005–2006 the civil war started, and we moved to the Nineveh area. I discovered there that I had a history

and my own language. The Arab-Israeli conflict 'helped me because if I am a nation I had to have my own language.' So, since I was not allowed to speak my own language, I started to invent one, a Christian not an Arabic one. At that time perhaps to fill in the hours I spent at home and not in school, I was also writing a novel 'The Dracula of the World'. I do not recall much of it except that the main character, a vampire, was actually Saddam. It is a pity I had to leave the copybook behind when I fled Dora with my family.

For R., as for many other Christians living in the capital, he was caught up in the fire during the war between the Sunnis and Shi'as. The disruption to their daily lives meant that a generation of children missed educational opportunities while the security situation deteriorated. Testimonies recall that many times children had to go through corpses left in the streets after an attack. Each day, going to school or to work became a dangerous gamble. Most Christians living in Baghdad dwelled in the neighbourhood of Dora, sharing their lives with Sabean Mandeans,[35] who traditionally worked as goldsmiths in the bazar. Also, Kurds from Sulaymaniyah lived along with Christians mainly from Nineveh plain who fled from Duhok in the 1970s during the Kurdish resistance. Dora was built by the British as an oil-refinery station and it hosted Assyrian levies in the British Army since the 1920s. For this reason, some areas were called Athuri, a modification in Arabic of the Assyrian Ashuri. Until 2003, it was politically controlled by a Sunni minority.

In the memory of Christians who left the capital, Dora was a place where they could enjoy relative peace. It was a middle-class neighbourhood and most of their inhabitants were merchants or worked for the refinery operating in the vicinity. After Al-Qaida started targeting people and facilities in this neighbourhood, very few observers recognized that Christians were a target, thereby ignoring the religious character of the conflict. Christians were seen as 'collaborators' and 'traitors' because they worked for foreign companies or because they were seen as supporting Western powers. In any case, many families were targeted, and people were kidnapped or killed while churches were destroyed. Entire Christian communities were torn apart. In September 2006, the *New York Times* published an article which discussed how the US military had finally provided security in the one of the 'bloodiest' mixed neighbourhoods of the city. Praising the work of the US military, the article reports that finally 'the odor of death on the streets has eased'.[36]

Thanks to the new security situation, the number of dead fell from 126 in July to 18 in August. Even the number of Sunni and Shi'a killings dropped from 73 in

July to 14 in August. The presence of the security forces could not deter the complete disintegration of the community. Houses left by those who fled the violence were occupied by complete strangers and those who dared to return after the situation became normalized could not tell friends from enemies. The result was that not even the army knew who moved into the neighbourhood and this compromised all the security measures put in place by the US military. After many years, it is evident that the mistrust of the Dora residents was justified and that the efforts to win over the Iraqi population remained part of a sterile rhetoric, impossible to implement on the ground and that this was only a truce between waves of renewed violence.

As reported by many witnesses, whole families started to be threatened and ransoms had to be paid for the release of kidnapped relatives. The violence led to the mass exodus of Christians from the area and, as denounced by some members of the clergy, on many occasions this caused a religious cleansing, with homes that had not yet been expropriated by force being increasingly legally signed over by family members of hostages in exchange for the release of their relatives. The situation was so critical that by 2007, entire Christian neighbourhoods were under threat.[37] With a rhetoric which anticipated ISIS in April of the same year, Al-Qaeda took over a mosque in Dora and from there ordered Christians 'to convert to Islam, pay a pool tax to stay or die.'[38] As a result, and without any help either from the Iraqi government or from the US Army, Dora was completely transformed to the point that as Mar Addai II, patriarch of the Ancient Church of the East, said to the Assyrian International News Agency (AINA), 'only the families that agree to give a daughter or sister in marriage to a Muslim can remain, which means that the entire nuclear family will progressively become Muslim'.[39] The Church authorities begged both the Iraqi and US forces to provide them with security but their appeals have been largely ignored.

Many of the Christians living in Baghdad never lost their link with their villages of origin. The Nineveh region became for them a place to flee to from the violence engulfing the capital. One particular family I met fled back to their original village of Batnaya, a few kilometres from Mosul. One of the family remembers that they arrived on 15 July 2006. That day, as every year, Batnaya was celebrating its patron saint, St Kriakos. Batnaya in 2006 was full of Christians coming from Baghdad and other places who had fled the violence and had begun to restore the old houses previously abandoned and the area started to be revived again. The population increased rapidly, and more building construction and services were needed. There was no hospital and for everything it was necessary to go to Mosul, which was not a safe area, or Duhok which was part of the Kurdish Region but still too far away. It was for this reason that, starting in 2006, the returnees to the Nineveh Plain resumed an old project in an independent Christian area where they could finally live in peace and profess their own religion without being persecuted. However, those who thought they had fled to a safer place found themselves caught up in the fight between the KRG and the Iraqi government for control of the area. In addition, the vicinity to Mosul affected relations between these traditional Christian villages and the neighbouring area, making the prospect of peace very fragile. Despite all this, many returnees remember the years between 2006 and 2010 as their 'stability years' before 'like during the Ottoman empire they came to take men to fight in their army and our women for themselves'.[40]

Mosul in the crossfire

After 2014, many people talked about the culture of coexistence prevailing in the Nineveh Plain and in particular in Mosul before ISIS's intervention. However, the testimonies of the survivors now in the diaspora coincides with reports released through the years by different NGOs monitoring the level of sectarian violence in the area. At the beginning of the twenty-first century, Mosul was very far from being the example of peaceful coexistence often mentioned after 2014. On the contrary, the second largest city in Iraq equalled Baghdad in its sectarian violence. It was by chance that attacks were carried out simultaneously in both cities after 2003. For the Christian community and for the other religious minorities sharing their destiny, the capture of Mosul by ISIS was the culmination of a persecution that had lasted more than ten years. Most of the media and historians have neglected to see a link between past and present when dealing with the unbelievable violence inflicted by ISIS.

Some of the testimonies gathered by the Schlomo Organization for Documentation[41] show that the threat began before 2014 with the advent of ISIS. One of the testimonies from Mosul, victim code D.S.N., says:

> We had [been] exposed to several abductions, threats, murder attempts, and the death of my father as a result of fear in 2013. I used to work in Grains Manufacturing Department in Mosul and as a goldsmith after work. After I have been threatened for many times, I moved my goldsmith's to Tillskoff and I left my job for thirty days. After that I was warned to be dismissed from my job, so I went back to my job. Later, my brother (N.S.N.), was a university

student, was abducted in 2013 and was released for 20,000 US dollars ransom after torturing him.

This happened before 18 July 2014, when:

> all the Christians in Mosul were threatened either to leave the city, be Muslims, tribute, or murder so we fled heading to Tillskof. In Alarabu Quarter, we had been robbed. They took our money, gold and our car, too. We fled again on August 6 as a result of ISIS terrorist Organization invasion in that area.

The violence inflicted by ISIS on the Christian community and other religious minorities suddenly plunged the area back into the seventh century and the Pact of Omar. According to the *Oxford Dictionary Online*, the Pact of Omar is a 'Treaty attributed to the second caliph, Umar ibn Khattab (d. 644), regulating the activities of non-Muslims, and it served as a model for contemporary revivalist groups seeking to control non-Muslim social and religious life.' One of these revivalist groups is definitely ISIS since 'in 2007, the Islamic State of Iraq, forerunner of ISIS, issued a series of ideological guidelines for jihad. Among them there was an unprecedented cancellation of traditional Islamic tolerance for "Christians"' and for the other "People of the Book".'[42] Al-Aliyani, quoted by Daniel Williams in his book, identifies in Christians, Jews and other similar sects such as the Sabean Mandeans, a common enemy with their Muslim religious and political enemies:

> We believe that the factions of the People of the Book, and those of their ilk such as the Sabeans and other are today, in the Islamic State a people of war not enjoying a status of protection ... If they desire security and safety, they must create a new pact with the Islamic State and accordance with the conditions of the Pact of Omar that they violated.[43]

But what did this pact provide for? And in which sense did Christians violate it? The Pact of Omar was a pact which defines the interaction between Muslims and non-Muslims living in the same territories. Non-Muslims were called *dhimmis* and were required to pay an extra tax, but usually they were unmolested. This pact was proposed by Christians and signed by Muslims on the conditions reported below. Christians accepted limitations to their freedom in the territories administrated by Muslims in exchange for protection. The letter sent to the Caliph began with the following words:

> In the name of God, the Merciful and Compassionate. This is a letter to the servant of God Umar [ibn al-Khattab], Commander of the Faithful, from the Christians of such-and-such a city. When you came against us, we asked you for safe-conduct (aman) for ourselves, our descendants, our property, and

the people of our community, and we undertook the following obligations toward you.[44]

Despite this, the request for protection seems to come from the Christians, the different Muslims caliphates that came to power in the years and centuries that followed have always read it as a blank cheque to persecute Christians and other religious minorities in order to establish the unquestionable predominance of Islam. Christians and every *dhimmi* were condemned to pay a tax to live in Muslim lands. David J. Wasserstein, in his book *Black Banners of ISIS: The Roots of the New Caliphate* (2017a), refers to it as a remnant from the medieval past, when Christians, conquered by Islam, looked for protection.

The pact itself does not reflect an actual, formal agreement. What it does do is represent attempts, centuries after the Islamic conquests, to attain two objectives. First, Muslims sought to establish the status of the Christians under Islam as settled at the moment of conquest. And second, they aimed to express that in ways that made sense in terms of how Islam existed in relation to other faiths at the time when the Pact was first set down in writing. The real history behind the text was forgotten or ignored.[45]

However, this almost forgotten pact has been revived by ISIS and with it the pretence of agreed terms of coexistence between Muslims and Christians which is vague and it does not imply that violence will not be used against them. Starting from the constant position of inferiority in which Christians were kept and ending with the repeated attacks to which they were subjected to, the idea of a special treatment of 'The People of the Book' should actually be revised. When Al-Aliyani refers to the Pact of Omar, he is actually referring to a piece of Islamic jurisprudence which appears to have been subscribed only by Muslims and hardly accepted by Christians. Wasserstein also states that:

> Yet its understanding of its relationship with Christians and Christianity is actually more complex. It reflects the movement's desire to take Islam back to the patterns of the seventh century. For ISIS history lives and is a model for the present. If tradition shows Christians and Jews subservient to Islam in the seventh century, then so they must be also today. That is why Mosul and Raqqa under IS rule both offer us versions of the medieval document—the only concessions to modernity in it are the addition of numbers to the clauses and a reference to electrically operated loudspeakers. Otherwise, the Pact of Umar lives on in the Islamic State.[46]

As has happened in other historical moments, a good example is the Armenian Genocide. Christians have always been seen as allies of Western powers and for this reason they had to be persecuted and eliminated. What is new in ISIS's approach is the identification of non-Muslim with Shi'as since they followed the path of the Jews and Christians in lying and infidelity. Christians and other minorities, together with Shi'as, have betrayed the agreement of submission to Muslims inherent in the Pact of Omar.

In the shadow of the Christian Cross

It was in mid-October when we finally arrived at the small Christian village of Teleskof. It was unusually hot and sunny for the season. It might not sound very familiar to Christians living in the West, but this small Christian outpost in the Nineveh Plain, together with Alqosh, Bartalla, Baqosfa, Qaraqosh and Karamless, has become a symbol of Christian resistance and rebirth after the destruction caused by ISIS. Located just 30.5 kilometres north of Mosul, this village has become the focus of international aid due to the constant threat of attacks, a threat which now comes from the new deadly militia of Al-Hashd al-Shaabi. The village is announced from the road by the crosses that in any size and colour from the roof of each house seems to defy the enemy watching from a few miles away with the sole power of faith.

In October 2019, I had the opportunity to visit the Church of St George in Teleskof which had been hit by ISIS's mortars. The village remained under ISIS control for twenty days during 6–26 August 2014, when it was liberated by Peshmerga forces. Father Salar, the young priest in charge of Teleskof's parish since 2017, accompanied us to the building site. On our way, the signs of reconstruction were already evident: 'This is a youth hall,' he said, pointing at the cask of a new building still in construction. 'That is a playground for the children.' It is new, with a kids' slide and a swing still immobile, waiting for the first happy children. Around these two new buildings is the debris of the old church: 'That is the dome destroyed by the mortars. We are trying to restore it.'[47] However, the archives of the church have been destroyed, 'everything has been destroyed, but we want to open a museum in order to preserve what has been left.'[48] A few metres further down, a small metallic door opens onto the building site. A series of columns are still standing, indicating the original perimeter of the church. The architect and project manager came with us and immediately explained that everything in the church was destroyed, including the altar and apse. The roof had almost completely collapsed. A thick layer of debris prevented visitors from taking a picture of the collapsed rear of the church (Figure 2.2).

Figure 2.2 Courtyard of St George Church, Teleskof, October 2018. Photo by the author.

The reconstruction was also an opportunity to unearth the oldest strata of the church and to discover its original floor by making a hole at the base of one of the columns. Also, old inscriptions and graves were exposed thanks to the most recent destruction. 'We can rewrite the history of this church,' says Father Salar. 'This is our history, our faith. Christians here are ones who more than others in the world live deeply with their faith.'[49] In the courtyard of the church, an old confessional damaged by the mortars had stopped listening to confessions. Next to it, the improbable blue eyes of a destroyed statue of Jesus Christ stared at the rabble around it in dismay and disbelief.

A few hours later, a mass starts in St George's Church, recently restored thanks to a donation. The mass is preceded by vespers. The chants in Aramaic fill the church, establishing what looks like an unbreakable link between past and present. The exchange prayers among the congregation recalls centuries past, when the Church was at its beginning, here, in this part of the world, before spreading its faith to the West. In the meantime, faithful of all ages joined the rite. Among the congregation was a woman wearing a hijab, perhaps in an effort to build a bridge between communities. 'I stayed until the end, I wanted to.'[50]

After mass, the crosses, which earlier seem to defy an invisible enemy, are now glowing with colours in the dark from the roof of each house. One of the villagers must have read our surprise and indicated the tallest cross on a hill at the edge of the village. 'They just erected it,' said one of the villagers. The main street of the village had now come back to life. Shops were open, men were sitting talking in loud voices in the tea house close to the church. Families walked down the street buying groceries, entering and leaving shops. Some of them took the opportunity to talk to us in their broken English and tell us their stories. M. is a former Internally Displaced Person (IDP) who had fled the village when ISIS attacked it, and he was now back. He reopened his barber shop in which two of our activists were enjoying a full treatment. Words of hopes and fear. People here thought that ISIS would attack again as soon as they had the opportunity. This meant that all those crosses would fall again, that the church would have to be rebuilt again and that people would be displaced again. This could be a story of courage and endurance, but it could also be the last breath of life of a millenarian civilization, a threat exorcised, at least for the moment, by the existence of a safe haven for Christians, the ancient town of Ankawa on the outskirts of Erbil. The Christian community in Erbil has grown considerably due to the refugees from the territories occupied by ISIS. Their sudden arrival is still posing a huge burden on the Christian churches in Erbil. All the churches have been very active in providing food and shelter for all Christians; however, most of them are still living in refugee camps with little hope of going back to their villages, let alone to Mosul. Only a few families are now returning permanently to their places of origin. Funds for reconstruction are still scarce and security is still a deterrent to going back to the liberated territories.

Erbil 'Pinnacle of Towns'

The region surrounding the city of Erbil lies where the north-western edge of the Zagros Mountain range meets the Tigris and the Mesopotamian plains. This geographical position made Arbela, Erbil, one of the most important crossroads between the rich plains of Mesopotamia and the valleys of the mountains leading to today's Iran. After 2003, the fall of Saddam's regime and the creation of the Kurdish Regional Government made possible the implementation of international archaeological projects aimed at restoring, protecting and promoting the antiquity of city. In 2006, the Citadel of Erbil, heart of the Autonomous Region of Iraqi Kurdistan, was added to the UNESCO World Heritage List as a protected site. Archaeological field surveys revealed that the original settlement of the citadel can be traced back to the middle Neolithic period (5600–5000 BCE). Further archeological studies have revealed that it was only in the Chalcolithic period (4500–4200 BCE) that the pottery found in the citadel is comparable to that of Nineveh and Gawra. This made the archaeologists think that by that time, Erbil was probably one of the main urban centres in northern Mesopotamia.[51]

It was around 2300 BCE when an unknown messenger recorded on a cuneiform tablet the receipt of 5 silver shekels to pay for his journey to Irbilum. We do not know what was the reason for his travel nor the nature of the journey and to whom he had to deliver his message. However, these few words enshrine the entrance of Erbil in recorded history. It is possible that, already at this time, the city had become a very important crossroads between Mesopotamia and Asia. Its position and importance led to its capture by the Gutis, a barbaric population threatening the stability of Mesopotamia. 'In a single day he captured the pass of Urbilum at Mount Murnum and captured Nirishhuha, the governor of Urbilum.' This is the text of another cuneiform tablet, dated around 2200 BCE.[52]

This was just the beginning of a trend which saw Arbela increasing in importance and power and consequently as a target of looting and destruction. In 1975 BCE, King Amar-Sin, who belonged to the third Neo-Sumerian dynasty of Ur, looted the city. Amorite Shamshi-Adad I (1812–1780 BCE), after usurping the throne of Assyria, conquered the city of Erbil and its territory, leaving testimony of his endeavour in a stele AO 2666, now at the Louvre: 'I crossed the river Zab and captured all the fortified cities of the land of Urbel.'[53] But it was in the thirteenth century BCE, under the Assyrian Empire, that the city enjoyed what it was probably its apex. It is at this time that we get to know that the city hosted an important temple Egashankalamna, or 'The House of the Lord of the Earth', dedicated to the goddess Ishtar. There is no archaeological record of this temple, but a small votive bronze statue conserved at the Louvre Museum is scribed, Šamši-Bēl, dedicated to Ashur-dan I (1178–1133 BCE) King of Assyria. However, it must have been a very important centre of worship if Esarhaddon's cylinder (681–669 BCE) reports on some restoration work being carried out in it: 'He clothed Egashankalamma, the Temple of Ishtar of Arbail, his lady, with electrum and made it shine like the day. He had fashioned lions, lion headed anzubirds, bulls, naked heroes and griffins of silver and gold and set them up into the entrance of its gates.'[54] What is certain is that its role as a centre of worship favoured the ideology of the Assyrian kings and helped them to unify their territory under their political and religious power.

Erbil, 'pinnacle of towns', was also spared from defeat by the Assyrians by the Babylonians and their allies. The presence of the Temple of Išhtar is probably the main reason for its survival, together with its cosmopolitan character and for being an important commercial crossroad linking Mesopotamia with the Iranian Plateau, a position of prominence which was to last throughout the Persian Empire, established by Cyrus the Great (558–530). In his *Histories*, Heraclitus travels in the region of Arbela and Karka (Kirkuk), where:

> Now the nature of this road is as I shall show. All along it are the king's stages and exceeding good hostelries, and the whole of it passes through a country that is inhabited and safe [...] From Armenia the road enters the Matienian land, wherein are thirty-four stages, and a hundred and thirty-seven parasangs. Through this land flow four navigable rivers, that must needs be passed by ferries, first the Tigris, then a second and a third of the same name [the Great and the Lesser Zab], yet not the same stream nor flowing from the same source; for the first-mentioned of them flows from the Armenians and the second from the Matieni; and the fourth river is called Gyndes [Diyala], that Gyndes which Cyrus parted once into three hundred and sixty channels.[55]

The land visited by Herodotus had 'exceeding good hostelries' and was 'inhabited and safe' and part of an efficient system of communications put into place by the Persian Empire and which led from the Aegean Sea to Iran, 2,400 kilometres, connecting Susa, Kirkuk, Nineveh, Edessa, Hattusa and Sardis.[56] Erbil's prominence in the following centuries was recorded by other historians from antiquity such as Strabo (Geography, XI, 13.7) and Xenophon (Anabasis, IV, 1) until Alexander the Great's expedition to Asia (334–326 BCE). In 331, Alexander fought the last battle against Cyrus III at Gaugamela, about 60 kilometres north-west of the Citadel of Arbela.[57]

Alexander the Great's victory over the Persians inaugurated the Hellenistic period for the whole of this region and for Arbela as well, with the establishment of new relationships between East and West. Arbela became part of a wider zone called Adiabene. But what is important for Arbela and for this region is that through the sophisticated routes, the pride of the Persian Empire, inherited by the Macedonians a few centuries later, Arbela was drawn into the long wars between the two conflicting superpowers of the region: Rome and Parthia. Arbela and the citadel appear in the chronicles of the Roman Empire during the Sassanian period (224–651 CE). The dramatic event of the campaign of Caracalla in 216 CE saw the devastation of the Citadel in 216, described in a few words by Dio Cassius in his Roman History:

> After this Antoninus [Caracalla] made a campaign against the Parthians [...] So Antoninus now ravaged a large section of the country around Media by making a sudden incursion, sacked many fortresses, won over Arbela, dug open the royal tombs of the Parthians, and scattered the bones about.[58]

Despite all the dramatic events, thanks to its geographical position Arbela maintained its cosmopolitan and multi-ethnic character. Under the Roman Empire and later under Byzantium, this whole region had always been a place where frontiers vanished to leave space for merchants and travellers looking for ways to reach remote parts of the globe. Among them, it was also inevitable to find believers of different confessions, old and new, confronting old and new political powers. Old and new doctrines found a common ground of confronatation between them: Judaism, Zoroastrianism, Christianity, Manichaeism, all of them coexisted in not always a pacific way. Conversions from one religion to another were common. Already in the first century CE, the ruler of Adiabene, Izates II, vassal of the Parthian king, converted to the Jewish religion, gaining a place in ancient Jewish history. At the same time, we can see the firm presence of Zoroastrianism as the main obstacle to the inevitable expansion of Christianity in the region. The struggle between the two religions is wonderfully depicted in the *Legend of Mar Qardagh*, where Qardagh is appointed by the King to govern over Arbela and its surroundings, transforming from a traditional Persian hero to a defender of the Christian faith (Walker 2006). At the beginning of this legend, Qardagh entered his home in the city of Arbela and made a great festival for the pagan gods, honoured Magianism and gave gifts to the fire temple. After a few days, he began to build a fortress and house on a hill called Melqi. Within two years, he built and completed a strong fortress and beautiful house. At the foot of the hill, he built a fire temple at great expense and appointed magi to it for the service of the fire (ibid.).

This legend is just one of the many which rose to explain the passage from the old religion to the new one, Christianity. The stories show how leaders of West and East Syriac traditions encountered one another and their rulers from rival Christian and Zoroastrian traditions.[59] There is a long thread which links the history of the Church in Iraq with the birth of the Church of the East. All the denominations of the Church of the East, in their effort to distinguish themselves from the West, trace their origins directly to the Apostles and, in particular, to the missionary work of Saint Thomas who is believed to have converted local people to Christianity. Saint Thomas arrived in the East before Saint Peter went to Rome. This is something that local religious figures and parishioners told us with pride: 'We are the first Christians,' 'this is our homeland'. This sense of belonging was passed on from generation to generation through a missionary tradition which directly connects Thomas with Christ. The first apocryphal text is the *Acts of Thomas*,[60] which is the starting point of a missionary narrative that would accompany all the difficult phases of the Church of the East in its effort to defend itself from internal and external attacks. Divided into thirteen acts in which the Saint operates miracles and converts others to the true religion thanks to his vicinity to Jesus, his acts resemble the mandate Jesus gave to all of his Apostles in Acts 1.8. Saint Thomas is the first one to challenge the powerful and the heretics living in the East, causing the inevitable turmoil, war and death that comes with the conversion of pagans along his route to India and then in India itself. His deeds closely resemble his kinship with God. He operates miracles, baptizes new Christians, and challenges the institutional power by facing the wrath of the rulers. This point is very important for the future of the Syriac narrative because 'Christianity arrives in the Syrian Orient through the conversion of the royal household.'[61]

Legitimation of the new religion can come only from power. The anonymous author of the *Acts of Thomas* lives in a very unstable world. In the early third century, the Roman Empire was suffering from a major crisis along all its frontier. However, it was the Eastern frontier which challenged the power of Rome. The end of the Parthian Empire and the rise of the Sassanid Persians threatened the very stability of Roman rule. In 226 CE, Ardashir, an Iranian prince from Sassan, declared himself Shahanshah, 'King of Kings'. His intention was to restore the Persian Empire, expanding his power in the territories controlled by the Romans. His successor, Shapur, followed his father's plans. By the middle of the third century, the Sassanids had defeated three emperors and established themselves as a new, unbreakable power in the area. The collapse of the Roman Empire and its capillary administrative and legal apparatus caused a power void in the territories. To worsen things further, the Edict of Milan, an agreement between the two Roman emperors, Constantine for the West and Licinius for the East, concluded in Milan in 313, which established the religious tolerance of Christianity in the Roman Empire, had the effect of converting Christians and Christianity into an enemy of the Sassanids. This edict, promulgated in the middle of the Roman–Persian Wars, also granted Christians full legal rights and the restitution of their confiscated properties.

Ankawa: The largest Christian enclave in the Middle East

In August 2014, Erbil fell victim to another invasion. This time, it was not by a foreign army thirsty for conquests, but by a long trail of desperate men, women and children fleeing from ISIS's violence. They left their villages, their houses, their jobs, their churches, the lands that have been theirs for centuries (Figure 2.3). In Father Michaeel Najeeb's words, they were forced not only to: 'Abandonner un jardin, un arbre que l'on côtoie depuis l'enfance. Mais aussi l'odeur d'une rue, la couleur d'un portail, tout qui fait la vie d'un homme' (Najeeb).[62] The then Archbishop of Erbil, Bashar Warda, would later describe it as a 'biblical flood. First, you heard the rise of noise. Then the first few showed. And then, almost at once, the streets were filled, and it was like a sea, a sea of people washed up from the desert' (Rasche 2020).

This unprecedented number of IDPs suddenly filled the Christian enclave of Ankawa, where originally around 30,000 people lived with around 13,200 families for a total of around 70,000 refugees.[63] Overnight, the Chaldean Catholic Archdiocese of Erbil, together with the other leaders from the Syriac Catholic and Orthodox churches, became the only interlocutor of the KRG, which found itself in the unwelcome position of dealing with an unprecedented emergency without having the human and economic means to face it. When an agreement was finally reached, the KRG was to guarantee lands and basic security for the Christians, but everything else, including food, shelter, medical care, housing

Figure 2.3 Chaldean Catholic Cathedral of Saint Joseph (Mar Yousif) in Ankawa, Arbil. Source: Wikimedia Commons.

and education, was the responsibility of the Church.⁶⁴ This agreement had the power of transforming almost overnight a religious entity into a humanitarian organization expected to lead an extremely difficult refugee crisis. Archbishop Bashar Warda remembers those days in an interview in Erbil in April 2019.⁶⁵ In this interview, the Archbishop of Erbil revealed the extent of the tragedy and urgency suddenly unfolding in front of their eyes. He remembered that the first, most pressing need, was to provide food and shelter for those who came having lost everything they owned. It was clear almost from the beginning that this was not going to be a transitory situation. With ISIS in control of the territories, the IDPs' precarious situation was likely to last for months, if not years. Even if there was no time to think, concern for the future was always present in every action and decision made in those first days of emergency.

From the beginning, it was clear that providing food and shelter was not enough. Further action was needed in order to deal with the inevitable consequences of the trauma caused by this mass exodus. Archbishop Bashar Warda insisted on opening schools in the camps so that the children from Mosul and the Nineveh Plain could have some kind of sense of continuity in their lives. It was not the first time that the Archbishop of Erbil referred to education to heal tensions in the community. In May 2010, a convoy of twenty buses taking Christian students from towns and villages of the Nineveh Plain to Mosul to attend classes at the university was hit by bombs. Around 70 students were wounded, and one Iraqi lost his life (Sam 2010). In response to this deadly attack, Archbishop Bashar Warda founded Al-Hamdaniya University, located in Bakhdida/Qaraqosh so that students do not have to make the dangerous journey to Mosul. This university, inaugurated in 2014, currently hosts 60 per cent of non-Christian students, including Muslims, and Shabak among other minorities.⁶⁶ The foundation of the Catholic University in Erbil in 2016 also shows the commitment of the Church to invest in education in order to contribute to the much needed healing process of the Iraqi community, with an outreach programme which includes granting scholarships to Yezidi women.⁶⁷

From 2014, the Church found itself transformed into a humanitarian agency, without having the personnel and the knowledge to deal with such delicate and complex issues that were involved (Rasche 2020). However, despite the high number of Christians who left the country, it is focusing on being part of the solution and collaborating with other forces in the reconstruction efforts, using its knowledge and skills principally in the field of education, but also of health, creating jobs and opportunities for all. The establishment of schools and clinics, sectors in which Christians have the trust of the Muslim population, is a way to be involved in the construction of a new society. In Archbishop Bashar Warda's words: 'Survival is not a goal for me, you can survive everywhere. I do not want to present my community as a victim, because playing an effective role in the society will give us dignity.' And then, almost evoking the words of the refugee family interviewed a few days earlier in Alqosh, 'Never give up hope. Be part of hope. As long as we have life there is a new day to breath. We are people of hope, but this hope is not a wish, it's a responsibility, a call.'[68]

This same call to support the future of Christians and beyond, has led the Church to speak out, in front of the international community, of the need to recognize the violence perpetrated by the ISIS as genocide with the establishment of new organizations that would be tasked with documenting these atrocities. Schlomo Organization was established just after ISIS's intervention in Iraq. In 2014, all of a sudden, Ankawa, the Christian stronghold in Erbil, received thousands of IDPs fleeing from ISIS. Its original function was to document, through the gathering of interviews with the survivors in refugee camps, the atrocities they had suffered. For a long time, the territories conquered by ISIS were inaccessible and it was important to understand how much of the millennial Christian heritage had survived this umpteenth persecution against them. The first time I visited them in the headquarters in Ankawa, all their interviews were kept in very organized files, divided by town in a camper just outside a refugee camp on the outskirts of Ankawa. All efforts possible to compile the documents were made by volunteers who worked without any support from the government or other entities. However, almost immediately, the original purpose of the organization evolved towards a demand for justice and compensation for the abuses suffered which could only come about through the international recognition of genocide against Christians and other minorities who had been affected, in particular the Yezidis.

In this context, Schlomo was preparing all the useful documentation in order to demand justice and bring the perpetrators to the competent courts so as to provide reparation for the victims. This is a doubly difficult fight because, if on the one hand Iraqi law does not contemplate crimes of genocide, on the other hand Iraq has not signed the Rome Statute and therefore the international community cannot intervene as it did, for example, in Rwanda and the former Yugoslavia. However, since its establishment in 2016, Schlomo has managed to raise international awareness of the fate of the Christians in Iraq by sharing information and collaborating with local and international organizations, despite some of the activists saying that their impact on Iraqi society has been very weak and that it is still extremely difficult to carry out reconstruction projects in the Christian areas affected by ISIS. One of the other interviewees told me openly that now, when you enter Bartalla, the village she and her family come from, it is very difficult to see the flags of Hashd al-Shaabi militia flying on the roofs of their now occupied houses and places of worship. A situation which in most cases prevents Christians from returning to their ancestral lands.

Since those days of emergency, it was clear that the Church was not called only to care for its faithful. Among the Christian refugees there were also Yezidis and members of other minorities in need of food and shelter. They, too, had lost everything and, without an organized structure as the one the Church could provide, were left completely abandoned to themselves once they reached Erbil. Father Michaael Najeeb, Archbishop of Mosul, remembers those challenging days, in which he had to explain to Christians why it was important to welcome others. Remembering those days, he said: 'L'installation a été d'autant plus difficile que cet immeuble de réfugiés a vite pris l'allure d'une sorte d'arche de Noé. J'ai absolument tenu à faire un peu de place à plusieurs familles yézidies' (Najeeb 2017).[69] This is because, 'Ne pas aider quelques familles survivantes de ce massacre, c'était devenir le complice du mal' (ibid.).[70] Taking this step, Father Michaeel Najeeb built a bridge between the Christians and Yezidis, who now call him Baba Sheikh, from the higher authority of Yezidis. This tragedy seems to have acted as a catalyst for a renewed reciprocal recognition of the two communities since, as Baba Sheikh tells Father Michaeel Najeeb, 'Nous avons le même ennemi et nous portons tous les deux un habit blanc' (ibid.).[71]

Father Najeeb was living in Qaraqosh when the exodus caused by ISIS began. It was also thanks to him, and to his sensibility towards the Christian heritage of the Nineveh Plain that, along with human beings, he could save the invaluable manuscripts that ISIS had sworn to burn and that he had been digitizing for years. To avoid the disaster that had already happened in Palmyra and the destruction of the tomb of Jonas in Mosul, Father Najeeb entrusted centuries-old manuscripts to families fleeing the violence that once again struck the most sacred and ancient plain in the world. Saving these books from destruction is saving memory and heritage and with it the wisdom of those who had to face similar distressing circumstances. Among the historical memories, or destinies as he calls them, Father Najeeb was able to save one very important one from the end of the eighteenth century. It is the story of Monsignor Tappouni, who, realizing the imminent fall of the Ottoman Empire, in the wake of the massacres against Chaldeans and Syriac, travelled mainly to France, Great Britain and Germany in order to try and convince the European powers of the need to establish a

Syriac–Chaldean state in the north of Iraq. This idea, which at that time, if pursued, could have changed the course of events, and now resurfaces in many speeches by Christians who feel the need to protect themselves from external enemies by having the responsibility of administering their own territories.

Pope Francis: An unexpected visit

In 2019, in an outspoken effort to open an interfaith dialogue, Pope Francis and the Grand Imam of Al-Azhar, Ahmed el-Tayeb, signed a Document on Human Fraternity for World Peace and Living Together, during a global conference on the subject in Abu Dhabi. Besides deploring terrorism and supporting a 'Dialogue among believers means coming together in the vast space of spiritual, human and shared social values and, from here, transmitting the highest moral virtues that religions aim for. It also means avoiding unproductive discussions,'[72] the document also stressed the importance of a 'concept of *citizenship* based on the equality of rights and duties, under which all enjoy justice. It is therefore crucial to establish in our societies the concept of full citizenship and reject the discriminatory use of the term *minorities*, which engenders feelings of isolation and inferiority. Its misuse paves the way for hostility and discord; it undoes any successes and takes away the religious and civil rights of some citizens who are thus discriminated against.'[73]

When in March 2021, Pope Francis made his historic visit to Iraq, it was the first time that a pope had paid a visit to the country of the origin of Christianity. In the message prior to his visit, the Pope addressed the Iraqi people, saying that he was going as a pilgrim to bring a message of peace and coexistence. Each stop of his intense journey had been carefully planned and came after the Iraqi president, Barham Salih, visited the Vatican on 25 January 2020 with the purpose of discussing the Pope's agenda for his visit to Iraq. Pope Francis was scheduled to visit Baghdad, from where the Christian community was uprooted well before the advent of ISIS, and then continue to Ur, Najaf, Mosul, Qaraqosh and Erbil. Every stage of his journey fulfilled his wish to reach all the communities, and to advocate for peace and communal understanding. Vatican News and many other media broadcast this event live, while the Iraqi government declared 6 March, as National Day of Tolerance and Coexistence, the day of the Pope's visit to Ur and of his encounter with Grand Ayatollah Ali al-Sistani, spiritual leader of most of the world's Shi'a Muslims, including Iraqi Shi'a, who make up 60 per cent of the population. According to some, the unlikely encounter between these two men, had the immediate effect of ceasing all hostilities by the Shi'a militias. Father Ghazwan, interviewed just a few days after the event, said that Pope Francis appreciated the humility in which al-Sistani lived and who agreed to leave his isolation to receive Pope Francis in his humble house, a privilege the Grand Ayatollah had for years refused to grant to any Iraqi politician because of the harm they have inflicted on the country. It is very difficult to estimate how influential al-Sistani is with the Shi'as in Iraq, who seem more prone to follow the dictates from Iran. The interpretation of the impact this encounter had on Christians or on the future of interfaith dialogue in the country is still very contradictory. However, the message of peace and reconciliation from the debris in Mosul, sent with the support of the local Muslim authorities and in front of an audience that was majority Muslim, conveys a meaning that goes beyond formalities, because all ethnicities and confessions are victims of ISIS's violence.

On 6 March 2021, protected by the millennia-old Ziggurat of Ur, Pope Francis met the representatives of all the religions present in Iraq. In the city indicated in Genesis 11.27–8 as the birthplace of the Jewish, Christian and Muslim patriarch Abraham, he re-established a common link between religion and the memory of a time where coexistence was the norm. Pope Francis' purpose was 'to rediscover the motives for coexistence among brothers, so as to rebuild a social fabric that goes beyond factions and ethnic groups and deliver a message to the Middle East and the whole world'.[74]

Despite the strong symbolism of these two visits, people from different faiths interviewed just after this apostolic journey stated that the most significant moments were not the ones broadcast by the press. Most Christians, remembering the edict with which ISIS forced them out of Mosul, experienced feelings of disbelief, joy and consolation in hearing the Pope's voice in the same city after so much suffering. Some of them until the last minute were very sceptical about this visit, which they expected the Pope to cancel because of the lack of security and the threat posed by the two missiles launched from the Nineveh Plain towards Erbil just a few days before. The image of the Pope visiting and then leading a prayer of suffrage for the victims of ISIS's violence among the debris of one of the most ancient cities in Iraq, struck many chords and reminded everyone of the futility and short-lived gains obtained from extreme violence. The fact that Pope Francis' words of peace and reconciliation resounded among those stones that testify to the pain of the women and children sold off by ISIS was only the first act in an extraordinary journey which had the effect of stimulating the presence not only of Christians, but also of other minorities living in the country. Father Amman, in his interview, wanted to stress the fact that most of the audience in Mosul were Muslims, as Muslims were the city's authorities and all the people in charge of his security. His visit to Qaraqosh, the historic Syriac where, 'Les bergers souvent musulmans fournissaient la laine et les familles chrétiennes la travaillaient' (Najeeb 2017),[75] had the purpose of celebrating its martyrs while finding the strength to endure, persevere and nourish a hope for change.

Beyond the formality of the rite, Pope Francis' message was subversive, because talking about peace is always revolutionary, especially amidst the recurring violence that has engulfed Iraq. This is the first Pope who chose the name Francis in honour of Saint Francis of Assisi, and his message refers to that of the Saint of Assisi, who, defying the violent and corrupt life of his times, adopted the greeting, 'May the Lord give you peace.'[76] As in the case of the humble monk who, during the fifth Crusade, crossed the enemy line to be received by Sultan Malik al-Kamil, Pope Francis approached the representatives of Islam and of all of the other religions as friends, appealing to the pacific tradition existing in Islam. Pope Francis followed the rule that Saint Francis wrote in 1221, just after returning from Damietta in Egypt, where he witnessed again the horrors of war. This new rule was introduced, that never received the imprimatur of Pope Honorius III and that was written when incomprehension, greed and violence determined Christian–Islamic relations, and was meant to be an orientation for the monks approaching Islam. It stated:

> The brothers who go can conduct themselves among them spiritually in two ways. One is to avoid quarrels or dispute and to be subject to every human creature for God's sake, so bearing witness to the fact that they are Christians. Another way is to proclaim the word of God openly, when they see that it is God's will, calling on the hearers to believe in God almighty, Father, Son and Holy Spirit, the creator of all, and in the Son, the Redeemer and Savior, that they may be baptized and become Christians.[77]

Be humble and have respect for one another is at the base of this revolutionary message. Not only Christians, but Muslims, too, have 'to be subject' to every creature, and they also have to respect the preaching of the Christian faith when they are ready to receive it, without resorting to violence. Only in this way can different communities live together. This is the legacy of the Beatitudes according to Matthew, 'Blessed are the peacemakers, for they shall be called sons and daughters of God' (5.9). If everyone, no matter what is their condition on earth, is a son or a daughter of God, it means that we, as Christians, have the duty to live in peace with them because every offence against them is directed at ourselves.

Despite this, the original message of peace has been undermined by Saint Francis' contemporaries, the seeds he planted regarding the possibility and the need of a peaceful dialogue with Islam fell on infertile ground. In 1965, the Second Vatican Council (1962–5) ushered in a new era in the relationship between the Catholic Church and the other confessions. With *Nostra Aetate* (*In Our Age*) proclaimed by Paul VI on 28 October 1965, the Catholic Church opened up a series of initiatives aimed at establishing long-lasting relationships with all religions that are 'found everywhere':

> try to counter the restlessness of the human heart, each in its own manner, by proposing 'ways,' comprising teachings, rules of life, and sacred rites. The Catholic Church rejects nothing that is true and holy in these religions. She regards with sincere reverence those ways of conduct and of life, those precepts and teachings which, though differing in many aspects from the ones she holds and sets forth, nonetheless often reflect a ray of that Truth which enlightens all men. Indeed, she proclaims, and ever must proclaim Christ 'the way, the truth, and the life' (John 14:6), in whom men may find the fullness of religious life, in whom God has reconciled all things to Himself.[78]

The overt reference to the Second Letter of Paul to the Corinthians and specifically to Chapter 5 and the Ministry of Reconciliation talks about the commitment of the Church to act as a bridge between the different ways of thinking and living the Truth, including Islam, is because:

> They adore the one God, living and subsisting in Himself; merciful and all-powerful, the Creator of heaven and earth, (5) who has spoken to men; they take pains to submit wholeheartedly to even His inscrutable decrees, just as Abraham, with whom the faith of Islam takes pleasure in linking itself, submitted to God. Though they do not acknowledge Jesus as God, they revere Him as a prophet. They also honor Mary, His virgin Mother; at times they even call on her with devotion. In addition, they await the day of judgment when God will render their deserts to all those who have been raised up from the dead. Finally, they value the moral life and worship God especially through prayer, almsgiving and fasting.
>
> Since in the course of centuries not a few quarrels and hostilities have arisen between Christians and Moslems, this sacred synod urges all to forget the past and to work sincerely for mutual understanding and to preserve as well as to promote together for the benefit of all mankind social justice and moral welfare, as well as peace and freedom.[79]

In order to avoid the demonization that always originates from each other's ignorance, the only way to bridge the gap is through personal relationships. This is what Pope Francis meant to do with his visit to Iraq, the first one of a pope in the land where all the most ancient Western religions were born.

The Church advocated by the Pope is a global one, in which all faiths can live and work together for the realization of peace and against any injustice. In *Hosh al-Bieaa* (Church Square) in Mosul, he said before his prayer:

> If God is the God of life – for so he is – then it is wrong for us to kill our brothers and sisters in his Name.
>
> If God is the God of peace – for so he is – then it is wrong for us to wage war in his Name.
>
> If God is the God of love – for so he is – then it is wrong for us to hate our brothers and sisters.
>
> Let us now join in praying for all the victims of war. May Almighty God grant them eternal life and unending peace, and welcome them into his fatherly embrace. Let us pray too for ourselves. May all of us – whatever our religious tradition – live in harmony and peace, conscious that in the eyes of God, we are all brothers and sisters.

Politics of divisions in the Christian community

The political spectrum of the Christian community is also not helping the Christian minority to stand up against the evident 'Kurdification' of their areas. It is as if the original fragmentation of the Church of the East has transferred to the political sphere. Evidence for this is the number of Christian or Assyrian political parties that represent the different visions that the community has of itself which, of course, have to be added to Christians who identify with the main Kurdish political parties, the KDP and PUK. People interviewed in Ankawa regarded this proliferation with increasing diffidence. Most of them considered these new parties as a vehicle to build personal political fortunes and accused their representatives of jeopardizing their cause. This is also true since most of these parties are actually financed by the main Kurdish parties such as the PDK and, for this reason, they are not independent. The persons interviewed did not have any problem in sharing the fact that these parties are considered by most of them as 'grocery stores' because they buy everything that is available to fill up their shelves. It is a humorous way to define them, but this shows how the divisions inside the community are actually fomented by the main parties. There are currently around ten different political parties, all of them representing the Christian community. Some of them are supported directly by the main political parties, the KDP and PUK, and therefore are hardly an independent voice.

This, of course, has consequences when the political process is ongoing both in Iraq and in the Kurdish Region. According to the Iraqi Constitution, Christians have the right to a quota as with other minorities. According to the 2018 Kurdish Constitution, 11 seats out of the 111 seats constituting the Kurdistan Parliament are reserved for Assyrian-Chaldeans, Turkmens and Armenians. Other minorities do not have the right to a quota and consequently do not have any participation in Parliament. In the run-up to the Kurdish elections, and since most of the minorities live within the borders of the Kurdish Region, the discussion about how to change this situation has been very passionate, with each community advocating for a quota due to the new demographic changes which altered the map of the region due to the intervention of ISIS. On 16 August 2018, the Open Think Tank (OTT) and the Konrad-Adenauer-Stiftung (KAS) Syria/Iraq Office held a conference in Erbil to discuss the inclusion of Turkmens, Arabs, Yezidis, Kakais, Shabaks, Zoroastrians, Sabis and Muslims in a new, revised quota system to change the current situation, in which 11 seats are reserved for Assyrian-Chaldeans, Turkmens and Armenians. Among the requests for the political recognition of all minorities, the participants advocated for a real representation, independent from the traditional parties, with the participation of representatives voted directly by the minorities themselves. The report of the meeting, published a few days later, states that:

> In conclusion, opinions about the quota system as the only chance for small minorities to be represented and be able to protect their rights were rather positive. However, the majority supported its reformation to achieve effective participation and to reflect the actual importance and societal contribution of minorities.[80]

This think tank comes after the Assyrian parties gathered in front of the Kurdish Parliament in order to protest against the interference of the main parties and to advocate for a separate vote and candidates to be chosen and elected only by Christian voters. It also came at a moment in which the components were more sensitive and more aware of their rights and of the danger of assuming a Kurdish identity that does not represent them. For this reason, the recognition of the components has to go through a revision of the way in which the KRG had dealt with them until now. The fact that most of the communities do not have access to a quota is in itself a deterrent for a peaceful and constructive coexistence, in particular after the conflict against ISIS. This need for being recognized independently on their actual number comes, first of all, from the sorrow and the horror experienced by the communities in the last conflict. Recognition means protection against further violence and engaging in an interfaith dialogue could help to restore the trust compromised with the advent of ISIS. It is very difficult to anticipate the outcome of these requests due to the volatility of the political situation in the country; however, it is evident that if the KRG wants to keep its territories, including the disputed ones, under its control, it cannot afford to ignore them. Furthermore, it cannot ignore the claims of the communities for an active participation both in the legislative and in the executive power, in particular in the Council of Ministers. During the same meeting, in order to achieve this goal, some of the participants suggested that the elections of minorities should be 'separately regulated' and 'led to some recommendations made to the parliament, including special registration, special ballot stations or ballot papers for minority voters, as well as a separate election day'.[81] In a perverse repetition of Saddam Hussein's Citizenship Law of 1978, it looks as though, until now, security was guaranteed to most of the minorities by offering them the option of being either Arab or Kurdish. Instead, what all of them are increasingly asking for is to be citizens of a secular country as the only way towards peace and equality.

3

Survival

Yezidis and the power of testimony

Starting from August 2014, an until then virtually unknown religious group called the Yezidis gained international fame. Suddenly, the West woke up to find out that words such as massacres, sexual enslavement, slave trade and mass graves were as real as the images that the media around the world broadcast about the Yezidis. In addition, the perpetrators, ISIS, itself engaged in a public display of violence through the social media which, on an initial superficial analysis, seemed to make efforts to prove the charges against them futile. However, very few in the West knew about the Yezidis and that they were a small religious group whose origins were not clear, that their knowledge has been transmitted mainly orally and that its membership to the group can only be transmitted by birth. Neither was the West aware that they had been the object of fierce persecution because they were considered 'devil worshippers' both by Christians and Muslims because of their devotion to the Peacock Angel Tasûsî Melek, considered the mediator between God and the Yezidi people.[1] The world was also ignorant of the fact that their social organization was very strict, and they were divided into endogamous religious castes: Sheikhs, Pîrs and Murîds (Açikyildiz 2014; see Figure 3.1).

Women and children, but first of all women, were sold on the market. Each price corresponding to each type of good. A virgin was obviously more expensive. When a woman had been married and remarried various times, her value could drop considerably, it could be as low as US$50. In this way, everyone could access the war booty. This was another term we often heard in those months: 'war booty'.

It was in October 2018 when we interviewed two sisters, who asked for anonymity, who had just returned from their captivity in the hands of ISIS. We met in the Yezidi city of Ba'adrie, whose name of Syriac origins means 'The Place of Help, or Refuge'. Both of them had been kidnapped at the same time when

Figure 3.1 Celebrating the Yezidi New Year on 18 April 2017, Lalish. Source: Wikimedia Commons.

they were very young. When they were released after the payment of a ransom, they did not recognize each other. At the time of the interview, their mother was still in captivity. When we reached the house, their father and other members of the family greeted us. He was crying. The girls were waiting for us in a big room, heated by a gasoline stove. Their father and other members of the family did not join us. It was a very different interview from the one with Jawaher and her son. Jawaher and her son screamed their tragedy and their cries contrasted with the painful silence of these two young sisters. The interview did not last a long time. The elder sister told us how she was abducted while on her way home. She said that she did not recognize her sister when she was finally rescued. All this was said in an almost imperceptible tone of voice, as if wanting to retract the words immediately after having said them. The younger sister did not say a word. Any attempt to get them to talk seemed like a violent intrusion into their lives.

The intervention of ISIS and the tragic destiny of this pacific population hit by ISIS violence, sparked a huge media coverage which lasted for some time. They explained to us who the Yezidis are and why they were targeted so cruelly. All the political and social causes of the formation of ISIS were studied and published in the press as well as in academic journals and books. The ISIS attacks on the Yezidis had the effect of attracting the attention to this community. What is different in the case of the Yezidis' experience is not only the level of violence they suffered, but the fact that this violence gave rise to the publication of testimonies which constitute a sort of counter-information, an alternative view of events that until now has been the exclusive prerogative of the media and the perpetrators.

Alessandro Portelli's, *The Order has Been Carried Out* (2003), gathers testimonies of the massacre of the Fosse Ardeatine in which 335 men were executed in Rome by the German SS in 1944 as retaliation for an insurgent attack on German soldiers, killing 33. The interesting part of this investigation lies in the exposure through testimonies of the individual histories which provide the background to this event. Without this effort to understand the lives of those involved, the official narrative provided by the Germans and supported then by the Catholic Church that assigned the responsibility of these deaths to the partisans would have never been questioned. Portelli talks about the importance of oral testimonies: 'Oral sources are never anonymous or impersonal, as written documents may often be. The tale and the memory may include materials shared with others, but the rememberer and the teller are always individual persons who take on the task of remembering and the responsibility of telling' (2003: 14). In the case of the Yezidis as well, personal testimonies are an integral and important part of the story. The individual, with his/her memory and the emotions inevitably attached to it, provides us with a side of the story that enriches and complements the official one which is necessarily anonymous.

Giving a name to violence creates a strict bond between the researcher, the reader and the general public. This bond can become very strong because an individual testimony refers specifically to places and people who are close to us. In addition, a testimony repeated many times, even if from different perspectives, can make us reflect on the individual behaviours of victims, perpetrators and bystanders. Where would I be in a similar situation? What would I do? Would I survive? What would be my life after this? Testimonies have the power to create an empathy between the victims and whoever is listening in a way that official history cannot offer. The purpose of oral history is not to establish a correct chronology of the events. All the testimonies reported here, from the two young girls interviewed in Ba'adrie to the most famous ones such as Nadia Murad's, provide a piece of truth that cannot be ignored. Talking about Holocaust survivors, but applicable to all the victims of mass violence and genocide, Geoffrey Greenspan says that they are in a cruel condition that forces them to feel torn apart in two different worlds, 'before' and 'after'. It is only with the process of telling that they integrate their two worlds. This process is hardly linear and survivors never achieve a total integration into everyday life, no matter if they seem to have found a new identity in another social and cultural context.[2]

Portelli's approach to oral history in addition has another innovative position. Talking about the massacre of the Fosse Ardeatine, he says that oral testimonies also have the power to move the focus of attention from the specific time and space when the event took place and link it to events that preceded and followed it. Events do not just have a beginning and an end for the individuals who experience them. They are part of a wider existential thread that has a beginning before the fact and an inevitable continuity after the story is told. This thread is not linear, it is full of knots that have to be untied through an exorcism to avoid its tragic repetition.

The background to the last, tragic event in 2014, was the seventy-two previous genocides of which the Yezidis were victims. It is very difficult to establish the historical events of all these attacks, however. As well as the Christians, Kakais, Turkmen, Shabak and other minorities, the Yezidis have been subject to discrimination, forced deportation and killings. Historians such as Kreyenbroek[3] and Birgül Açikyildiz[4] studying this particular group have discovered, already in the thirteenth century the Yezidis were present in a vast area, between Sulaymaniyah to the far east and Antiochia to the far west. In addition, they occupied the area between Diyarbakyr and Siirt while Sinjar was already considered their stronghold. In *The Other Kurds*, Nelida Fuccaro (1999) points out that Yezidism also became the official religion of the semi-independent principality of Jazira.[5] Their influence was obviously opposed by the Muslim rulers of the region, who considered them apostates and in the fifteenth-century pogroms forced on them conversions to Islam, which became a very common threat in the relationship between the two religions. It was in 1414 that a coalition of forces was organized against the Yezidis and that Sheikhan, the very centre of their power, was attacked. From the sixteenth century onward, the territorial power of the Yezidis waned, and their destiny was tied to the struggle for power between the Persian and the Ottoman empires competing for the same territories that once belonged to them. The conquest of Diyarbakir and Mosul by the Savafids, for example, meant the beginning of persecutions that involved the arrest and killings of Kurdish chieftains among those Yezidis.[6]

It is not surprising, though, that the Yezidis' memory of these events is still embedded in their songs, granting the possibility to historically record at least the most recent ones, thereby establishing a possible chronology. In 1832, the

Kurdish chieftain of Rowanduz destroyed several villages, killing many Yezidis. Only five years later, in 1837, in retaliation for the booty taken by Yezidis, the Ottoman governor of Diyarbakir surrounded Sinjar and after three months forced the Yezidis to surrender. He kidnapped a number of Yezidi women and sold them on the slave market in Mardin, setting a disturbing precedent.[7] Another massacre took place in 1892, after the members of a Yezidi delegation in Mosul were called to convert to Islam. Those who refused were beaten while the rest, including the prince, were forced to pronounce the Mohammedan profession of faith. On that occasion, the attack against the community was particularly cruel. Many villages were destroyed, and the Ottomans could boast that they had pillaged the main temple of the Yezidis, Lalish (Guest 1993 and Galbraith 2007).[8] In the twentieth century, the history of the Yezidis continues to parallel the history of the Kurds, the ethnic group to which the Yezidis belong. The Sykes-Picot Agreement and the arbitrary creation of Iraq in 1921, the Arabization campaigns and the genocides committed by the Ba'ath Party and later by Saddam Hussein's regime in particular during the 1980s against the Kurds, have also badly impacted on the Yezidi population.

Women victims of the past, protagonists of change

The absence of a durable peace has always prevented the victims and the whole country to come to terms with the events that destroyed the fabric of its society. Nadia Murad in, *The Last Girl* (2017), and Badeeah Hassan Ahmed in, *A Cave in the Cloud* (2019), talk about the simple life they were leading prior to their kidnapping. However, neither of them can avoid remembering how the fear of persecution was always with them. There is always an uneasiness in their words, a sense of non-belonging that can only derive from a condition of disadvantage lived for generations. Young people were not given the chance to forget the past because even if 'Kocho was a young village, full of children. There were few people living there who were old enough to have witnessed firmans firsthand, and a lot of us lived thinking those days were in the past, that the world was too modern and too civilized to be the kind of place where an entire group could be killed just because of their religion' (Murad 2017: 29). However, by Nadia's admission, the tales handed down from generation to generation were all stories of tragedy. As seen above, official history tells us that even before ISIS, the Yezidi community was the target of various deadly attacks by Iraqi military forces. Nevertheless, if we follow Portelli's ideas about oral history, Nadia's testimony has the same value of macro-history. Before being a tale of unbelievable atrocities, Nadia's is one of disappointment and betrayal. Disappointment because the Iraqi government and the KRG were not able to defend them and abandoned the Yezidis to ISIS. Betrayal because, together with the whole of the Yezidi community, she was denied their fundamental rights also guaranteed by the 2005 Iraqi Constitution, to belong to the Yezidis' traditional lands and to lead the peaceful lives they were entitled to. Instead, they had to witness the destruction of all the religious, social and human values on which their community was based.

ISIS carried out what Daniel Feierstein would call a genocide as a social-engineering project, with the breakdown of old norms and hierarchies while creating new ones in every aspect of life and for every member of a given society.[9] Feierstein was talking about the plans carried out by the Nazis during the Second World War and by the Military Junta in Argentina. However, the comparison is legitimated by the fact that, as for ISIS, the Nazis and the military in Argentina had the purpose of dismantling a cultural and social fabric that they considered harmful and therefore had to be destroyed, dismembering families by separating the children from their parents at the birth to give them into adoption to families faithful to the regime. In both cases, the goal was the destruction of family ties, together with the memories and the tradition they hold.

History teaches us that these strategies of destruction have the opposite effect. In the case of the Nazis, they triggered a self-consciousness of what being Jewish meant, even in those who admitted to not being aware of their being Jewish. On the other hand, the discovery of the serious breaches of human rights perpetrated against the 'communist enemies' during the dictatorship of the military Junta in Argentina sparked a renewed consciousness among the citizens of the need to uncover the truth through the creation of a strong civil society net. It is this renewed self-awareness that gives individuals the opportunity to retell the history of their own community through their own individual experiences. In the case of the testimonies of some Yezidi women, this amounts to a recognition of their Yezidi identity. Badeeah Hassan Ahmed remembers that just before she left her house in Kocho towards what they believed was safety:

> with her bony, arthritic hands, Adlan untied her apron. Just outside the living room hung a small package wrapped in white cloth made from trees found at Lalish. This package was what we called the Berat. Inside the cloth was soil that had been collected at the foot of the Shikefa Berata, or the Cave of Berat. The Shikefa Berata, we Yazidi believe, is from another planet. The cave is only opened

once a year, when the energy inside has reached its peak. At this time, the earth in the cave is culled and placed in packages for each Yazidi family. The Berat is considered to have great healing properties.

Ahmed 2019: 29

In her memories, Nadia Murad is more explicit when she says in her book that she 'did not know a lot about my own religion', because 'only a small part of the Yezidi population are born into the religious castes, the sheikhs and the elders who teach all other Yezidis about religion' (2017: 27). It is only after ISIS, though, that a deeper knowledge of the most important aspects of religion become crucial for shaping an identity and therefore for survival. Nadia Murad offers a universally comprehensible version of the basic beliefs of Yezidi religion:

> Yazidis believe that before God made man, he created seven divine beings, often called angels, who were manifestations of himself. After forming the universe from the pieces of a broken pear-like sphere, God sent his chief Angel, Tawusi Melek, to earth, where he took the form of a peacock and painted the world the bright colors of his feathers. The story goes on that on earth, Tawusi Melek sees Adam, the first man, whom God has made immortal and perfect, and the Angel challenges God's decision. If Adam is to reproduce, Tawusi Malek suggests, he can't be immortal, and he can't be perfect. He has to eat wheat, which God has forbidden him to do. God tells his Angel that the decision is his, putting the fate of the world in Tawusi Melek's hands. Adam eats wheat, is expelled from paradise, and the second generation of Yazidis are born into the world.

Ibid., 2017

All these details prepare the readers for the incontrovertible reality that this genocide was not perpetrated as it is widely believed on a population without any knowledge of the outside world. Between the lines, the message Nadia conveys is that schooling, their exposure to an international reality, together with the input they received from the community of Yezidis living abroad are all elements that give the image of an already changing community dealing with the violent product of a colonial and postcolonial history.

Women constitute the litmus test that is a key to reading and interpreting the progress of a country; a country advances and grows if women grow, and it retreats when women retreat. In this context, the concepts of purity and honour are fundamental because: 'Honour and respect are the result of the observance of social rules and the avoidance of Sherm. In Yezidi society in the homelands, a family honour is crucial to its social and economic survival' (Kreyenbroek 2009:

54). Central to honour is the chastity of family women who are forbidden to marry out in order to keep the purity of the blood of the community (Açikyildiz 2014). However, together with the tradition, the isolation and the lack of education, it is the activities and behaviours of a wide range of female intellectuals who in different times moved with ease in the territories of the sciences, the arts, culture in general, politics, economics and society as a whole. These women offered a reinterpretation of tradition that, exposing the violence and marginalization experienced by all women re-tied the threads of events which, through the dense weave of the most diverse experiences, led them to question patriarchal concepts such as the purity and virginity of women shared not only by closed and traditional communities such as the Yezidis, but also by a patriarchal system that wants to nullify them. For this reason, the following poem written by Nazik al-Malaika is a denunciation of the violence suffered by all women in Iraqi society:

To Wash their Shame Away

'Ah! Mamma!' the fateful cry pierced the air,
A pool of blood submerged the head, the ebony hair,
A final shiver from the corpse, lying inert,
'Ah! Mamma!' Only the executioner heard.
Tomorrow dawn will peep and roses will awake,
A call to youth, to dreams, will be heard at daybreak
But the green fields will answer,
The red poppies will say:
Yea! She is gone! To wash their shame away!
The executioner and his friends will meet again.
He'll say, wiping his knife:
'We've done away with shame!
We're again free and honest, our honor is restored!
Bring the cup, barman, fill it and take my gold! Call the perfumed, the languid, the sweet cabaret girl,
Her eyes are more precious to me
Than gold or pearl!'
    Fill the cup, O assassin,
    Be merry and be gay!
    Thy victim's blood will surely wash
    Thy shame away!
O women of our quarter! O maidens far or near,
Tell your lords, tell your men to

Be good cheer
With the tears of our eyes we'll
Knead the bread we eat,
We shall cut off our locks and skin
Our hands and feet,
So their clothes may remain pure,
Shining and white.
No smile, no laugh, no sign, no look
To left or right,
And tomorrow who knows? How can we ever guess
How many of us will be thrown in some wilderness,
   To wash their shame away![10]

Nazik al-Malaika (1913–2007) was a well-known Iraqi poetess, famous for breaking away from the European models of poetry of Byron and Shelley, to return to the vast tradition of Arabic poetry (Rubin 2007). This poem is also the result of an epic effort made by Iraqi women to free themselves from a sort of slavery imposed by men and never questioned by any structure of power ruling in the country. In 1921, British power in the country, established through the Sykes-Picot Agreement, was based on three main pillars: a British-backed Arab monarchy, a treaty to legitimate their presence in the country, and a constitution that even if aspiring to democratic principles actually gave space to 'religious, sectarian, geographical and class gender-based divisions and exclusions' (Efrati 2015). All this was sanctioned by the introduction of the Tribal Criminal and Civil Disputes Regulations (TCCDR), with which British authorities sacrificed the development of a unified civil society on the altar of safety, security and control of the country. This Customary Law had a very detrimental effect on how gender issues were dealt with by the succeeding governments. Decentralizing the judicial power into the hands of local sheiks and tribal leaders definitely helped the British to maintain their idea of law and order in a country and territory that was very difficult to control without a constant and expensive military presence, in particular after the tragedy of the First World War.

The result, from a gender point of view, was that tribal customs which provided for the exchange of women to settle tribal territorial conflicts, laws regarding honour killing, rights to children's custody, were de facto encouraged. The strengthening of these tribal customs under British rule could not go unnoticed. In 1927, the political officer, Stuart Edwin Hedgcock, and his wife, Monica Grace, under the joint pseudonym of Fulanain, published with Chatton

& Windus a book entitled, *Haji Rikkan: Arab Marsh*, in which they denounced the enslavement of women in a society which considered women only as property to be exchanged and completely subjected to the will of men. Set in the Arab Marshes, this is a very personal account, in the form of a novel, of life in the marshes at that time. The book saw different editions through the years. Along with the difficult life led by the protagonist, Haji Rikkan, and his family, the book exposes the violence and loneliness experienced by women because, 'Not even the humblest Arab of the marsh would deign to eat with his wife. "We sleep in the same bed as our womenfolk," said the Haji once, "but eat with them? No, that were too great a disgrace".'[11] Hedgcock and Grace belonged to that minority of British officials and common women citizens who were very aware of the real situation of women in the countryside where they were considered to be property by their guardians, who could dispose of them as they liked, including selling and buying them like animals. The custom of *mahar*, a sum of money or other property given by the husband to the wife as an obligation to marriage according to Islamic law, also made women's guardians force them to divorce their current husband so as to be sold off to another man in marriage. Having daughters was considered very profitable at the expense of women's freedom and well-being. For this reason, any attempt to break these rules by women or others could result in her death and the perpetrators were sure of their impunity, as Nazik al-Malaika suggests with her poem.

Hedgcock and Grace alias Fulanain also introduce the reader to a woman belonging to Haji Rikka's family. In a moment in which her brothers are whispering, calling her *majnuna*, crazy, she whispers him her story:

> So far, beyond the ordinary common places of greeting, she had said nothing; but now, as the brothers talked in low voices over their tea, the word *majnuna* reached my ears, and hers also.
>
> 'Effendim,' she said, 'in thy country if a great sorrow fills all a woman's thoughts and all her life, is she counted mad?'
>
> I had no answer ready, and she appeared to expect none, but stared into the glowing embers of the fires.
>
> 'He was a man!' she said, as if to herself. Then she turned to me with a swift question. 'Thou hast heard of him?'
>
> 'No,' I replied, not knowing of whom she spoke.
>
> 'Thou art but a youth,' she said, excusing my ignorance. 'Yet I remember, as though it had been last year, my first sight of him. That was the year of the great hailstorm, and he sat talking in my father's house. From behind the women's screen I looked at him: what strength, what mighty limbs! Ah, he

was good to look upon, bold of eye, and full-bearded. My heart loved him as I looked.

'Then one day his brother's daughter came to me. "Ruwaidhi desires thee, he desires thee," she whispered, and I feared to believe her. But the next day I passed him by the water's brink, and as I passed I heard him say low, "O beautiful, thou hast killed me!" And drawing my cloak over my face I hastened on.

'After that day we met, no matter how not once but several times. He wanted to take me to wife, and I was ready, but I feared to tell him. And then, as our custom is, I was bidden with another woman to his house; and I knew that he would watch, and if I ate nothing take the sigh that I desired him not. Trembling I stretched forth my hand to the food, and when I had eaten he kissed my mouth.'

Her voice died away, and I feared that I should not hear my story after all; but in a few moments she began to speak again.

Gold, gold! Who made gold? Allah, or the Evil One? When they came to ask for me in Ruwaidhi's name, my father wanted seventy golden liras for my price; for he was a pround man, and I was beautiful. How could they close with so high a price, when Ruwaidhi was penniless? For only a few months before he had given all he had to buy him a wife; but that before he saw me. All he could borrow and pledge they offered, and one said, 'For my sake, reduce the sum by ten liras,' and another 'For my sake abate yet another ten'; but my father refused them all, So returning to Ruwaidhi they said 'All thou didst offer we have offered, and more, yet her father refused, What is thy wish?'

'Return again,' said he, 'and whatsoever her father asks, accept that.' And they agreed upon seventy liras.[12]

In the years to come, despite many calls by officials favouring the transference of tribal criminal cases to the civil courts, the TCCDR remained in force for many decades, surviving the end of the British Mandate in Iraq, the end of the Second World War and the following British invasion of the country, 'Abd al-Karīm Qāsim's revolution and the end of the monarchy, the advent of the Ba'ath Party and Saddam Hussein's dark dictatorship. Nobody in all these decades questioned the legacy of this Custom Law which left women at the mercy of the tribes. Even enlightened observers like the Hedgcocks, despite his insistence on the inhumanity of this situation, questioned the opportunity of risking to compromise the control of the Iraqi countryside by challenging old, but 'working', tribal laws. Between the lines it can be uderstood that both husband and wife accepted that despite the violence, Arabs seem to have learned that the way in which they deal with women as property is very effective and that ensures 'future amity between the tribes hitherto at feud. More surely than the payment of money, this inter-marriage brings about a lasting and real reconciliation.'[13] This attitude is at the root of the perpetuation of the slave conditions of women in the country, but it is first of all the result of a colonial ideology handed down from Hegel, which considered non-Westerners as people not able to govern themselves according to Western principles. In addition, it is fair to notice that it was not until the Equal Franchise Act of 1928 that women over 21 were able to vote and women finally achieved the same voting rights as men, correcting the previous Representation of the People Act of 1918 which virtually excluded two-thirds of all women from voting. At the same time, many women all over Europe had to wait until after the end of the Second World War to gain citizens' rights.

We have to wait until the 1950s for the issue of the condition of women to enter a broader discussion on the legacy of colonialism. Women activists such as Naziha al-Dulaimi realized that the state abandoned women to their destiny by leaving the administration of justice in the hands of religious and tribal leaders. In the years to come, despite the insistence of an urban intellectual elite who tried to appeal for the transfer of these powers to civil courts instead of to Shari'a courts, the governing powers could not reverse the TCCDR for the same old reasons. An attempt to amend it was also left again in the hands of religious and tribal leaders and all calls for a modernization of society, which would have involved a change in gender relations, was always jeopardized by the strong class division. An Iraqi Women's Union was established in 1945 and the League of Defence of Women's Rights started to operate underground in 1952 and was legally recognized six years later. Until 1963, under the republic, this organization enjoyed support and reached '42,000 members, 53 branches, 87 literary centres, and 111 housework-training centres'.[14] Unfortunately, these achievements were short-lived and suffered a huge decline with the end of 'Abd al-Karīm Qāsim's power.

The period of strict nationalism under the Ba'ath regime and later protracted by Saddam Hussein did not do anything to improve women's lives. The idea of a patriarchal state embodied by the head of the state and sanctioned with blood by a militarized society, considered women to be just a means of reproduction for the sake of the new Arab state. All religious and ethnic minorities were oppressed, and the succeeding wars, the Iraq–Iran War (1980–8), the invasion of Kuwait (1990) and the 1991 First Gulf War, suffocated any possibility of dissent. The embargo that followed ended by corrupting the last vestiges of civil coexistence, already strongly compromised by the conflicts that preceded it. Women had to undergo a further wave of conservatism which further jeopardized their ability to affect and change society, their activism reduced to women's organizations such as the General Federation of Iraqi Women (GFIW), founded by the regime and in charge for overseeing the application of the new law regarding women's observance of Islamic rules which were advanced in the Faith Campaign initiated at the beginning of the 1990s by Saddam Hussein. This campaign coincided with the most difficult decade for Iraqis in general and for Iraqi women, in particular.

Shayma N.'s testimony comes together with those of other women who, in the decades before ISIS denounced, sometimes shouting, but more often whispering, their anger at the pain inflicted on them:

> I believe that, after the 1991 war, when the soldiers came back from the front, the regime needed women to go back to domestic life. It launched the Faith Campaign, instrumentalizing religion to get women back home. I think that it also represented the fall of a system of thinking, due to the loss of war and the general impoverishment. I think the regime was responsible for the rise of conservatism in society in the 1990's, because its political emptiness and its inability to provide anything for society. People became inclined to believe in the invisible. Religious practice is encouraging for people who live in despair. I think women came to the hijab for reasons that were, at the beginning, very practical and not really religious. It was difficult during the sanctions to look after our hair. It became more difficult to maintain a good hairstyle and nice clothing. It was a financial charge as well. It became more convenient to wear something over the head.[15]

Women in Iraq perceived the 2003 US-led invasion as a new opportunity to resume their fight for civil rights. Unfortunately, this was not to be because, in almost a century, the priority of invading forces masked behind the façade of bringing democracy and civilization, did not change. The TCCDR and with it its spirit was translated into the Transitional Administrative Law (TAL) 2004, introduced by the occupying forces after the end of the Iraq War of 2003. It came into effect on 28 June 2004 and enacted the official transfer of power from the Coalition Provisional Authority (a division of the United States Department of Defense) to a sovereign Iraqi government. When in 2003, George W. Bush intervened in Iraq, the complete shambles of American-led post-war Iraq and the distrust towards Iraqi people and culture very quickly transformed what was supposed to be an army of liberation into one of occupation. This process was extremely damaging not only for the Americans, but also, and more so, for all of the country.

The mantra of the administration which pursued a unified and democratic Iraq repeated on the occasion of the referendum for independence held in the Kurdish Region of Iraq on 25 September 2017. This preference for a united Iraq made even less sense then, when it was obvious that the central government in Baghdad was unable to make the already shaky idea of federalism work after the fall of Saddam's regime.[16] The war between the Shi'as and Sunnis, which caused so much bloodshed, heavily compromised any attempt at nation-building and dramatically reaffirmed the idea that Iraq was very far from having any sense of unity. The 2005 Constitution itself was based on the Transitional Authority Law imposed by the Americans and Paul Bremen and, as Peter Galbraith comments: 'There was no opportunity for public comment or input, an omission unheard of in modern constitution writing, and this angered many Iraqis.'[17] The birth of the 2005 Iraqi Constitution which should have paved the way to a new country, already contained all the contradictions that led to the war and to a new authoritarianism, of which the eight years of Prime Minister Nouri al-Maliki (2006–14) have been the authoritarian, inevitable consequence.[18]

Despite the constitution itself providing for 'robust protection against discrimination and guarantees equal treatment of all Iraqis irrespective of gender, race, ethnicity, colour, religion, creed belief or opinion, or economic or social status',[19] the insistence on obedience to Islamic law constitutes a serious obstacle to its implementation. In general, 'almost all these laws resulted in potential discrimination against minorities, because they were rooted in Islamic Shari'a principles that did not account for non-Muslim communities'.[20] This distinction put in danger the survival of non-Muslim communities themselves and, in case of war, fails to provide them with any kind of protection. In addition, on a basic level, the adherence to the Shari'a law does not allow non-Muslim citizens to identify with the culture of the country.

This was very clear during the debate that a new law proposed by Baghdad on 31 October 2017 sparked, and led to a huge controversy in Iraq and in the rest of the world. The Iraqi government proposed an amendment to the country's personal status law, which would allow men to marry 9-year-old girls. It was the second attempt at changing this law, which dates back to 1956. This draft law, withdrawn due to strong internal and external opposition, would have reverted the situation of women in the country. It provided for Muslim clerics to decide on marriage contracts, and would restrict the rights of women regarding the custody of children and inheritance. This law would in theory only have applied to Muslim Shi'as. However, since according to the constitution Shari'a Law applies to all Iraqi citizens, it would also have affected minority groups and would have caused even more divisions among them. This is also because of other amendments included in the bill which provided for the legalization of marital rape and the prohibition of Muslim men from marrying non-Muslims.[21]

This is only one of the latest examples of how the 2005 Constitution of the country fails to protect minorities and are the consequences of the inconsistencies present in the constitution itself. A constitution should not be written with a specific group in mind, on the contrary it should reflect the country's diversity and the similarities shared by all the religions practised in its territory. If this does not happen, there is the risk of hindering the free exercise of religion freedom.

The Kurdish Regional Government: Transition or change?[22]

Something would change in the country with the creation of a no-fly zone in 1991, which saved the Kurds from the widespread killings ordered by Saddam Hussein's regime. Until then, deeply intertwined factors such as nationalist and ethnic ideologies, patriarchal tribal norms and traditions, together with religious conservatism were the main obstacles that women had to overcome and refuse the violence their own society subjected them to (Alinia 2013). The creation of the autonomous region had the side effect of allowing within the limited borders of its territory the birth of agencies and NGOs who started to deal with individual rights. Going back to see the evolution of the impact of women's activism in the Kurdish Region, it was possible to see that the first decade after the establishment of the region's women's rights were not recognized. The first Kurdish parliament refused to repeal the law which criminalized honour killing. It is thanks to women's activism that almost ten years later both the PUK and the PDK, the main political parties in the Kurdish region, agreed to reform the 1969 Iraqi Penal Code and to criminalize honour killing (ibid.). This was an historic move because starting from this moment, 'the legal status of Kurdish women has improved and their opportunities for activism and participation in public and political life has greatly increased' (ibid.: 49). Alinia talks about the creation of shelters where women can hide and the development of reconciliation and negotiation tools to educate the families of the victims to overcome their mentality. However, despite these improvements, violence against women is still very much a way to solve problems within the family and the community, even though it has been criminalized and this acts as a deterrent.

From the testimonies gathered by Alinia, it is evident that women have become in general more conscious of their rights in a society 'going through a rapid, and at times violent transformation, in which "normal" and "taken for granted" gender roles are being questioned by many more young people' (2013: 107). Thanks to women's activism in 2007, the Kurdish Regional Government took the first step towards the annulment of child marriage by allowing families to cancel those marriages if they wanted to. Just a year later, in 2008, the same parliament ratified Law 15 and reformed Law 188 of the Iraqi Personal Status Law with the purpose of forbidding child and forced marriages (Begikhani 2010). Nadia and Badeeah are among those young women who are questioning their role within a traditional society whose survival and patriliny depends on the 'pureness' of its women and on the pride of its men to defend it. These ideas are so embedded in the society that one of the main challenges for women, as Frantz Fanon (1967) told us talking about black minorities, is that the process of seeking liberation from a condition of oppression starts from the recognition that the ideology of the oppressor dwells also in the mentality of the oppressed.

The violence perpetrated by ISIS had the effect of catapulting young Yezidi women into a nightmare which belonged to the past. Suddenly, the changing community in which these young girls grew up and that some of them probably thought of changing was forced to return to an image of itself which belonged to that time frozen in the past that their enemies wanted to recreate. ISIS intervened at a time when the community was already heading towards a series of changes, in particular in the traditional relationships between men and women inside and outside the family. Another very interesting nuance that can be grasped by reading all of these testimonies is the continuous insistence of women to no longer be seen as victims, but also and above all as beings able to earn their freedom in the worst conditions and, as in the case of Nadia's mother, the awareness of the injustice suffered in their relations with men. Talking about her birth at the beginning of chapter 2 in her book, Nadia says plainly that her mother 'loved me, but she didn't want to have me'. And then she goes on saying that her mother managed to buy pills for three months, trying to avoid another pregnancy. Nadia Murad goes on to explain the life of a Yezidi woman who was married when very young to a farmer:

> Like many Yazidis, whose mother tongue is Kurdish, she didn't speak much Arabic and could barely communicate with Arab villagers who came to town for weddings or as merchants. Even our religious stories were a mystery to her. But

she worked hard, taking on the many tasks that came with being a farmer's wife. It was not enough to give birth eleven times – each time, except for the dangerous labor with my twin brothers, Saoud and Massoud, at home – a Pregnant Yazidi woman was also expected to log firewood, plant crops, and drive tractors until the moment she went into labor and afterward to carry the baby with her while she worked.

Ibid., 2017

No society can overcome a tragedy like the one the Yezidis are still suffering from without going through dramatic changes. The world was not the same after the two World Wars. Societies had to rethink themselves, class, gender, generational relationships, were subject to huge pressures to break with the past. The end of the Second World War saw the birth of the idea of human rights, children's rights, women's rights. There was a new awareness of the rise of a new balance of power inside and outside the family sphere. The post-war meant an inevitable clash between the generations. In the case of Yezidi victims of violence, it is important to ask how their experience contributed to end the isolation of the community and transform their experience into a wider fight to raise awareness of women's rights around the world. By doing this, Yezidi women paved the way for a comparative approach with similar experiences in other genocides around the world.

In the turmoil of a genocide, women are frequent, but not always, collateral victims of violence, paying a heavy price for violence almost always devised and orchestrated by men.[23] Given the vulnerable position of dependence women find themselves in within patriarchal societies, they are invariably the victims when a society turns violent. In times of peace, women in society experience many levels of violent behaviour because of their gender, even in societies considered advanced in terms of recognition of women's rights. Taking this physical and verbal abuse against women into account is a clear indicator of how, in extreme situations such as war and genocide, violent predispositions can assume very dangerous levels with a very specific kind of gender-based violence.

In the case of ethnic cleansing and genocide, where a dominant group intends to remove or destroy another group in whole or in part, women are targeted because their reproductive abilities endanger an ideologically driven future society envisioned by the perpetrators, where the victim group does not reproduce. Attacking women can be seen as 'a deliberate and often official strategy of the perpetrators as a way of exterminating a culture and an ethnicity'

(Warren 2018).²⁴ Gender violence inflicted on women in the victim group is therefore not peripheral to the main events, but a central pillar of the ideological goal.

The Geneva Convention of 1949 and the Additional Protocols of 1977²⁵ stated rape and other forms of sexual violence are crimes against humanity. Yet, very rarely are they reported or even recognized as having occurred. The International Criminal Tribunal for Rwanda (ICTR) was 'the first ever international tribunal to deliver verdicts in relation to genocide, and the first to interpret the definition of genocide set forth in the 1948 Geneva Convention. It also is the first international tribunal to define rape in international criminal law and to recognize rape as a means of perpetrating genocide.'²⁶ In the wake of the ICTR's decision, the International Criminal Tribunal for the Former Yugoslavia (ICTY) charged seventy individuals with crimes of sexual violence, including sexual assault and rape, of which, as of early 2011, almost thirty of those tried have been convicted.²⁷

Shame and the fear of rejection from their own societies often leave many women without any psychological, familial or economic support. Bina D'Costa identifies that the *Birangona*, the Bangladeshi women and their babies who were victims of Pakistani soldiers, often faced insurmountable difficulties reintegrating into their own society in 1970s. The term *Birangona* means literally 'war heroine' and the intentions of the authorities in naming them as such was to recognize the sacrifice made by the women who suffered violence during the war. However, in so doing, the victims of rape were identified and categorized, and because of the cultural norms of the community, they were deemed to have brought shame on the entire society. This triggered a rejection of these women by their families because they were a stinging reminder to the state of how the culturally desirable norm of *purdah* (female seclusion) collapsed during a time of war, when the men were unable to defend their own women (D'Costa 2018). Not only were women refused by their own society, but also their children conceived through rape were abandoned by their families as they were perceived to be the children of the enemy. The Bangladeshi government responded to the issue of wartime pregnancy in a way in which it perceived to be legitimate per the norms of laws and religious culture, and so exercised its authority over women's bodies and their maternal role through abortion and forced adoption (ibid.).

In cases where rape has been used as a weapon of war, in Rwanda, in the former Yugoslavia, in Darfur and in other places, the reintegration of women victims of sexual violence is not uniform and is highly dependent on their community's culture and faith. In the communities where their return was more difficult, the main obstacle victims faced was the stigma associated with their situation. This cultural background forces silence and a lack of recognition, and has, in turn, been very detrimental to initiatives directed at recognizing sexual violence, and the eventual identification and trial of those responsible. On the contrary, the focus has been always more on concealing the wound from other people's eyes than on having it out in the open, seeking justice and healing for its victims. Impunity for the crime of rape was sanctioned by law in Italy until the 1970s. The law provided that a 'rehabilitating marriage' between the victim and the offender was enough for the rapist to avoid prosecution.[28] This law supported the custom, according to which a woman would lose her honour if she did not marry the man to whom she had lost her virginity.

The examples sketched out above happened in very different social and cultural contexts. The cases of the former Yugoslavia and of Bangladesh and Rwanda are very different, especially in the intentions of the perpetrators. In some cases, the perpetrators aimed at completely destroying the other group, in others the idea was to assimilate the opposing group into their own race or vision of how the future of the country should be. According to eyewitness testimonies, Pakistani soldiers would tell women that this way they would have had Pakistani children, giving no importance to whether this would mean mingling with their Bangladeshi ancestry and heritage. Similar sentiments were expressed in the former Yugoslavia, and, in Rwanda, the long-term consequences of sexual violence was infection with HIV and/or Tutsi women bearing Hutu children (D'Costa 2018).

For the religious and ethnic minorities sharing the same land as that occupied by ISIS, its attack on the Yezidi people was not a surprise. It was one of many invasions they have suffered in distant and recent memory. The question is in what ways the ISIS genocide against the Yezidi was different to previous genocides.[29] ISIS aspires 'to organize society along puritanical lines of seventh-century Arabia, a worldview that imposes the distant past on the present' (Fawaz 2016: 30). In order to fulfil its goal, 'ISIS sought to dismantle the diverse social fabric made up of Sunnis, Shias, Kurds, Yezidis and Christians that has developed and persevered since the ancient civilization of Mesopotamia, today's Iraq. Broadly, their wrath is directed at minorities whom they view as infidels without human rights' (ibid.).

It is in this context that their treatment of the Yezidis has to be interpreted and understood. It is ISIS's delusional desire of purification that feeds their extreme violence. What happened to the Yezidis is a dramatic example of how a small, unarmed community can be overwhelmed by such violence. Religion provides a very powerful message of cohesion and identity, a sense of belonging to a specific time in history. Mahmoud Hussein says that ISIS's members cannot stop being violent because they 'would have to accept explicitly the fact that the Revelation contains both timeless teachings and circumstantial prescriptions. In other words, they would have to question the dogma of Koranic imprescriptibility' (Hussein 2017).[30] This means that since the 'Koran is the Word of God, and God being infallible, all the verses of the Koran must necessarily have eternal and universal scope' (ibid.).

Religious or ideological extremism makes easy the dehumanization of the 'other', usually identified as the enemy in times of conflict. Both the Spanish Inquisition and the Holocaust were expressions of the will to set up an alternative, uniform world, in which there is no space for whoever dissents or is different.[31] Otherwise, it would be difficult to explain the horrors of the bloodshed of the Inquisition which lasted for centuries,[32] or the extermination of Jewish civilians carried out during the Second World War, especially when Germany was losing the war.[33] Later in the twentieth century, the cases of Rwanda and the Balkans can also teach us about the elements that can trigger a genocidal response in different societies.[34]

In the case of ISIS, the most disturbing element is the religious discourse underpinning their actions. The existence of a multifaith, multicultural society does not fit with the focus of a strict collective identity based on the particularistic interpretation of Islam professed by ISIS. ISIS thinks of its new conquered lands in exclusionary terms without conceding to any kind of dissent. The new Caliphate had to be an exact replica, frozen in time and space, of an idealized past when Islam was pure. In the case of ISIS, there are all the factors and variables of a genocidal intention: an absolute conviction of following God's will and the parallel intent of imposing the realization of a political and physical space where this new society can thrive and in which each member has to fulfil a specific role. ISIS wanted to re-establish a Sunni Caliphate which in its intentions had incorporated the rules and laws of seventh-century Arabia into the twenty-first century',[35] and in order to realize this it had to eliminate any obstacles in its path, including the decimation of populations resistant to their ultimate exclusive religious domination. The violence inflicted by ISIS, which included the murder of members the Yezidi population, as well as other acts defined by the Genocide Convention of 1948, is well documented by the United Nations and shows a detailed plan to make possible the absorption of Yezidi women and children into ISIS's new world (UN 2016). At the core of any attempt to obliterate the 'other' as an enemy group, irrespective of who the enemy is considered to be, violence is inevitably inflicted on women as a subgroup of that population (ibid.). ISIS aimed at the destruction of an inner world, an ancient one, whose paradigms are not acceptable in the new imagined world longed for by its members. In order to destroy any competing world, their strategy aimed at weakening the most vulnerable members of the group by kidnapping, deporting and killing their families and relatives. The absorption of women and children became a 'structural component' aimed at the total obliteration of the Yezidi race.

It is estimated that around 6,000 Yezidi women were sold to Muslim families or forcibly married after converting. Nadia Murad's memories of the events and the threats endured in captivity confirm this (2017). It is well documented that the kidnapping and deportation of Yezidi women was planned well in advance.[36] ISIS itself in its online propaganda made public its policies regarding the treatment of women as war booty (UN 2016; Murad 2017). Also, the number of women abducted reveal the extent of ISIS's willingness to destroy the community by compromising the Yezidis' long-standing tradition of honour and pureness through the violation of its women and children. ISIS was in need of recruiting more combatants. The promise of rape was a powerful recruiting tool for this purpose. The establishment of a department of war spoils (Fawaz 2016), in which the distribution and management of resources such as oil went hand in hand with the sharing of sex slaves is a stark indication that indiscriminate rape was at the core of ISIS's strategy. A strategy not directed exclusively to Yezidis constituted ISIS's prime target but shared with all religious minorities in Iraq.

Just after the fall of Mosul in 2014, from the pulpit of the now destroyed Al-Nuri Mosque, Abu Bakr al-Baghdadi gave Christians the following ultimatum: 'Leave, convert or die' (Najeeb 2017).[37] In reality, Christians and Yezidis shared a common destiny. ISIS's rage towards Yezidis has constituted only the first half of a drama that, without any external intervention, would have involved all the minorities trapped on the path of the reinstated Caliphate (Omtzigt and Ochab 2019).[38] Contrary to the narrative of a choice granted to Christians as 'People of the Book', ISIS in *Dabiq* no. 4, in an article entitled, 'Break the Cross', threatens them, stating: 'We will conquer your Rome, break your crosses, and enslave your women, by the permission of Allah, the Exalted. This is His promise to us; He is glorified and He does not fail in His promise. If we do not reach that time, then our children and grandchildren will reach it, and they will sell our sons as slaves at the slave market' (2019: 5).

Did ISIS manage to destroy the Yezidis? Strategies of survival in the Yezidi community

Targeting women through sexual violence and forcible removal is considered a premeditated act of genocide, clearly identified in Article II of the United Nations Genocide Convention of 1948, but equally important is to understand how the targeted groups react to this violence and are able to reverse the attempts to destroy their link with their religious and cultural past in order to ensure a future. As observed in the Bangladeshi case, deep patriarchal values can condition a community to marginalize women whose rape is perceived not as a personal trauma, but as a trauma for the whole community. They are marginalized because they bring 'shame' which needs to be forgotten before it can be forgiven.[39] Honour, purity and female chastity are fundamental to the Yezidi community. Due to the considerable number of women affected by sexual violence, after the violence concluded and some women returned to their communities, recovery and social reintegration became one of the most important goals.

In 2016, the German Federal state of Baden Württemberg inaugurated a special programme called 'Special Quota' (*Sonderkontingente*) Humanitarian Admissions Programme (HAP). The programme aimed at receiving 1,000 vulnerable women and children from northern Iraq to help them in their recovery and reintegration. The programme was 'a rare experiment in terms of a humanitarian admissions programme for a) targeting internally displaced persons (IDPs) rather than registered refugees and b) being administered on the local (federal) level rather than by the central German government' (McGee 2018: 87). The programme gave the opportunity to analyse conflict-related sexual violence and its associated traumas (ibid.). In addition, it offered the unique opportunity to envisage the fundamental changes in the Yezidi community caused by these tragic events. Dr Ilhan Kizilhan, a Yezidi transcultural psychologist based in Germany in September 2016, in an interview, talked about the fundamental changes already in place in the Yezidi community as a consequence of the enslavement of Yezidi women by ISIS. He said that:

> since August 2014, the Yezidis have become a different society than before the genocide. Their culture now needs changes and an acknowledgement of their new realities. In this context, Baba Sheikh, their spiritual head, has shown great courage by being the first to proclaim that the raped Yezidi women are still part of their community and are not to be discriminated against. They are still

allowed to marry Yezidi men and continue to be members of the Yezidi community of faith.

Omarkhali 2016: 152

Before they left for Germany, Baba Sheikh, the higher Yezidi religious authority, received the 1,000 women for a blessing in the Yezidis' main temple in Lalish. On this occasion, he formally welcomed all women into the community. He said:

> You are part of us and you are part of you, we share your pain. We are proud that you managed to escape and return to us despite the severe experiences you went through. You are courageous and strong women and I am proud to be here with you today. I bless you and wish you a good and blessed life in Germany. Be sure to behave well in Germany, to obey the laws and to continue living as Yezidi women.
>
> Omarkhali 2016: 152–3

Given the traditional patriarchal culture of the Yezidis, this was a very courageous statement as it recognized the end of the status quo within a society which had barely changed in the past few centuries. Baba Sheikh's blessing was an act of humanity which looked to the future. He confirmed the reintegration of Yezidi women kidnapped by ISIS in an official document. For some Yezidis, this means the extinction of the community because of the introduction of new, impure blood, for others this tragedy offered an opportunity for a fundamental change which could save it. It is probably too early now to estimate future developments, but the establishment of the reacceptance of the victims of sexual violence in Lalish was a first step towards survival. From a religious and psychological point of view, this blessing meant a lot for Yezidi women because it reversed the forced coercion of the sexual voice of ISIS and re-established the principles of honour and purity that had been lost in the tragedy. At the same time, this blessing for the whole community meant the readmission of their defiled womenfolk and with it their survival as a group despite the genocide.

After 2003 and the fall of Saddam Hussein, the freedom the communities experienced in the Kurdish Region in northern Iraq allowed them to develop more rapidly than the rest of Iraq. This translated into the formation of civil society through the establishment of local NGOs and non-profit organizations, which after the ISIS attacks developed the clear purpose of documenting the atrocities committed by ISIS, in part with the help of women who had survived.[40] In the beginning, their main function was to document what happened to the

Figure 3.2 View of Shrines of Sheikh Adi, Sheikh Hassan, and Sheikh Bakr at the Yezidi holy site of Lalish in Kurdistan Region. Source: Wikimedia Commons.

Figure 3.3 Yezidi women (18 April 2017) celebrating the start of the new year which begins the following day at Lalish. Source: Wikimedia Commons.

victims with the purpose of gathering evidence against the perpetrators. NGOs such as Yazda gave the Yezidis the opportunity to have their voices heard in the international arena. The Nobel Peace Prize granted to Nadia Murad in 2018 helped to globalize the recognition of the tragedy that had impacted Yezidi women, in particular. In her courageous speech of acceptance, Nadia Murad expressed her astonishment at the lack of intervention in defence of the approximately 3,000 Yezidis women and children still in captivity at that very moment, but she also placed the tragedy to the Yezidis in a wider international context, as she showed in her acceptance speech:

> Every day I hear tragic stories. Hundreds of thousands and even millions of children and women around the world are suffering from persecution and violence. Every day I hear the screams of children in Syria, Iraq and Yemen. Every day we see hundreds of women and children in Africa and other countries becoming murder projects and fuel for wars, without anyone moving in to help them or hold to account those who commit these crimes.[41]

Nadia Murad, in *The Last Girl* (2017), using women's language and with a wide exposure, changed the traditional idea of 'shame' to a humanitarian one based on the adoption of international law as a tool for the protection of all minorities. In this way, the drama lived out by Yezidi women during the ISIS's genocide is no longer only their trauma but is universalized as a tragedy experienced by all women who, around the world, have been victims of sexual violence. This new awareness of being part of a wider community had the consequences of snatching the Yezidi community from its secular isolation, to engage in an internal discussion about the role of women in Yezidi communities at home and in the diaspora, a discussion which involves a revision of who belongs and who does not belong to the community, and who can be excluded or reintegrated into it (ibid.).

In 2009, only five years before the tragedy, Philip G. Kreyenbroek published a book of interviews with Yezidi members of the German community. Kreyenbroek's research demonstrates how the subjects of honour and the opportunity to mingle with the hosting society turned into a discussion about the inequality with which men and women are treated in the community. In addition to a redefinition of the relationship between men and women, there is also the awareness that the caste system divided into Sheikhs, Pîrs and Murîd on which the community has survived until now, is not protecting it as probably might have been its original intentions, but is actually compromising its own survival.

In the 2009 Kreyenbroek interviews, both male and female interviewees believed that no changes were possible. However, despite the evidence documented in Kreyenbroek's interviews supporting the fact that the community was rejecting women who had been captured and forcibly married during their captivity with ISIS, data gathered by Jordan Greaser and published in 2018 disproved this assumption. The full set of participants in Greaser's study agreed with the need to accept the women who had been captured by ISIS and returned. This applied to women who were never impregnated as well as to those who had been impregnated but no longer had the child (Greaser 2018).[42]

On a local level, in Iraq, the experience of Yezidi women, in particular, had the effect of challenging the traditional isolation of the community with the inauguration of an interfaith dialogue and the creation of a civil society working towards a future of peaceful coexistence. Women's retelling of their past experiences with ISIS also helped trigger a discussion within the community about how to live the Yezidi faith outside of the traditional ethnic and cultural norms that had existed for centuries.

4

Unheard Muslim voices

The Sunnis

Among all the voices contained in this book, the ones belonging to the different Muslim communities cannot be silenced. Wars and persecution left their marks on every community and the level of arbitrariness that ideologies and extremism always carries with them very often ends up engulfing in its violence those who also thought they would be immune. In reality, and contrary to what the Western media tends to depict, the Muslim world is not a monolithic entity, but a very complex reality that is sometimes difficult to decipher. In Iraq, being Muslim in itself never saved individuals or communities from persecution. In search for a universal consensus for their cause, first the Ba'ath Party, later Saddam Hussein and most recently ISIS, killed, imprisoned and tortured whoever they perceived to be their potential enemy regardless of their ethnic, religious or political affiliations. This is the case of the different ethnic groups with a majority of Muslim adherents such as the Kurds, Shabak and Turkman. With the advent of ISIS, this became even more evident. Sunnis living in the areas occupied by ISIS were not spared the fanaticism and violence of this group. ISIS's violence lacerated their social fabric at a family and individual level with the result of creating divisions that would be very difficult to overcome in the future. Fathers against sons, brothers against brothers, these communities found themselves trapped in an unstoppable spiral of violence, in which they assumed simultaneously or in turn the role of perpetrators, victims and bystanders. This makes very difficult every attempt of a dialogue and reconciliation within them and with other communities.

The almost schizophrenic situation has another, very detrimental, effect on the relationship that the Muslims have on the perception that other communities have of them. Minority groups such as Christians, for example, consider themselves as the victims of the bloody war between the Shi'as and Sunnis. The destruction of the Christian churches in Baghdad as well as the persecution of

Christians and other minorities has reinforced the perception that Islam is the sole source of the country's instability. This awareness does not distinguish between Shi'as and Sunnis, but strengthens the idea that Islam is inherently violent because it is the only religion that preaches violence from its inception, denouncing in this way the absolutistic readings that ISIS does of the Quran. Mahmoud Hussein says that the difficulty of Muslim people in openly denouncing their refusal of ISIS's ideology comes from the fact that 'they would have to accept explicitly the fact that the Revelation contains both timeless teachings and circumstantial prescriptions. In other words, they would have to question the dogma of Koranic imprescriptibility.'[1] This means that since the 'Koran is the Word of God, and God being infallible, all the verses of the Koran must necessarily have eternal and universal scope,'[2] it becomes difficult for any Muslim to concede that some verses had a meaning only in seventh-century Arabia. It makes it difficult for most Muslims to condemn ISIS on religious grounds, even if most of them are against the horror unleashed by this extremist group.

From the point of view of the religious minorities' victims (Callimachi 2015) of the violence perpetrated by ISIS, this reticence in condemning ISIS and its ideology is a clear sign that Islam is synonymous with violence, discrimination, slavery and intolerance. It is also the origin of the deep mistrust they have towards all Muslims, even in the most favourable circumstances. ISIS has definitely compromised the relationship between the communities in the Kurdish Region which, in the last twenty years since the establishment of the Kurdish Regional Government in northern Iraq, has become a safe haven for all religious minorities. Many activists interviewed talked about the aggressive nature of Islam based on the Quran's verses which exalt war and intolerance towards the *kafirs*, infidels. The support that some Muslims granted to ISIS had the effect of strengthening this perception among minorities, thereby compromising intercommunal relations, even in the Kurdish Region where they enjoy more freedom.

Kurdish society remains a deeply religious one, in which Islam is practised by the majority of the population. In the KRG, alone, in the three governorates of Erbil, Sulemaniyah and Duhok, there are 5,537 mosques, while Mosul and Kirkuk, belonging to the disputed territories between the KRG and the central government in Bagdad, count around 3,000 mosques for a total of 10,000 imams. In this context, the religious intolerance preached and practised by ISIS found fertile ground in the areas it occupied as well as in some of the most extreme Muslim populations in the rest of both Iraq and the Kurdish Region. A renewed religious intolerance reflected in the recrudescence of hate speeches delivered by different imams in the mosques was also supported by some of the media.

This situation alarmed not only religious minorities which feel threatened by the possibility of renewed violent attacks against them, but also the most moderate sections of Islamic representatives who are working for the establishment of a more stable and peaceful society through a constructive inter-religious dialogue. The situation is so alarming that, in 2018, Kakai Chraw Organization for Documentation saw the need to organize a series of ad hoc workshops to educate imams in the fields of human rights, peace-building and coexistence. In particular, the project aimed at targeting the areas recently liberated by ISIS as well as the disputed territories, in the belief that this will contribute to the process of stabilization and peace-building in Iraq and in the Kurdistan Region. The workshops were to run in Erbil, Sulaymaniyah and Dohuk for all the imams operating in the KRG and in Shekhan and Kalak for the imams coming from Mosul and in Chamchamal and Taqtaq for those operating in Kirkuk.

By that time, the Islamic Forum, an organization based in the Kurdish Region and set up to link Islam with respect of human rights and for inter-religious dialogue, committed itself to providing already trained teachers to deliver these workshops, including experts in Shar'ia law providing a reading of Islam that would be different to that of the extremist interpretation offered by ISIS and other similar groups. The target was to reach all the 10,000 imams operating in those areas, with the help of 20 teachers who would run fifty-two week-long workshops with a maximum of 25 participants. Reaching out to the imams is a very courageous act of faith in the possibility of establishing trust among communities.

The tragedy of the Sunnis

Among the different voices that cry out to be heard are those coming from the Muslim communities living in Iraq. Most of them are ethno-religious minorities, divided between a conformity with the main groups in the battlefield, Sunnis and Shi'as and their regional allies, and their identification with their ethnic origin. The war between the Shi'as and Sunnis that dismembered the country between 2006 and 2009 has inevitably caused a divide in the Shabak and Turkman communities difficult to heal. The presence of both Shi'as and Sunnis in the two communities has destroyed their social fabric and the advent of ISIS further complicated the situation.

In October 2018, a visit to the refugee camp of Garmawa revealed that the violence did not only affect non-Muslims but also Sunni Muslims. The camp was situated in the Duhok Governorate, between Duhok and al-Shikhan, in the vicinity of a small village whose Christian faith is announced by the crosses on the roofs of the small houses. The person responsible for the camp had announced our visit and a few people gathered at the entrance. Children and some women were also present during the whole time while we asked questions to the men. All of them were from small villages around Mosul and told us about how their lives had been destroyed by ISIS. They felt abandoned by both the Iraqi and Kurdish governments as well as by the international community, which, through the United Nations Refugee Agency (UNHCR), opened these provisional camps for them without taking care of them. Trapped between competencies, these families are living on charities and on the meagre contribution from the UN, around US$20 per person per month. They claim that they do not receive any support neither from the Iraqi government because they are told that they can move to a camp close to Mosul where they can receive help from the Iraqi government, nor from the Kurdish government which tells them that the Mosul area is now safe and that they should move there since they are not responsible for their safety.

Their tales, until now virtually ignored by the press and researchers alike, are not different from those of the Christians. They talked about how their lives were good and they had everything in Mosul, of how they could live in peace with everybody until the situation started to deteriorate following the intervention by ISIS. The women remembered their previous lives as happy and plenty in comparison to the squalor of the camps and the uncertainty of their future.

This visit to the camp was an opportunity to understand how the intervention of ISIS and the violence to which the different groups were subjected started with the gradual tearing of the social fabric of the people living in Mosul and in the surrounding areas. The men and women we met in this camp were afraid to go back to their original villages. This is because, after the fall of Saddam Hussein in 2003, Sunnis have been 'imprisoned within a cycle of upheaval and violence'.[3] ISIS was able to exploit the vacuum of a Sunni identity and sense of belonging to the new Iraq. Sunnis, suddenly removed from power, saw themselves lacerated by different souls which could not be translated into a unifying political, religious or social idea. Transformed into pariah in the same country they governed, excluded from official posts by a Shi'a authoritarian government, it is not surprising that ISIS in its rapid conquest of mainly Sunni territories was able to recruit so many Iraqi Sunnis in its own ranks. This, however, caused fractions

Figure 4.1 Refugee children in Camp Garmawa near the city of Dohuk in Northern Iraq. Source: Getty Images, Ullstein Bild.

and incurable sectarianism within a community already disenfranchised from the new, US-made Iraq, in which Sunnis saw themselves forced to negotiate their loyalty either with Erbil or with Baghdad. Denying Sunnis the possibility to participate in the political, social and military post-war reconstruction was only one of the numerous mistakes committed by the Bush administration first, and then by the decision to withdraw the US troops from the country during Barak Obama's presidency. Failing to engage with Sunni sheikhs turned out to be a boomerang because, left without any interlocutor in 2014, the Sunnis were forced to choose between a hopeless present and the 'promising' future offered by ISIS. Some, many of them, chose the only movement that would allow them to regain possession of their own history, to rediscover their lost identity. In an article by David Ignatius published in the *Washington Post* in October 2014, during the first months of war, the journalist interviewed one of the Sunni sheikhs. After attributing Sunni collaboration with the Islamic State to the persecution of al-Maliki's government, Jalal al-Gaood said that the Sunni community has two options: 'Fight against ISIS and allow Iran and its militias to rule us or do the opposite. We chose ISIS for only one reason. ISIS only kills you. The Iraqi government kills you and rapes your women.'[4]

These words reveal a history of discrimination and violence but, at the same time, they suppose a unified reaction of the Sunni community towards a common enemy to justify support for ISIS shared by the whole community. In reality, ISIS was also an opportunity for internal revenge and unsolved disputes within the community itself and between different tribes. The choice al-Gaood talks about in this interview was not that of every Sunni. The intervention of ISIS had the effect of dividing the community even further between those who supported it and those who fled. During the liberation campaign, the Sunnis who fled the advance of ISIS had already nourished motives of revenge against those who stayed and who were identified as members of ISIS. The result was that tribal leaders were able to form new militias made up of Sunnis who had escaped from ISIS with the purpose of attacking and punishing those who supported it in an effort to claim back their houses and lands. Only violence, in the mind of these displaced people, could solve the rift opened up in the community. Or this was the opinion of Sheikh Nazhan Sakhar al-Lehibi, a Sunni Arab sheikh from the village of Hajj Ali talking about his tribal cousins who decided to support ISIS in a town near Mosul, 'because it will teach their wives, children, sons, and relatives'.[5] Four years have passed since the liberation of the areas previously occupied by ISIS. According to some analysts, traditional sectarianism in Iraq has been replaced by a less acrimonious environment, shared by all the main actors involved. Kirk H. Sowell offers a political analysis of Sunni politics between 2014 and 2020:

> While the dramatic reduction in sectarian conflict is welcome, the sectarian polarization of 2003–2014 has been replaced by a system in which posts are still allocated on an ethno-sectarian basis, and Sunni leaders are fully integrated members of a kleptocracy that lurches from crisis to crisis and has done little to actually develop Iraq.[6]

Politics does very little to explain the real situation on the ground. In reality, most Sunnis who did not take part in the atrocities committed by ISIS are now ostracized on a local level. The sheikhs of the tribes are the ones who have to deal with thousands of people like those in the Garmawa Camp, who are not able to go back to their lands. The people interviewed in Garmawa Camp lost everything, their homes, their businesses and every possibility to see their lives starting again. When asked how their lives were before ISIS, most of them replied that they had their houses and their businesses. One report summarizes the devastation to the Sunni community more succinctly: 'Most of the 5 million displaced persons in Iraq are Sunnis. And most of the tens of thousands of Iraqis who were killed, raped, or kidnapped by ISIS jihadists are Sunnis. Nearly every city left in ruins by the fight to expel ISIS – from Fallujah and Ramadi to Mosul – is predominantly Sunni.'[7]

Despite this, the people from Garmawa Camp as well as other thousands of Sunnis spread all over the world, are trapped in narratives which are not their own. For the Iraqi government, for the Kurdish Regional Government, and most importantly for all the minorities, in particular the Yezidis from Sinjar who were attacked and enslaved with the help of local Sunni tribes, being Sunni became synonymous with being complicit with ISIS. The consequence was that in the areas surrounding Mosul, once ISIS was declared defeated, reconstruction projects promoted by the Iraqi government failed to include them. Villages were not rebuilt, the lack of infrastructure and the impossibility of reinstating the industries thriving before ISIS, prevented Sunnis in refugee camps from going back to their cities and villages. And 'as a result, Mosul has been gripped by "reverse displacement," as up to twenty-five families per day leave the ruined city to head back to camps, its migration office said last year'.[8]

It is because of the persistence of their association with ISIS that Sunni voices have not been heard. Their voices showed the anguish of those who feel completely abandoned by the only interlocutors indicated to them by the international community, namely the Iraqi government and the Kurdish Regional Government. Even their current geographical location, within the Kurdish Region, seemed to play against them. According to the person responsible for the camp, since their villages have been liberated from ISIS and therefore considered safe, the Kurdish Regional Government, following the advice of the UN, invited them to leave this camp and to move into another one, close to their destroyed villages, out of the Kurdish Region. The families living in the Garmawa Camp preferred the life in limbo that they led in the camp, where they could access food and shelter to the uncertainty of a life back in their villages, with no home, no jobs and also with the lack of security.

Most of the children who surrounded us during our visit were either born in the camp or were spending most of their childhood there. They did not have any place to call home apart from those tents with the symbol of the UNHCR, which probably did not tell them much. They were not likely to develop a sense of belonging to that country called Iraq, on the contrary they are like loose cannons who will probably bring more disorder, war and violence in their desperate quest for recognition.

Shabak: From victims to persecutors

It is the etymology of their own name, Shabak, which determines their shifting religious and ethnic identity. Some suggest that this name comes from the traditional overlapping of this groups with others living in the same area. Shabak means 'mix' or 'overlapping'. Others think that this name comes from Persia and 'consists of two syllables: *Shah*, which means the king and *bek*, which means the lor or the glorified. Thus, it means the glorified king' (Sa'ad 2013: 156). Whatever the etymology, their survival as a distinct group is remarkable in an area, the Nineveh Plain and in particular in the area along the Mosul–Eski Kalar Road,[9] that they shared with Christians, Yezidis and Kakais. To add to the mix and to the various interpretations of their origins, the Shabak have a sacred book called *Buyruq* of *Kitâb al-Manâqib*, which means 'The Orders', written in Turkmen. This means that, as in the case of the Yezidis and the Kakais, only a few members of the group have access to their sacred book since their language is mainly Gorani Kurdish, while the 'Shabaki' vernacular language is spoken only in private. The fact that they have a sacred book has been one of the reasons for the Shabak to be considered different from the mainstream Shi'ism, to which around 70 per cent of them belong. In reality, these are not holy books but are 'merely religious poems and hymns read by Sufis on religious occasions' (2013: 161). The shifting of their religious identity drove them towards Shi'ism; however, in the 1990s, Michiel Leezenberg reported after carrying out fieldwork among the Sarlî, a community located in Eski Kalak close to Shabak villages, that some of them had embraced the Kakais' faith and beliefs:

> I quickly found out that these Sarlî were Ibrahimî Kaka'is, whose sayyid lived in nearby Erbil. When I asked whether there were any Shabak living among them, my Sarlî hosts said that they, and a number of others, were Shabak themselves.
> Leezenberg 2019

Their syncretism also includes elements found in Christianity such as confession. Their social structure has a defined hierarchy of Pīrs with a Baba at the top, which recalls the one we found in both the Kakais and Yezidis. The Shabak were born from the conflagration of the Ottoman Empire. The instability caused by this event and the need to find an equilibrium within the new state of things, led the Shabak tribes to convert to Shi'ism since the end of the First World War and at the time of the British Mandate. The Shi'as provided the Shabak with a new narrative, new heroes, a new identity. Arabic poetry was introduced to celebrate the heroic deeds of Husayn ibn 'Ali in the Battle of

Karbala. They promoted a sense of unification through the cult of their saints. All this was done without compromising either the tribal laws which still governed the tribes or their genealogy (Nakash 1994) – a process carried out with the blessing of the British authorities. The Shabak study and read the poetry written by Ismail I, who ruled Iran from 1501 to 1524 and who converted the country to Shi'a Islam with the establishment of the Safavid dynasty. Already in 1950, the Shabak made pilgrimages to the main Shi'a shrines in Kerbala and Najaf, a fact which confirms the conversion of most of them to Shi'ism (Leezenberg 2019).

Their religious syncretism, together with their open adhesion to Shi'ism, caused their systematic exclusion from power, in particular during the Ba'ath regime. Despite their constituting a numerical majority in the country, due to their existing or alleged links with Iran, the Shi'as had to endure massive persecution. Trapped between religious and ethnic wars, the Shabak share the same destiny of their Yezidi and Kakai neighbours, in the endless war between Shi'as and Sunnis that has torn the country apart for decades. The failure of a unified Islam in Iraq and in the Middle East in general that could have meant a straightforward and painless insertion into the Iraqi nation-building process, had to come to terms with the gradual exclusion of the Shi'as by the Sunnis who, beginning in the 1930s, started the Arabization Campaign which reached its culmination during Saddam's regime. Their alleged 'Persian connection' led to their banishment from Iraq by succeeding Sunni governments. In addition to their massive presence in the ranks of the Communist Party, this weakened their political participation and, by the end of the 1970s, most of them had already abandoned the path of secularism to undertake that of religious extremism, probably in an attempt to regain their space within the Iraqi political scene. However, despite this and their massive participation in the Iran–Iraq War in the ranks of the army, their Iraqi citizenship was never recognized, and the war between Sunnis and Shi'as between 2006 and 2009 questioned the call for a unified and democratic country boasted by American propaganda after 2003. Between 2003 and 2014, the majority Shi'a Shabak have been persecuted by the Sunnis: attacks, kidnappings and killings claimed more than 1,000 victims and added to the terror that all religious minorities living in the Nineveh Plain had to endure. It has been reported that in 2009, Al-Qaeda sent two truck bombs to the village of Khazna Tappa close to Mosul during the dawn prayer. The detonation was so violent that it caused 'a square kilometre of complete destruction' (Kimball 2017). As for the other minorities, the situation had a very tragic turn in 2014 with the advent of ISIS. The various Shabak villages around

Mosul have been destroyed and many of their inhabitants had to flee for their safety. Similarly to what happened to the Christians whose houses were marked with an 'N' for Nazarens, Shabak homes were marked with an 'R' to signify 'Rafida', a term ISIS militants use to designate Shi'a Muslims and others who do not conform to their dogmatic religious perspectives.

Currently, the Shabak community is calling for an investigation into the serious crimes committed by Al-Qaeda and ISIS against the community. In an article published in August 2020, the Shabak Member of Parliament, Salim Jumaa, estimated that there were around 2,300 victims of terror. He also called for an investigation into the fate of young Shabak abducted by ISIS, never to return (Taie 2020). Together with other religious minorities, Shabak think that the remnants of ISIS are the cause of the precarious security situation affecting the Nineveh Plain and other vulnerable parts of the country, in particular the disputed territories between Erbil and Baghdad.

Many Shabak have been displaced and, even if they started to return to their villages and to Mosul, their community is still largely living in refugee camps. They are too scared to go back to their villages, with their future depending on the constant, exhausting game of responsibilities between Baghdad, Erbil and the UNHCR. By that time, the UN had declared the area around Mosul free from ISIS. Of course, the reality on the ground was very different. ISIS was very much still in control and attacks against civilians in the area of Mosul constitute a constant threat to their safety. On the other hand, their presence in the Kurdish Region was just tolerated. The general conviction that both Shi'a and Sunni Muslims in Mosul had at the very beginning welcomed ISIS made them complicit in the tragedy that hit the country. The perception that in the past few years the attention of the international community has been driven to other religious minorities to the detriment of their community has also exacerbated their historic resistance to identify with Arab or Kurdish ethnicity. At the same time, the Iranian-backed militia, Hashd al-Shaabi (Popular Mobilization Forces), with its military interventions against minorities, in particular in the disputed territories between Baghdad and Erbil, exacerbated the situation.

The use of special militias by the Iraqi government in order to control internal and external military interference was not a novelty before ISIS's intervention. However, the formation of the Hashd al-Shaabi supported by Maliki to face the threat from ISIS further complicated the situation on the ground. These militias, previously called Special Groups Fighters, were set up with the intention of speedily forming local brigades in charge of defending their communities from external attacks. The Iraqi Constitution stipulates that the prime minister is also the commander-in-chief of the Iraqi Army and that all of these militias were officially integrated into it. However, this proved to be wishful thinking, in particular after the so-called defeat of the Islamic State and the definitive withdrawal of US troops from Iraq.

In reality, since the beginning, different forces worked towards their total independence from any control.[10] As a result, the security situation deteriorated further, with brigades fighting along ethnic and religious lines. In Mosul and the Nineveh Plain, two local militias, in particular, defied the central government, openly acting against it. On 15 July 2007, Haider al-Abadi tried to remedy the situation by issuing Executive Order 1388. This order stipulated the redeployment of the Hashd al-Shaabi out of Mosul and Nineveh Plain and, in particular, from the Christian areas. One of the two militias openly refused to obey their reincorporation into the Iraqi Army. Both militias Liwa al-Shabak/Quwat Sahl Nineveh, also known as PMF 30th Brigade, led by Waad Qado, and the other, called Babiliyun, also known as the 50th Brigade, led by Rayan Khaldani, refused to obey their reincorporation into the Iraqi Army.[11] The impunity with which all of these brigades act in the area and their clear religious and ethnic affiliation have raised concerns in the Christian population and have seriously undermined the efforts of pacification of the area. In many of the conversations with members of the different communities, the abuses committed by these brigades undermine every credibility of a future dialogue with the Shabak community.

Bartalla: From Christian stronghold to Shabak headquarters

Bartalla is a small Christian village 15 kilometres from Qaraqosh, and was almost completely destroyed by war in which 30th Brigade has its headquarters at Bartalla. Father Beham Benoka, the Bartalla parish priest in 2021, is very active in denouncing the worrying situation of Bartalla, a village that until the 1980s was completely Christian and that since then has witnessed continuous demographic changes with the consequent taking over of Shabak supported by Iran. Father Beham Benoka's reconstruction of the history of the village traces back the beginning of the changes to Saddam Hussein's Arabization policies. In the 1980s, Saddam Hussein confiscated thousands of hectares of Christian lands and distributed them to Muslim soldiers as a reward for their service. In this way, Saddam Hussein created a subdistrict completely dependent on a Muslim administration headed by a Muslim mayor. This move interrupted an unbroken historical Christian presence in the territory that dated back to the fourth century BCE, when the original Assyrian population converted to Christianity. After 2003, in order to guarantee security in the Nineveh Plain, the population did not try to challenge Saddam's legacy and, without listening to Christian voices, imposed a local council composed of eight members, of which three were Christians, three were Shabak and two were members of the PDK, effectively giving power to a Muslim majority.

The war between the Shi'as and Sunnis began to claim its first victims almost immediately. The consequence was that, in agreement with the American and Kurdish forces at that time responsible for the security of the area, Shabak families started to move from Mosul to the villages around it, including Bartalla. In order to give a legal bases to their ownership claims, these new families were granted permission to change their IDs, which now listed Bartalla as their place of birth. This worsened the situation for the Christians living in the area. The approximately 15,000 families now living inside and outside of the walls of the old town constituted a real strain on the infrastructure and on the availability of jobs as well as the possibility of running a business. For example, the new Muslim administration acts completely independently from any central control from the Iraqi government, and also administers the bids to allocate shops in the town. Since this happened, the price for a licence has gone up by 500 per cent, preventing Christians from bidding. Shabak also started to persecute Christians openly. Father Benham Benoka[12] remembers that on Christmas night in 2009, during Maliki's presidency and with the support of Kurdish forces, a group of Shabak Shi'as were celebrating Ashura in the streets of Bartalla. The procession stopped in front of St George's Church. They invaded the church with the intention of proclaiming it the first Christian church in the area to be transformed into a mosque. This reinforced the conviction among local Christians that when ISIS invaded the area, most of the Shabak welcomed and contributed to the looting, destruction and confiscation of Christian houses and properties. An act, Father Benham Benoka explains, against Article 23 of 2005 Iraqi Constitution, which prohibits the confiscation of properties with the purpose of implementing demographic changes.

When the Christians went back to Bartalla after the liberation, they found all the Christian houses burned inside as opposed to the Muslim ones which had been left untouched. Witnesses confirmed to me that these damages could only have been caused by locals and therefore could not be the result of the Western war against ISIS. Shabak claims to Christian towns and lands have become evident with the open proclamation, supported by Iran, for the formation of

Shabakistan. As it always happens, the idea of the establishment of a new political and geographical entity is accompanied by the birth of an ideological narrative that justifies it. Some Shabak militias, such as 30th Brigade, claim, some think without any evidence, that the blood they shed for the liberation of the area entitles them to retain the properties confiscated from Christians. At the same time, they work for the total annihilation of the Christian presence in the area by building Shi'a shrines next to Christian churches.

According to some witnesses, the 30th Brigade is responsible for sectarian abuses with the purpose of impeding the return of IDPs to their original homes. In addition, the 30th Brigade is jeopardizing any attempt at reconstruction by speculating with the checkpoints it has created on the highway between it and Mosul and by controlling the business of metal-scrapping, indispensable for reconstruction projects. The 50th Brigade has been accused of the same abuses and, despite both of them denying their belonging to the Badr organization, their actions in open defiance of the orders from the central government constitute a heavy burden on the country.[13] This situation has increased the mistrust of the other minorities and jeopardized attempts to find a common ground for a peaceful coexistence until the central government in Iraq takes on the responsibility of guaranteeing every citizen's right by controlling the militias and stopping the unchecked violence perpetrated by them.

5

The challenge of statehood and modernity for the Kurds

Baghdad vs Erbil

In March 2017, the American University of Iraq in Sulaymaniyah invited Francis Fukuyama to its annual Forum entitled, 'Durable Solutions for the Middle East', to debate prospects for governance reforms both in Iraq and in the Kurdish Region.[1] The interviewer was Dr Barham Salih, founder of the American University. In 2018, Dr Barham Salih was elected President of Iraq and in that capacity received Pope Francis I in his historic visit to the country. Fukuyama explained why he was in favour of the US intervention in Iraq; however, he also pointed out that elections do not make a democracy, and that the myopia of the American Administration failed to see what the construction of the state involved. After the toppling of Saddam Hussein, says Fukuyama, the United States became responsible for a post-war period that failed to export Western democracy because this could not be done without the existence of a working state, able to guarantee political order and security. To be functional, a state, wherever it is, has to fulfil three main requirements: first, the ability to deploy security and grant equality to all of its citizens; second, it has to guarantee the existence of the rule of law which limits the power of the state itself; third, it has to guarantee the accountability of its leaders. This is a major task, which would be difficult to undertake with success by a foreign power.

In his article, 'The Kurdish Spring', Michael Gunter talked about a Kurdish Spring in three countries: Turkey, Syria and Iraq. In three of them he states that we witness a 'sudden demands for meaningful democracy along with cultural, social and political rights and their immediate implementation before the window of opportunity closes' (2013: 442). He also notices that the difference between the situations in the three countries is that in the case of the Kurdish region, the KRG represents a government constitutionally recognized and the only attempt, in fact the 'most successful one, at Kurdish statehood in modern times' (ibid.: 441). Many observers (Bengio, 2012; Mansfield, 2014; Galbraith, 2007), together with many officials of the KRG seem to share this vision. It is undeniable that since its official establishment in 1992, the KRG that inherited a land and a people plagued by war, mass deportation and genocide, had to start the process of state-building in a very challenging reality. In addition, and this is one of the elements that distinguishes the KRG's experience from similar ones in contemporary history, the imposition of a no-fly zone together with the heavy intervention of NGOs and other organizations in the internal affairs of the newly formed 'state', happened in a context in which the perception that the population had of the state was understandably negative when not frightening.

However, it is important to remember that an embryonic Kurdish Parliament, called the Revolutionary Council was already in place since 1966. This Revolutionary Council 'held a wide range of powers, including command of the guerrilla army, administration, jurisprudence, tax collection, and supervision of the local police and prisons' (Bengio 2012: 31). This movement depended heavily on the KDP and included some of the Kurdish tribes, besides some independent figures (ibid.). It was in those years that the drift of support between the KDP led by Mustafa Barzani and the PUK led by Jalal Talabani compromised the unity of the Kurdish movement that arrived divided at the negotiations with the Ba'ath Party in 1970. The 1970 agreement with the Ba'ath Party was one of the most significant steps on the path to Kurdish autonomy.

The negotiations included a series of clauses aimed at the establishment of 'independent organizations for Kurdish women, youth and students; the appointment of a Kurd to the post of Vice-President; and agrarian reform to be carried out "immediately" in the Kurdish area' (ibid.: 48). Despite these clauses, the deal with Baghdad was highly detrimental for the Kurds because, while it provided for some degree of autonomy, at the same time in the clauses which remained secret, the agreement stated that the Kurds were to keep a force economically dependent on Baghdad, while the Iraqi troops were going to withdraw from their 'normal' position in the Kurdish North and the forces of Jalal Talabani were to be disbanded. The KDP was allowed to operate freely in the Kurdish Region and to publish its own newspaper.[2] The secret clauses also provided for a referendum to be held within a year, the purpose of which was to define the region of Kurdish majority (Record, 2 April 1970; Bengio 2012). These points are important because, in future and inevitable negotiations and in clashes with Baghdad, the Kurdish authorities always referred to these agreements when claiming their rights within the Iraqi state. These divergences also meant that the KRG did not have all the freedom to act and that its survival as an independent region was always subject to endless negotiations.

Unfortunately, the basis on which these agreements were made were very weak, indeed. The Ba'ath government did not intend to respect the agreements whose clauses were essentially not implemented. It is also important to say that in the 1970s, the Ba'ath regime had already embarked on the path of the Arabization of the whole of Iraq and that its pan-Arab ideology was shaping all political and social intervention. The Kurds did not have a state, but they were forced to deal with a very powerful one, which was increasingly isolated from the international community and with an authoritarian agenda that it was eager to implement at any cost, a tendency that would increase year after year. As an example, exactly at the same moment when the Ba'ath Party signed the agreement with the Kurdish authorities, the Iraqi government started the persecution of the Kurds, targeting a specific group of citizens, for example the Faylee Kurds. There are reasons to say that this attack on the Faylee Kurds was not motivated only by political reasons but also by economic ones. The Faylee Kurds were targeted because they constituted a very successful business community.[3] In July 1970, some of its members were summoned to the Chamber of Commerce in Baghdad, where they were rounded up and stripped of their documents, arrested and deported without any communication with their families. All their properties and belongings were confiscated and redistributed to other Iraqi Ba'athists (Al Failyon 2012). The Chamber of Commerce in Baghdad was directly involved in this, the same Chamber of Commerce established in 1936, by a combination of Iraq, Arab and Jewish merchants that saw a Kurdish president in the 1950s (Castellino and Cavanaugh 2013).

Another means that the Iraqi government employed in order to curb the Kurdish aspiration to autonomy was the nationalization of the oil fields in Kirkuk in 1972, 'putting an end to Kurdish claims to the oil of the region' (Bengio 2012). This was in complete breach of the 1970 agreements and the Kurdish authorities saw themselves without any possibility of having the revenue that would have ensured their autonomy from the central government. Their dependency on the Iraqi state exacerbated the economic situation in the traditionally Kurdish areas, which saw their income fall by this decision. The attempt to assassinate Mustafa Barzani, leader of the PDK, in July 1972 also contributed to the Kurdish people's distrust of the central government (ibid.). The process of isolation and persecution carried out by the Ba'ath Party and the Iraqi government against the Kurds continued because the persecution escalated, with an intensification of the Arabization programme, the massacre of the Barzanis (1983), the Anfal Campaign (late 1980s) and the chemical attack on Halabja (1988).

The year 1970 saw an intensification of internal conflicts within the Kurdish movement, in particular between the KDP and the Talabani movement which was banned from publishing its newspaper *Al-Nur* and whose members were forced to surrender military equipment to the authorities. The following merger of the Talabani's forces with the KDP required a process of reconciliation between the two groups (Bengio 2012). However, the imminent war (1974–5) against the regime put aside for a while the disputes internal to the Kurdish movement which in the face of danger seemed to have overcome tribal loyalties in order to achieve unity. However, as would become clear in the future, the rivalries would often emerge throughout Kurdish history. What is important is that throughout this painful and bloody path to autonomy, all the conflicts both those fought against the Iraqi government as well as the civil war (1994–8) that hindered the first years of the KRG, served simply to strengthen Kurdish national identity.

Starting from the 1970s, though, and despite the political and social turmoil caused by the Ba'ath Party and Saddam Hussein's dictatorship, when the KRG was officially established in 1992, with the decision by the Western allies to impose a no-fly zone in the northern part of Iraq, the Kurds had already gained some experience of government, mostly at a local level.

Did the Kurds have the capability to build a democracy? According to Sardar Aziz, 'Democracy requires a defined territory and people as well as a cohesive state. However, in 1992 none of these existed. The absences resulted in roadblocks to democracy, which remain in the region today' (Aziz 2014: 76). Despite the lack of basic conditions to build a democracy, the Kurdistan National Assembly chose to hold an election in a move that had almost no precedents in that part of the Middle East. Most of the studies consulted talk about the fact that the elections were considered fair by international observers and that the results, almost a 50–50 split between the PDK led by Massoud Barzani and the PUK led by Jalal Talabani, constituted the basis for the looming civil war. In sum, which was the narrative used on the ground in order to reach or actually 'define' what the people needed to build a democratic state? Unfortunately, proving Fukuyama's point that elections and democracy are not synonymous, the most recent Iraqi history teaches us that elections are not enough in order to guarantee a smooth transition to democracy and that a rigorous implementation of a constitution, together with the normal functioning of Parliament and the government would instead guarantee it. Thus, the elections did not only present an opportunity to reach a population disbanded by war and forced displacement, but they also confirmed the need to distinguish the Kurdish people from Iraq and the state repression of the Kurds by Saddam Hussein. From this, a constitution was drafted in 1992, in which the basic rights of the citizens were protected and the participation in the political life of the Kurds by all those living within the region was guaranteed. This stance has lasted until today.

After the intervention of ISIS, Massoud Barzani said in an interview that the differences between the KRG and Baghdad are not personal, but 'rather conceptual, and related to the core philosophy and culture of state administration of caring for Iraqis' interests'.[4] Even if these words do not match the reality on the ground, they show the Kurds' ambition to be different from the Iraqis and their politics of terror, strengthening in this way their sense of belonging. Another interesting point to be explored in this regard, and in consequence of the attitude introduced above, is that the KRG, in particular starting from 2003, in its inevitable and endless negotiations with Baghdad, assuming a posture very unusual in the Middle East, tried to solve disputes using legal means and not by overt military confrontation. It is undeniable that the negotiating skills of the KRG had to improve if they wanted to be accepted not only by Iraq, a country to which they were attached in 1992 and upon which they are still undeniably dependent, but also by the neighbouring powers such as Turkey and Iran, at that time opposed to the very existence of an independent Kurdish region in the area.

Legislating for the Kurds

Due to the devastating experience of genocide and war and also to the specific time in history in which it was drafted, the Kurdish Constitution was outlined on the model of Western democratic constitutions: which means that its main concern was to guarantee all citizens' fundamental rights and responsibilities before the law. First of all, it guarantees freedom of speech, free circulation of ideas and minority rights for all ethnicities within Kurdish society. It also establishes three main powers: the legislative, the executive and the judicial. It stresses, too, the prominence of civil and political rights. Article 21 states that: 'the privacy of every citizen, as well as his dignity and his honour have to be respected'. Article 22 states that: 'an accused is presumed innocent until proven guilty in a court of law. No one shall be sentenced to death for a crime committed for political reasons. No one shall be sentenced to death for a crime committed while less than twenty years of age'. Article 23 states that: 'Punishment is personal; no one shall be punished for another person's crime.' In addition, Article 1 establishes the geographical boundaries of the region and, in Article 4 it is stated that it will: 'enter into a voluntary partnership with the Arab part of Iraq within the framework of a federal Republic of Iraq including two federated regions enjoying equal rights'.[5] The KRG, therefore, has presented itself since the beginning as a democratically elected state, born to change the traditional politics of the Middle East. After twenty-three years, it is possible to envisage whether or not this has been achieved and if it has, what its impact has been in the region and also in the neighbouring Kurdish communities.

Herish Khali Mohammed and Francis Owtram have been exploring the efforts of the KRG between 2003 and 2010 in the field of international relations (Mohammed and Owtram 2014). Given the 'quasi-state' condition of the Kurdish Region and the need for recognition, the KRG was historically forced to open itself to the external world. This exposure increased with the humanitarian crisis that developed during the First Gulf War of 1991, and it was realized that something had to be done to protect the Kurds. However, with the establishment of the KRG just one year later, the challenge of the new government was not only to achieve international recognition, but also to obtain this within a legal international framework. In Mohammed and Owtram's study regarding the legal provision of the para-diplomacy developed by the KRG, 'all the respondents concur that the status of the Iraqi Kurdistan region is constitutionally entrenched and guaranteed. Furthermore, they assert that the Kurdistan Region has been granted legitimate powers to implement foreign relations but not to formulate foreign policy' (Mohammed and Owtram 2014: 69). However, from the answers of the high-level officials of the KRG, it is clear that there is also an attempt to build a tradition of foreign policy which legitimizes even more strongly the legal framework provided for in the 2005 Iraqi Permanent Constitution.[6] Nevertheless, with the ambiguity that always permeates the relationship between Erbil and Baghdad, the former representative to the United Kingdom, Abdul Rahman, interviewed by the authors of the article, said that the Kurdistan Regional Government representations abroad existed before the Iraqi constitution.

The extent to which foreign relations have developed prior to and after 2003 is still to be analysed in detail. An insight into the difference between the two phases can be deduced by considering the state of the quasi-total dependency of the KRG on international agencies and NGOs analysed by Denise Natali in her study on the state of dependency of the KRG from international agencies which invigorated the development of the Kurdish Region. During this time, in which the KRG established its basis 'influenced by democratic norms imported from abroad' (Natali 2010), the KRG had to reflect on the drafting of a new constitution and the establishment of a modern parliamentary political system (ibid.). This parliament was not only responsible for the creation of ad hoc ministries of Reconstruction and Development, Humanitarian Aid and Cooperation, Peshmerga affairs, and Culture, but was also in charge of negotiating with all the international agencies the economic and future development of the region, thus strengthening the presence of a de facto Kurdish state (ibid.). This situation had the effect of improving the experience of foreign relations of the KRG, with the result that the KRG, due to the isolation in which the rest of Iraq then existed, became the only country maintaining its international relations. An admission that things had changed after the fall of Saddam Hussein and that the diplomatic efforts of the KRG must be directed in a different way is fundamental.

Another important step taken by the KRG to obtain international recognition was to make themselves willing to explore the dramatic past of the Kurdish people in Iraq. This had two main purposes and effects. The first was that, in this way, the people would feel united in their recent history and more inclined to recognize that they belong to the region. The second was that an insight into this painful history of suppression and neglect would inevitably provide the new 'state' with a proper narrative and legitimation. In the cases of Italy and France, for example, the new governments established after the Second World War based their legitimacy on the role of the resistance in the liberation of the countries from Nazi fascism. The acknowledgement and remembrance of the sacrifices made by the soldiers and civilians who died in the effort to build a new, free country constituted and, in some cases, still constitutes a powerful account of the events which contributed to the establishment of a strong link within the new state and the population. In the case of the Kurds, the KRG had to assume this narrative from the very beginning since its own birth was due to the deep humanitarian crisis caused by Saddam Hussein's persecution. However, in a region devastated by war, the recognition of the genocides was fundamental in two different directions, an internal and an external one. The internal direction was that the KRG, in order to establish its authority and presence in the territory under its control, had to show its new citizens that it had the means and the determinatin to alleviate the sorrow and pain of the people by re-establishing some of the rights denied by the previous regime. These included the restitution of lands and properties illegally confiscated and the compensation for the human loss suffered by the Kurds, provided for in Article 140 of the 2005 Iraqi Constitution. The negotiations on the disputed territories, and in particular on

Kirkuk, involve Article 140, which is controversial and has never been completely implemented. This caused and is still causing a major rift between Erbil and Baghdad, and is seen as the main reason for the political instability of Iraq and as the source of the still current security threat posed by ISIS.

Guaranteeing citizens' rights

The KRG kept distinguishing itself from the rest of Iraq by the inclusion of a Bill of Rights, forgetting the commitment to the Iraqi Constitution, vigorously claimed by its higher officials until 2010 (Mohammed and Owtram 2014). In fact, a Bill of Rights, at least in the Western tradition, supposes a net division between state and religion, a way to conceive the state in contrast with the Iraqi Constitution which provides for the incorporation of the Shari'a law into the judicial system, but perfectly in tune with the idea, referred to by Alex Danilovic (Danilovic 2014) that the Kurds' most recent history shows that their fight for independence and their identity comes before any commitment to Islam and its values. To confirm this trend, the KRG issued a series of bills, for example a ban on honour killing and a partial ban on polygamy, which distinguishes the KRG from the rest of the country. Women's and children's rights have also been addressed, even if, especially in the case of women, the implementation of the law is hindered by the resistance of a popular culture not in tune with the new changes, so that honour killing and violence against women are rarely punished (al-Ali and Pratt 2011). In 2012, the Supreme Council of Women's Affairs of the Kurdish Regional Government designed a national strategy to confront violence against women in the region, aimed at raising awareness about the problem of the 'abolishment of discrimination between men and women, and the activation of the women's role in the process of reconstruction and development' (KRG 2012).

At the same time, state intervention in education has been aimed at reducing the high illiteracy rate of the generation that survived the war. Since its establishment in 1992, the KRG supported a programme of compulsory education which involved every sector of the region. In 2011, in the Kurdish Region, there were 5,000 schools, and even if this number does not fulfil all the population's needs, in particular in the rural areas, the average number of pupils in each class is approximately 50; of the eligible children in 2001, 99 per cent attend schools and the proportion of girls enrolled was 89.9 per cent.[7] On the contrary, despite the fact that the Iraqi Article 34 of the 2005 Constitution provides that 'education is a fundamental factor for the progress of society and is a right guaranteed by the state', and that 'Primary education is mandatory for children aged between 6 and 12 and the state guarantees that it shall combat illiteracy,'[8] the number of children who are not in education is much higher in the Kurdish Region than in Iraq. In both cases, women's and children's rights, the disparity between the two parts of the country is due mainly to the fact that the Kurdish Region has been able to guarantee a certain degree of peace and development to its citizens.

This climate favoured the implementation of policies regarding children's rights that had an impact on the population of the region. For example, the data on violence against children in the two parts of the country together with the policies adopted in order to prevent it, show how two societies, one in peace and one at war, deal with the problem. Officially, in 2008, Iraqi sources indicate that 376 children were killed and 1,594 were injured. The following year, 362 children were killed and 1,044 injured. The year 2010 saw a slight reduction in the number, with 134 children reported killed and 590 injured.[9] However, it is fair to say that these figures are likely to be inaccurate. In fact, it is very difficult to compile such statistics during wartime. Some awareness campaigns were conducted whose success has been difficult to assess. During the same period, the data from the Kurdish Region confirms the trends of those in the education sector. Being a region safe from war and insurgency, in 2007, the Ministry of Education of the KRG banned corporal punishment in schools.[10]

Economic development also went hand in hand with the changes experienced by the Iraqi Kurdish society and the foreign investment in the region, in particular by Turkish and European firms, contributed to the strengthening of the regional and international relations of the region despite the KRG's budget still depending on the federal government. However, in 2009, signed contracts with foreign companies for the extraction of oil, in particular with Norway's DNO and the Canadian Addax Petroleum (Gunter 2011), a move which shows the KRG's aim of reaching economic, besides political, independence from Iraq, prompted a dispute with the federal government over the destination of the revenue gained from oil and on the always ambiguous interpretation of Article 115 of the 2005 Iraqi Constitution. This article provides for 'the supremacy of the regional laws over federal laws and can be invoked if no agreement is reached on the management of oil and gas resources and the distribution of proceeds' (Iraq Government 2005).

Despite the tensions with the federal government, the KRG, thanks also to the peace and stability enjoyed in the region, managed to attract foreign investments and to institute a free market policy to the point that, 'in March

2011 *FDI Magazine*, a subsidiary of the British publication the *Financial Times*, ranked Erbil fifth among the top Middle East cities in terms of the potential for foreign investment (FDI)' (Gunter 2011: 103). According to Gunter, at the international fair celebrated in Erbil in 2010, international firms from Turkey, Iran, Jordan, Germany, France, the United Arab Emirates, Austria, United Kingdom and others participated, opening a new opportunity not only for the oil industry but also for agriculture, tourism and manufacturing (ibid.). This is an economic development whose impact on society and whose sustainability have still to be analysed in all their magnitude, but at least until 2014, this was the image projected to the world, the image of 'the other Iraq', the title of a promotional campaign sponsored by the Kurdistan Development Corporation. Studies in the economic development of the Kurdish Region have been carried out to identify the weak elements of an economy whose success is only partial. It is also fair to say that due to the condition of dependency, the KRG was not able to set out a strategic plan and regulatory rules to develop an industrial sector in the region until 2003.

Between 2004 and 2014, the economic indicators of the region show that a relatively secure environment allowed in the KRG an economic progress which contrasted with the economic indicators of the whole of Iraq in the same period. This fast economic development was driven primarily by the revenue from the oil industry. However, construction, agriculture and services also contributed to 8 per cent of economic growth. From 2003 to 2011, the nominal GDP of the region increased from IQD20,954 billion in 2008 to IQD28,320 in 2011. Per capita, the nominal GDP increased by 12.1 per cent within barely four years. The prevalent oil economy in Kurdistan, as happened in other Middle Eastern countries, transformed the region into a rentier state, able 'to fend off pressure for sharing of wealth and consolidate oligarchic control by enhancing both the distributive, welfare and coercive power of the state' (Halliday 2005: 278). This dependency had the result of creating a workforce completely dependent on the state's revenue.

After 2014, most of the public employees saw their salaries dramatically reduced and the private sector struggled to fulfil the demand for employment (World Bank Group 2015). The situation deteriorated further after the referendum for independence held on 25 September 2017. The renewed military confrontation between the KRG and the central government for the control of disputed areas in Kirkuk and in the Nineveh Plain has worsened an already precarious situation with the arrival in the region's main cities of a new wave of IDPs.[11] In addition, the decision of the central government to ban international flights to the region caused further damage to the regional economy (KRG 2017).

The industrial policy adopted by the KRG until 2014 has definitely improved the economic situation in the region, in particular in comparison with the rest of the country; however, the industrial development needs to be based on different variables, currently very weak or almost non-existent, such as public infrastructure, human capital, a working banking system and rules to fight corruption and guarantee transparency, besides political stability. In addition to the Ministry of Industry and Trade, in 2006 the KRG established a Kurdistan Investment Board whose purpose was to attract investors and contribute to the economic development process in the Kurdish Region (Investment Board 2006). Despite this and the enactment of an investment law in 2010, the economic development of the region was not providing the independence and the job security that a more focused approach which takes into account a closer collaboration with other ministries would allow. What was needed was a more customized approach to the different parts of the Kurdish Region for an assessment of their economic potential. This would have led to a better understanding of the educational and training needs in support of the industrial development and to a more specific legislation on the matter based on the specific strategic needs of the region.[12]

Despite this, the establishment of the KRG and its policies happened both in a state of dependency on foreign countries and, most importantly, without a real change in the basic, tribal structure of Kurdish society being carried out (Natali 2010; Stansfield 2003; McDowall 2000). This jeopardized the formation of strong mechanisms for power control necessary for the development of healthy and robust democratic institutions mentioned by Fukuyama for the formation of a workable state. This lack of 'democratization' is also reflected in the relationship between the Kurdish Region and Kurdish and non-Kurdish minorities living in its territory. This is evidence that the prominence of two parties, the KDP and the PUK, tied to the Barzani and Talabani families, respectively, constitutes an obstacle to the development of a real participation of all the citizens in the political life of the region.

However, as with other countries which have lived through the atrocities of war and the incongruity of reconstruction, the process is not exempt from contradictions. Education and awareness of one's rights inevitably initiate organizations and associations that end up challenging the old order. The KRG will have to manage the discontent that an uneven economic development has caused. The formation of a government is hardly enough to forge a nation. The challenge is in organizing a partnership with all the parties involved. Participation is the key to political success. In the meantime, corruption is rampant and 30 per cent of the population is poor; the future of the KRG will depend on how any leadership will solve the problems of security, jobs, welfare and social identity. Without tackling these issues, the region will not have any future and will fall more and more into the hands of insurgent groups.

There are different events that draw attention to the path followed by the KRG in the past twenty-three years. For example, the fact that in 2009, with the emergence of the Goran (Change) Party, the KRG had to face what are probably the strongest demonstrations of dissent in its brief history. A new generation of Kurds was demonstrating against the monopoly of power exercised by the KDP and the PUK and the two families, the Barzani and Talabani, respectively, who have been dominating the political and social spectrum in the region. The protests, including that of intellectuals who demanded more freedom of speech, were often initiated by common citizens over the lack of services such as water and electricity. These protests, which erupted violently mainly in Sulaymaniya, constituted an interesting challenge for the KRG because they employed precisely the same democratic platform on which the KRG itself was built, that of democracy, equality and human rights. So, the question is how the KRG reacted to this wave of protests. Was it able to control them? But, first of all, was it able to restrain itself from exercising its power to silence the protests? The KRG was able to stop the protests from happening in Erbil by closing the universities and banning large gatherings (Gunter 2013). Is this a sign of a functioning state? In other words, is the KRG able to act internally in accordance with the democratic principles on which that state was allegedly built?

The leverage of the minorities

After ISIS, the presence of minorities and their participation in the decision-making process of the reconstruction and, in the wider discussion, about the future of the stretch of land called Iraq, are even more preponderant while raising concerns about their survival. It also constituted an opportunity to revise alliances that until that moment had been considered unbreakable and in so doing it was also the moment when the claim for an identity became more and more pressing with the increasing violence endured.

The most unbreakable alliance was definitely with the Kurdish Regional Government, which, between 2003 and 2014, constituted an indispensable point of reference for all minorities and for Christians, in particular. The increasing influence of the Kurdish Region meant that all minorities could find a space to act, to talk, to exchange freely their thoughts and their fears. A space where they can establish their NGOs, associations and media. Participation in the political and civil life of members belonging to minorities is also guaranteed, with Christians, Kakais and Yezidis working in the police force and other public services. However, according to some activists interviewed, this freedom is only superficial. In reality, distrust between the components and the KRG is running deep and has its own origins in the way the KRG, and with it the Kurdish element, imposed themselves on them. The origin of this distrust has to be found not only in the way their presence was exploited and misunderstood by conflicting forces during the process of nation-building of the Iraqi states but also, more recently, in the way the KRG has dealt with the distribution of land in the areas traditionally inhabited by minorities.

The 2005 Iraqi Constitution and the innovations introduced in the draft constitutions of the KRG advocated for a federal Iraq, and provided for freedom of religion and coincided with the idea that Iraq is a multicultural country. However, the reality on the ground answers to the biggest and more pressing factors and, in particular, on the political development of the Kurdish Region. The unstable situation of the minorities is due to the failure of the international community to confront 'the specific vulnerabilities of minorities communities', as reported by the Assyrian Confederation of Europe (ACE).[13] In this way, minority communities found themselves again as a minority within a majority, be this Arab or Kurdish, and their security situation did not change from the past, leaving them as negotiations tools between the KRG and the central government in Baghdad. The sectarian war between Shi'as and Sunnis which tore the country apart make them take refuge in the Nineveh Plain which, even if providing temporary relief from the dangers of war, was still part of the disputed territories between Erbil and Baghdad thanks to the claim on behalf of the KRG that it was part of 'Greater Kurdistan'. The report also states that in the draft constitution published by the KRG in 2004, there is no mention of the Nineveh Plain and, on the contrary, the draft published just two years later Article 2 which claims that it belongs to the KRG. Always according to the report this confirmed the expansionistic aspirations of the KRG in the Plain which has been carried out since then with a coordinated intervention that includes the use of military force, usually disguised as provision of security or infiltrating the political life of villages and cities while changing their demography, fuelling and incrementing mistrust already strongly felt in the communities (ACE 2017).

The same lack of trust is present in other testimonies. Nadia Murad, in her memoires, remembers her refusal to speak Kurdish to the soldiers controlling the checkpoint between the area controlled by ISIS and the KRG, because they were the same ones who abandoned all the Yezidis to ISIS, confirms this distrust: 'Suddenly the KRG was trying to repair its relationship with Yezidis and re-establish our trust in them, hoping they we would once again call ourselves Kurds and want to be part of Kurdistan' (Murad 2017: 247). Father Michaeel Najeeb also even admitting that the Kurds in this historical moment are offering Christians security and protection, he does not forget that they, as well as the Sunnis, Shi'a and ISIS, want to take over their lands. Therefore, 'Cela nous convient, même si personne n'a oublié ce qu'ils ont fait à nos arrière-grands-parents et que nous connaisson tous leurs arrière-pensées' (Najeeb 2017).[14]

The advent of ISIS and the violence suffered by Christians and other minorities put a further strain on the relationship between the KRG and the communities. After the Peshmerga failed in providing them the security they had tried so hard to build for themselves, they accused the KRG and the Peshmerga of having left them in the hands of ISIS in order to enter as liberators/conquerors once ISIS retreated. Documents provided by Assyrian interviewees and openly available on the Internet show how the Peshmerga, aware of the danger, issued an order which required all the inhabitants of the Nineveh Plain to turn over their weapons.[15] The video has circulated on YouTube and shows the original document, stating that: 'Those who have in their possession heavy or medium weapons or ammunitions are to turn them over to the security team.' This order was signed by the director of the security team based in Hamdaniya in July 2014. According to testimonies, the Peshmerga went door to door, disarming Christians and Yezidis and other minorities, denying them any possibility of defending themselves and leaving them with the only choice of fleeing to take refuge in safer areas. The KRG previously assured them that it would be responsible of their safety, however, villages and cities were abandoned to ISIS.

This caused an even deeper divide between the KRG and the minorities, who, as in the past, have been the contention between two more powerful forces, ISIS and the KRG, confirming the dangerous trend that after 2003, marginalized and, worse, ignored the presence of minorities and their impact on the political and social fabric of the country and of the Kurdish Region in particular. In Erbil, members of the communities admitted they feared reprisals from the government, and agreed to interviews only if they were guaranteed anonymity and confidentiality, thereby destroying in some way the idea of a 'democratic' KRG as a credible alternative to the opposite 'tyrannical' Iraq.

From interviews with exponents of the minorities living in the Nineveh Plain, it was clear that the security provided by the Peshmerga forces has not always been perceived as a blessing offered in moments of need. On the contrary, they have sometimes been considered as conquerors and as the armed wing of the KDP. It is not uncommon for a member of any minority community to make comments about the presence at the entrance of villages in the Nineveh Plain of big images of Massoud Barzani, now the former President of the KRG, but representative of the power of the KDP in the area. A power that, after 2003, has been a deterrent to the development of autonomous communities that did not always identify themselves with the Kurdish Region and its efforts to build a nation-state based on Kurdish ethnicity. Infiltration into the internal affairs of the single communities has been denounced on many occasions during elections or in the daily disruption of the attempts made by minorities to run their own communities.

Due to the precarious security situation of the Nineveh Plain, it was expected that the communities would actually try to organize their own security forces by forming their own police force. However, this always led to a direct confrontation with the KRG, which always preferred to deploy its Peshmerga to those areas. According to the report by the Assyrian Confederation of Europe, for example, all these attempts have been appropriated by the KDP that, through its Christian representatives and, according to some Christians interviewed, through the representative of the single churches, had imposed its own security forces.

The KDP infiltration into the regional politics of the Nineveh Plain was revealed in the pressure exerted on the population of this area on the occasion of elections when citizens have been forced, under threat to vote for the party supported by the KDP. This happened in the 2005 and 2009 provincial elections.[16] On those occasions, the protesters, mainly students, have been threatened with the suspension of the bus service while common citizens with the loss of their jobs if they did not vote according to their directions. Analysing the complicated and ever-changing political spectrum of the KRG, members of the communities reported that behind the quota, representation awarded to them in the elections was filled by candidates belonging to political parties formed and supported by the KDP, jeopardizing any attempt of a real local representation. The attempted removal of Faied Abed Jahwareh as Mayor of Alqosh in June 2014 when Mosul had already been occupied by ISIS reminded the communities of how the advent of ISIS has been instrumental in the expansionist aspirations of the KRG.[17] Just before the referendum for independence, the KRG succeeded in removing Faied

Abed Jahwareh on corruption charges, substituting him with Lara Yousif, an Assyrian member of the KDP and a schoolteacher without any political experience, who presented herself in a Peshmerga uniform despite never having served in the army.[18]

A Human Rights Watch (HRW) report dated 2009 denounces the heavy interference of the KRG in the Nineveh Plain. Shifting the attention from the battle for the disputed territories in Kirkuk, HRW wanted to draw attention to the silent battle and the violence tearing apart Nineveh Plain and the continuous attacks on its villages, allegedly by Islamic extremists. Memories of these attacks are still present in the population of the villages and the consequences of the attacks, which went on in 2008 and 2009. These extremists attacked minorities communities of Chaldo-Assyrians, Yezidis, Shabak and Kakais labelling them as devil-worshippers and infidels.[19] The Kakai community, still not recognized either by Baghdad or Erbil, also suffered from heavy damages. The villages of Sufaia, Wardak, Zangal, Kulabor, Tulaban, Kabarli and Matrad, all of them on the road between Erbil and Mosul and about forty-five minutes from the capital of the KRG, present the sign of the violence suffered in 2009. In one of the villages, it was still possible to see the crater caused by a huge explosion in 2009 set off by Al-Qaida. Very close to the crater there is the headquarters of both the KDP and the PUK, together with their respective armed wings, a constant in villages inhabited by minorities.

However, within the communities, there are different ways to perceive this presence. One of the members of the Kakai interviewed said in this regard that the Kakais are very happy to have the protection of both parties because the members operating in the area all belong to their community. He also said that Christian people consider themselves as a different nation and do not necessarily identify themselves as Kurds while, for the Kakais, it is totally different because they consider themselves to be the original Kurds.[20]

In 2010, in order to grant political representation to the Christian community, a quota system was introduced for some of the minorities. This provided for five seats for Christians and one seat for the Yezidis, Fayli Kurds, Sabean Mandeans and Shabak. It is clear from this that not all minorities are recognized since Kakais and Mandeans, for example, are missing. With the title of, *Iraq Stolen Election: How Assyrian Representation Became Assyrian Repression*, the report aimed at denouncing the frauds at the basis of the last political elections in Iraq regarding Assyrian votes. What is very interesting in this publication, besides reporting on the flaws of the quota system, is an analysis of the crumbling sense of identity within the community and of the strategies that main political parties, in particular the KDP and Badr Organization are having on it. The report states very clearly the difference between ethnic and religious recognition, implicit in the 'Christian quota'. This religious-based classification that has been imposed on Iraq's Assyrian community and used to define them in a political context has greatly contributed to the deliberate dilution of the community's ethnic identity. This sectarian label consequently weakens their rights to land and self-determination as an indigenous people – a legacy from the Arabization campaigns carried out by the Ba'ath regime which identified them as 'Arab Christians' or 'Iraqi Christians'. This reductive classification has effectively resulted in the erasure of modern Assyrian history. This is confirmed by some of the Assyrians who were interviewed and who denounced the lack of historical knowledge in the younger generation. But they also anticipated the consequences in terms of political representation on the ground.

The danger of irreparable divisions among the different Christian souls in Iraq has been confirmed in the 2018 elections, when the Chaldean Catholic Patriarch, Louis Sako, directly endorsed the Chaldean Coalition. It was the first time that the Chaldean Church officially entered into Assyrian political life. This caused a lot of anxiety because it meant total identification of the community with religion, thereby undermining the call for the unity of all Assyrians under a common ethnicity. 'The Chaldean Church is one of the official churches recognized in Iraq. It was like this before, during and after Saddam. I like the Church, but I do not want to be represented by it in politics.'[21] This is the opinion not only of Christian refugees, but also of many Assyrians who are currently seeking a secular representation. Their opinion echoed that of representatives of the Chaldean Church in Iraq, who underlined the sectarian intentions of the Patriarch. This intervention had very detrimental effects also because it further divided a community already torn apart. However, despite this, the majority of Assyrians rejected this sectarianism.

There is a loophole in the quota system which allows non-Assyrians to vote for this quota, leaving the possibility for non-Assyrians 'to vote in the very elections that determine the special representation of the Assyrians.'[22] This then allowed the main political parties to manipulate the elections to the point at which voters could be deployed to one area from another in order to support a particular candidate through proxy parties which do not necessarily represent the will of the Assyrians. What is actually at stake, therefore, is not the question of who will represent the Assyrians in an established political arena, but rather the very nature of that political arena. Rather than allowing this arena to remain Assyrian, KDP proxy parties serve to advance the objective of dismantling the semi-independent Assyrian political jurisdiction that is viable in Nineveh (and which has already been functional in post-2003 Iraq) and to annex the Nineveh Plain to the Kurdistan Region. This necessarily means subsuming the Assyrian political agency under Kurds and, specifically, the KDP's political control.[23]

In October 2018, just after the elections, a Christian activist from Teleskof reported that a small group of people led by the KDP claimed to be the new representative of the village and took control of it. Their presence was not welcome in the village because they did not allow women to vote and complaints were raised in this respect. 'How can we explain to our citizens that ISIS's mentality is wrong when we impose the same ideas on our women?' said our interviewee. The interference of proxy parties in Christian villages is also testified to by the results of the 2018 Iraqi political elections. For example, if we consider the Assyrian community, the comparison between the votes cast in different years reveals how non-Assyrians are voting for the Christian quotas. Considering the change in demography due to the massive exodus of Christians from these areas, it is striking how the number of Christian voters increased instead of declining, which would be logical. This visit opened a series of questions regarding the capillary presence of the KDP and its Peshmerga forces in the areas inhabited by minorities.

Some of the interviewees reported the strategies of intimidation and coercion put in place by the main political parties. 'We are not free to talk. If we try, we are subject to retaliation,' said one student in Erbil. One of the most powerful strategies in the hands of the main parties is threatening voters with unemployment. The economic crisis together with the emergency caused by forced displacement compelled many Christians to become victims of these threats. When talking about his community, one of the priests interviewed said that:

> People there are talking from their hearts because they are afraid, and they do not know where to go. I saw and heard in the same family between them divisions depending on where they are making their living and from where they are making more money. Sometimes I feel they lost their humanity. During a mass in the church, I say the respect they should have from each other and I make very close to the religious part including the gospel on the respect of the ideas. Nobody understands the other side. Everyone is caught from a side or the other side. The priority is to survive, they do not think about education and many of them lost their historical memory. Most of them even in the past did not know about the massacres, however there was a hidden memory transmitted through the generations made them mistrust the Kurds'. Now all this is in danger to disappear in the face of poverty and lack of education.[24]

A comparison between the ways in which the different communities dealt with the advent of ISIS gave rise to the need for a new approach to the minorities' perceptions and version of the events, perceptions which are more and more linked to their composite identities. This makes them very distrustful of Kurdish politics and claims for independence in the name of Kurdish ethnicity. The interference of Kurdish political parties favoured the fragmentation of Christian identities and alliances. Assyrians, unlike Christians, for example, do not have a centre of power. Through the centuries the Christians have been divided into ecclesiastical groups, a reality which influenced the way in which they are perceived externally. Assyrians have been even more 'Balkanized' in a way that, according to Sargon George Donabed, recalls how, in the former Yugoslavia, identity followed religious identity. However, in the past twenty years, the Assyrian identity is down to that of the Christians, to the point of speaking Aramaic, but they all speak 'Christian'.[25] Many young people are completely unaware of their own recent history and the mass atrocities that have been committed against their communities over the past few decades and most of them ignore their past history. This is why when asked to define themselves as a group, the majority of them say they are 'Christians'. As one of the Christians interviewed pointed out, 'Christian' is a religion, it is not an ethnicity.[26] 'You can be Kurd, Arab, Turkman. All these are ethnicities. On the contrary, saying that you are Christian, it just defines you according to your religion and transforms you into a number, not a citizen.'[27]

The infiltration of political parties is causing the fracturing of a people and their identity by artificially nurturing separatist identities and raises questions of cultural genocide. The KRG continues to engage in practices that deprive Assyrians, in particular, but not only them, of their identity by financially supporting the development and solidification of other identities rooted in religion and denominational affiliations. Their policies deny Assyrians the chance to heal artificial divides and reconcile, thereby recognizing their full political and social potential in Iraq.[28]

The creation of a Syriac identity from the Assyrian one is only one example of how the KRG managed to further ethnically divide the Christian community in the region. The Christian Chaldean Syriac Assyrian Popular Council founded in 2007 in Ankawa is one of the organizations supported by the KDP. Loay Mikhael, its representative in Washington, released an interview to the Washington Kurdish Institute, in which he answers this way to the question describing what the history of Christians in Iraq was:

Well, the Christians of Iraq, ethnically, they are Chaldeans, Syriac and Assyrians as well. So, we've been there before Christianity. We've been there before Islam. Before any emergence of other [religious] communities in the area. So, the Christians have been there since the founding of Christianity, 2000 years ago. There are many sects of Christians. There are Chaldean Catholics. There are Syriac Catholics and Syriac Orthodox. And you have Asyrian Church. So, all these together, they call themselves Christians. I know there are a lot of sects, a lot of ethnicities, but if you talk to anyone in these groups, they will tell you 'we are one people, one group.' We speak one language. We share one history. Because of the historical thing and the political backgrounds, everybody calls themselves different. Some, they call themselves Chaldean. Some, they call themselves Assyrian and some Syriac.[29]

This interview contains all the concerns expressed by members of the Assyrian community about the interference of the KRG in their own identity. The Christian Chaldean Syriac Assyrian Popular Council claims that all the components under its umbrella are one people and one group who speak the same language, and that, in the end, they are all Christians, almost denying all the ethnic groups the Council represents. The reduction in the ethnic and cultural diversity of the Christians into a sole, indivisible entity has the political purpose of denying their identity(ies) and also has the advantage of reducing the number of interlocutors to one who does not necessarily represent the vision of all Assyrians or Christians. In this respect, some members of the Assyrian community talked about the fact that the KRG prevents them from getting politically organized, in that the KRG liaise only with their religious leaders.[30] It is a diversification instrumental to their unification under a single identity and language since the idea of a 'Christian language' has now replaced the knowledge of the existence of different languages for Assyrians.

Some of the interviewees mentioned that the KRG, in its draft constitution, gives minorities space to administer their cultural life within the region. Chapter 3 of the 2009 draft constitution is entitled, 'Ethnic and Religious Rights of the Different Groups of the Kurdistan Region'. Article 35 states: 'This Constitution guarantees national, cultural and administration autonomy to the Turkmen, Arabs and Chaldo-Assyrian-Syriacs wherever they represent a majority of the population. This shall be regulated by law.'[31] In its comprehensive effort, this article strikes the absence of any concrete reference to the geography of the Assyrian population. There is no mention of the Nineveh Plain as the area where most Assyrians live, and there is no mention of Ankawa, the Christian enclave in the heart of Erbil. For this reason, they blamed their own community for not having taken full advantage of their legal rights. For example, very few Assyrians of the last generation know how to read and write in their mother tongue and this despite the fact that the KRG allows minorities to teach their students in their own language. Assyrians advocate for a school curriculum which not only provides for a space to teach in their mother tongue, but that it also provides teaching about other religions in all schools in the Kurdish region.

In the months running up to the referendum for independence, the official line of the KDP and other political forces supporting the referendum and shared by other members of the community, was that Kurdish people have always respected minorities and that independence from the central government would strengthen even further the tradition of tolerance and peaceful coexistence that Christians and other minorities have experienced since the creation of the Kurdish Region in 1991. Assyrian history does not agree with this interpretation. The inhabitants of Batnaya, a village destroyed by ISIS and now completely abandoned, remember that to the boy's school, established in 1921 and run by the Iraqi authorities in 1992, was added another one for boys and girls run by the KRG. In the same village, there were also two mukhtars, one for the KDP and another for the Assyrian Movement (AM).[32] On 1 June 1993, just one year after being elected to the newly established Kurdish Parliament, the Assyrian representative, Francis Yousef Shabo, was killed. A strong supporter of the unity of Assyrians beyond their religious differences, Shabo was fighting to reverse the Arabization policies implemented by the Ba'ath Party against the Assyrians advocating for the restitution of the lands confiscated and for their return to their original lands. He 'spoke openly about Kurdish encroachment on lands historically inhabited by Assyrians',[33] and for this he was targeted by the KDP. In 2017, twenty-five years after his death, Assyrians remember him through a call to action to stop the intimidations against the silencing of Assyrian leaders by Asaysh, the military and security branch of the KDP. The Assyrians also protested because of a massive mural unveiled near the Assyrian town of Enishke, honouring one of Francis Shabo's murderers. Koveli, one of the presumed killers, who died in 2016, was never brought to justice for his crime and he is revered as a hero by the Kurdish authorities. This mural has been interpreted not only as a direct offence to the Assyrians living in the area because of its chosen location, but also as a covert threat to their lives, a threat that some of them take very seriously and that undermine any possible coexistence under a common Kurdish flag.

In October 2017, activists belonging to a charity association based in Erbil, talked in the same terms of confidence towards the KRG and the future of

Christians in it. This organization offers support to refugees in the camps in collaboration with other international organizations, in particular American ones. The twenty-one members of this independent organization at the time of the interviews were all Catholic professionals, doctors and lawyers, all of them with the commitment to help the community to overcome the legacy of ISIS.[34] Their vision, though, does not sound completely optimistic in contrast with that supported by the PDK. During the interview, the president of the organization highlighted two main points regarding the way in which the KRG interacts with Christian organizations. The first one was that, in the past, it was the KRG that gave work to people who were involved in charities, now this work has been assigned to companies and the way in which problems are dealt with in the camps has completely changed. At that moment in time, the KRG only paid for the rent of locals for the organizations. This meant that many outlets of this organization had to close down and the few that survived have to rely on the help of the international community.

Some Christian activists claim that the Church has also continued to offer help. However, this help comes according to the number of each different group and each group thinks about itself, with the Church discriminating between different Catholic groups instead of intervening through the organizations working in the areas. This is a problem which arises from another important fact which characterized the daily relationship between the KRG and the Christian communities: the KRG's interlocutors in the Christian community are not Christian organizations run by citizens but the Catholic religious authorities.[35] This generates suspicions in some members of the community who do not feel represented and think that it can cause not only a mismanagement of funds which could be distributed more fairly among the different groups, but also because, by doing this, the KRG jeopardized any possibility for civil society to develop on a non-religious basis, as one of the interviewee put it, 'they kill the civil spirit'.[36] This preoccupation is shared not only by Christians living in Ankawa, but also by Christians living abroad, who, on more than one occasion, have expressed the fear that the KRG does not aim to create a constructive Christian representation.[37] A Christian activist refugee from Bartalla now living in Ankawa confirmed that many doubts have been raised regarding the way in which the Church is managing the money received from the KRG and other organizations. Rumours about the unwise use of resources allocated for the refugees by Church authorities have been going round, including regarding their use to restore buildings in Ankawa, instead of financing the reconstruction of the villages destroyed by ISIS.[38]

When listening to these juxtaposed voices, it is very difficult to avoid thinking that not even the referendum could engage the whole community completely in a shared vision of an independent Kurdistan. If there is something that those interviewed held in Ankawa made clear it is that the level of loyalty to the KRG is not compact within the community and that there is a huge discrepancy between the posture held by some Christian representatives supported by the KDP and Christians who regard with suspicion the interference of Kurdish political parties in their communities. When talking with people from the different sides, it is not uncommon to find the contrast between the official version of the status of minorities in the Kurdish Region dictated by political parties, in particular by the KDP, and the unofficial stand circulating through informal channels among the members of the community who are refugees or still live in villages.

In order to have an idea of how these contrasting versions are real, it is important to remember that the Christian identity is just one of the waves of identities imposed on the original inhabitants of this lands throughout history and that this perception makes them aware that they are not ethnically Kurds. This perception of not belonging becomes more acute at times in which identities, as occurred during the 2017 referendum on independence, are used and misused to offer internally and externally a unity that can be perceived as artificial, as though Christian identity could be sacrificed on the altar of Kurdish nationalism in its effort to build a nation-state. On the other hand, in villages, in particular in the Nineveh Plain, the presence of the two main Kurdish political parties is causing unrest and is experienced more as an invasion than as a guarantee of security. The situation just described means that the Christian community lacks a credible leadership and that only a few civil society organizations can claim an independence from both the Church and Kurdish politics.

The war with ISIS had substantial economic and social consequences for a region with already weak state institutions. Since 2014, the influx of refugees, mainly from Syria, has changed the demography of the region and, in particular, of the main cities of Erbil, Dohuk and Sulemaniya, dramatically. Initially, starting in early 2012 with the influx of Syrian refugees and later of IDPs in 2014, the situation turned into a full-blown humanitarian crisis. At the beginning of 2015, there were 257,000 Syrian refugees and 1,003,300 Iraqi IDPs in the KRG. In addition, there were around 250,000 IDPs who came to the region before 2014. Therefore, in early 2015, the total number of refugees and IDPs totalled 1.5 million, which constituted a 28 per cent increase in the KRI's population. Of the total IDPs and refugees, 60 per cent are in Duhok. The larger number of Iraqi IDPs and Syrian refugees reside in many of the same host communities, placing strains on the local economy and access to public services (UN 2014). This situation has prompted the need for a short, medium-term response in order to guarantee the security of refugees and IDPs and a decent life in the camps.[39]

ISIS's incursion caused a serious deterioration of security in Iraq due to the massive displacement of Syrian refugees and IDPs across the country. This situation created an unprecedented crisis and an unforeseen burden on host communities. The emergency was further exacerbated by the federal budget cut, which left many state employees in the Kurdish Region without salaries. The impossibility for the KRG to reduce this gap in the salaries due to the volatility of the oil market and also to the constant confrontation with the federal government, aggravated the situation. In 2015, the World Bank estimated that the unemployment rate rose to 14 per cent, and the poverty rate had reached 41.2 per cent (World Bank Group 2015). This required an effort to revise the whole economy by involving the private sector to find new ways to improve the region's economy and support access to the labour market (MERI Economic Forum 2016). The instability caused in the region could be seen on 17 October 2017, with the violence that engulfed the area of Kirkuk with the intervention of the Iranian-backed militia Hashd al-Shaabi, which again threatened the stability and security of the area, preventing many IDPs, in particular Christians and Yezidis, from returning to their own villages and participating in their reconstruction.

According to reports on the social cohesion of the region since 1992, 'Sixty/four percent (64%) of IDPs in Erbil and forty/one percent (41%) of IDPs in Duhok reported that access to income is their first urgent need due to job scarcity.' It has been estimated that, 'only 33% of young men (aged 15/24) in IDP, refugee and impacted communities are in employment' in Erbil (Iraq/3RP 2016/2017; Multi/Sector Needs Assessment, MSNA, of Syrian Refugees Living in Host Communities, April 2015 & Multi/Cluster Needs Assessment for Internally Displaced Persons Outside of Camps in Iraq, October 2015). The dramatic economic situation means that the affected communities are still relying not on income coming from paying jobs but rather on the accumulation of debts and the reduction of consumption with the consequent drop of the purchase of other long-term assets.[40] In addition, based on the lessons learned from the protracted displacement in the KRG, several interviewees reiterated the need for developing sustainable livelihood programmes that actively promote the self-reliance of the displaced groups in order to move forward from the state of near total economic dependency on oil. This is because a sustainable, market-oriented livelihood assistance that improves employability and increases employment opportunities may alleviate immediate tensions between host community members and displaced groups.

The 2017 referendum for independence constituted a watershed in the KRG's politics, a political strategy designed more to obey an old narrative of redemption of the abuses suffered in the past. Despite the high turnout and the overwhelming victory of the 'Yes', this move caused the loss of the control of territories gained in the war against ISIS, in particular the city of Kirkuk, always claimed by the Kurds as their own. This situation forced the KRG to reshape and restore its political and economic relations with Baghdad as well as its neighbouring countries, in particular Iran and Turkey, who strongly opposed this referendum supported in this also by the United States.

The winner of this shift was the PDK. In the 2018 elections, it consolidated its power, winning 45 seats in the parliamentary elections against the 21 won by the PUK and 12 by Goran.[41] Despite the PDK's victory, a new government took eight months to materialize and the KRG was forced to adopt a more pragmatic stand, with the aim of finding a solution to the more pressing issues pending with the federal government in Baghdad, including de-escalating the military confrontation in the disputed areas, for example in Kirkuk, as well as the reopening of the border crossings for trade with Turkey and Iran, lifting the flight ban and ensuring the transfer of the KRG's share of the budget to pay the public-sector salaries suspended by the central government in retaliation for the referendum.[42] The case of Christians is probably the most striking example of how the strengthening of the PDK in the region leaves a very limited space of manoeuvre to the minorities forced into the middle between two interlocutors, the KRG and its political establishment and the federal government in Baghdad. In order to have their voices heard, Yezidis as well as Kakais and other minorities organized themselves in local civil society organizations. Even though the need for civil organizations, as we saw it, is not new to Iraq and the Kurdish Region, the fall of Saddam first, and the advent of ISIS have acted as catalysts for the creation of civil organizations in as many fields as there are hardships, discrimination and traumas caused by violence. In this process, Iraq has been able to compare itself and its history with similar experiences from other countries in order to find a way out, or at least a relief from the endless brutality of its history.

Conclusion

After 2003, whoever had the intellectual sensibility of hearing the voices of Iraqi people found out the fascinating blending of history, ethnicity, religions and sects coexisting in the country behind the headlines and everyday politics fed to a Western audience too much used to the media that offers a comfortable oversimplification of reality. Ignoring the past and present sufferings of minorities in the country is an intellectual treason of all the people who, day by day, work to rebuild their lives torn apart by continuous wars, persecutions, deaths and, in many cases, by an unstoppable diaspora. Turning our backs on them means underestimating their history, culture and the possibility for them to resume the thread that united them in the past and can still save them.

The Kakais are the most vulnerable of the minorities considered in this book. However, their willingness to find themselves again in an effort to reforge their own history is an example of how a community can survive. Their commitment to save their cultural and material heritage against all odds, and to be locally and internationally recognized is a call for help but also a great lesson of humanity. It has been a privilege to participate in this process, sharing with them stories from the Saranjam, and through them to discover who they are and how they place themselves in the religious tradition of the area as well as in its past and present history. The Saranjam of the Kakais, echoing Genesis 10 and the Gospel of Luke 10: 1–5, says that God divided humanity into seventy-two religions and prophesies that: 'The seventy-two religions will be unified, and Benjamin will be their head.'[1] It is probably not surprising that the unified religion advocated by Pope Francis together with its message of peace coincides with the vision of the Kakais for a future of peace and harmony in God.

The Yezidis have been at the centre of international and national attention since August 2014, when ISIS hit the community with unprecedented violence. Since then, the main purpose of organizations such as the Yezidi Organization for Documentation has been to gather all the information possible on the serious breaches of human rights that does not affect only their own community. On

6 February 2021, after seven years, the Yezidis were finally able to give 104 Yezidi from Kocho an official burial in their homeland. It was an important step towards the recognition of the suffering inflicted by ISIS. At the same time, the Coalition of Just Reparations, a partnership of civil society NGOs, is supporting a bill which advocates for the institution of a 'Directorate for Survivor Affairs', overseeing a three-pronged recovery strategy: compensation, restitution and rehabilitation. Another major feature of this bill is that it recognizes and addresses Conflict-Related Sexual Violence (CRSV) and the terrible way in which it has been used against Yezidi women, with 19 June being proposed as a 'National Day to Eliminate Sexual Violence in Conflict'.[2] This is a very important move because it forces both the Iraqi and the KRG's government to take steps towards the healing and reconciliation of the communities. However, some activists, including Yezidis, have raised concerns about the fact that this bill ignores other minorities, creating further divisions between communities.

On Sunday, 7 March 2021, Pope Francis, as the last act of his historical visit to Iraq, celebrated a mass in the stadium in Erbil. Until a few years ago, it would have been impossible to witness a Christian rite in a public space in the country that ISIS conquered by force. Beyond the symbolism, this visit had the prerogative to include Iraq in the interfaith dialogue currently happening in particular between Christianity and Islam. At a time when the breach between rich and poor widened day by day in every corner of the world, Pope Francis came to preach solidarity, peace and citizenship. This call was also to include Sunnis, Shabak and all the communities sharing this land.

The minorities analysed in this book have one thing in common, a history of persecution and oppression that threatens to deprive them of the most important thing for any community, their roots. The forms that these have decided to adopt are different, because the starting points are different and, above all, their needs. Their survival in Iraq depends strongly on their ability to demand a seat at the negotiating table and, a very important factor in the chronic instability of the Middle East, in their commitment to stay involved in policy debate and decision-making long after the governmental consultations have ceased. Their future depends on the support they can receive both internally by creating spaces of discussion within communities and looking for support from the government, and externally by consulting and collaborating with international organizations. However, many activists and, as seen in the Assyrian cases, for example, overtly question the political parties in both the Iraqi and the Kurdish regional governments, accusing them of following sectarian logics harmful to minorities.

Many communities realized that successive governments both in Iraq and in the Kurdish Region had betrayed them by showing their inability to manage the urgency that arose after the violence inflicted by ISIS. Iraqi society had to find answers to its need to understand what had happened, to its longing for justice, peace and reconciliation.

Despite the need for representation uniting all the communities, the capacity of minorities to organize themselves into civil movements to advocate for their rights is not the same. In the Kakais' case, for example, the internal divisions between those who wanted to come out in the open and those who, afraid of retaliations and persecutions, preferred to blend in with the Islamic society put a lot of strain on any development of an organized group. Because of the secrecy in which they have been forced to live for centuries, their eagerness for recognition had necessarily translated into the courageous work of redeeming sacred texts hidden for a long time, in the rediscovery and protection of their most sacred shrines, and into an even more courageous reinterpretation of their rites, culture and unique vision of the world. It was a silent revolution which aimed at preparing the future generations to be aware of their rights avoiding violence and disruption. Kakais can count on intellectuals engaged in the study, transmission and education of a new generation which will have the task of preserving their culture and of working for a peaceful coexistence with all the other minorities of the country. The Chraw Organization for Documentation, whose principal aim was to document the atrocities committed against Kakais after ISIS, is now engaged in a conversation with both the governments in Baghdad and in Erbil to obtain recognition. The road for the Kakais seems much more difficult than for the Christians or Yezidis. For example, dialogues between Kakai representatives and the authorities is difficult since, not being recognized, they are sometimes invited to negotiation tables only as observers. They do not have a quota either in the Iraqi or in the Kurdish government and this is causing a great deal of frustration within the community itself. Recently, one of Kurdish Regional Government's officials denied even the existence of a Kakai community by saying that most of the people indicated by the representatives as Kakais were actually Muslims who could not be forced to convert.

Pope Francis, during the meeting he held in Baghdad with the bishops, in the Cathedral at Sayidat al-Nejat on 5 March 2021, urged all of them to be 'pastors, servants of the people and not civil servants. Never apart from the faithful of God, never apart as though we were a privileged class. Not to renounce that privileged lineage which is the holy people of God' (Vatican News 2021).[3] Until the time when religious leaders from every community in Iraq lives among their people, supporting them, there is still hope that their presence will continue to be an invaluable asset to Iraq and the rest of the world.

I began this book with the intention of giving a voice to communities and individuals whose stories rarely reach us. In the end, what seemed like dissonant sounds and tales turned into a single symphony that prayed only to become a single community, united in the memory of a common violent past but determined to rebuild a future of possible coexistence on new foundations.

Glossary

Adiabene Ancient name of Erbil, today's capital of the Kurdish region in northern Iraq.

Ahl-e Haqq (Arabic) 'People of the truth'. An extreme sect of Shi'ite Islam in western Iran, in the provinces of Luristan, Kurdistan and Azerbaijan. They also live in Kirkuk and Sulaymaniyah, in northern Iraq. They venerate 'Ali, whom they consider to be divine, and the imams who descend from him. They also venerate Baba Yadgar, whose tomb is a site of pilgrimage. They believe in successive manifestations of the Divine seven and in metempsychosis. In some circumstances, for the similarities of some of the principles of their beliefs, Kakai people are mistakenly believed to belong to this sect.

Akitu Celebration of new year, re-enacting Enuma Elish, the Sumerian epic of creation which will be incorporated into both Assyrian and Babylonian cosmology.

Arrapha Ancient name of today's Kirkuk before it was renamed Karka d-Beit Slok.

Baba (Arabic) Father.

Bawa (Gorani Kurdish) Father.

Beth Nuhadra Ancient name of Dohuk.

Diwan In Kakai, religion is called Diwan, the council composed of Mawla/God and angels before the creation.

Emāmah (Arabic) In Islamic culture, black or white turban-style headdress worn by men in emulation of the prophet Mohammed.

Enuma Elish Sumerian epic of creation.

Farsh (Arabic) Local stone used by the Assyrians in the construction of their palaces and temples.

Gnostics Followers of the thought and practice especially of various cults of late pre-Christian and early Christian centuries distinguished by the conviction that matter is evil and that emancipation comes through gnosis.

Gorani Kurdish Kurdish dialect.

Hashd al-Shaabi (Arabic) Popular Mobilization Forces.

Imam (Arabic) The term is applied to the leader of the prayers at public prayers, to the spiritual head of a congregation or school, and to the leader of the whole Islamic community.

Jacobites Name by which in Syria, Mesopotamia and Babylonia, the followers of Monophysite doctrine were known since the sixth century. Monophysites believed in an inseparable nature, partly divine and partly human, in the person of Christ.

Jamkhāne or Jam Kakai sacred communal rituals.

Kafir (Arabic) Infidel.

Kakai (Gorani Kurdish) Brother.
KaliGaKuzna Kakai sacred place in Hawar where the first Jam took place.
Karka d-Beit Slok Ancient name of Kirkuk.
Kubba Babylonian ancient dish.
Magianism Ancient Iranian religion.
Mandeans Keepers of an ancient religion. They claim to be the last Gnostics and place river baptism at the centre of their religious life. They also claim their religious roots trace to John the Baptist. Originally present mainly in Southern Iraq, there are also communities in the USA, Europe and Australia.
Manicheans Believers in a syncretistic religious dualism, originating in Persia in the third century CE and teaching the release of the spirit from matter through asceticism.
Maqamas Sacred verses included in Kakai chants.
Mawla (Gorani Kurdish) God.
Mollah (Arabic) Title of respect for a religious and learned man.
Murîd (Arabic) Somebody who receives the teachings of a master in Sufism. For Kakais, it indicates a person who does not belong to the religious caste but to the ordinary people.
Nestorians Followers of Nestorianism, a Christian sect that originated in Asia Minor and Syria, stressing the independence of the divine and human natures of Christ and, in effect, suggesting that they are two persons loosely united. The schismatic sect formed following the condemnation of Nestorius and his teachings by the ecumenical councils of Ephesus (431 CE) and Chalcedon (451 CE).
Ottoman Empire The Ottoman Empire was one of the most enduring in history. It replaced the Byzantine Empire and spanned three continents: Europe, Asia and Africa. It lasted from 1299 to 1922, when it was replaced by the Republic of Turkey.
Pīr (Kurdish and Persian) A venerable old man. It is also a Sufi term corresponding to the Arabic sheikh. In the Kakais' case it means spiritual chief.
Qawltas In the Kakai tradition it is the time of fasting that celebrates the importance of the third pillar, humility.
Qibla (Arabic) Direction of prayers. Originally Jerusalem, it was replaced by Mecca, currently in Saudi Arabia. For Kakais, the direction is towards the shrine in Pīrdwar, Hawamaran region, Iran.
Rudaw Kurdish newspaper and TV channel.
SajNar In the Kakai religion, this is the name of the mythical era before the big bang.
Saranjam Kakai and Yarsan holy book.
Savafids Belonging to the Safavid dynasty (1501–1736). The rule of Iran by this dynasty became important because it established the Twelver Shi'ism as the state religion of Iran. This contributed to the emergence of a unified national consciousness among the various ethnicities of the country. The Safavids were descended from Sheikh Ṣafī al-Dīn (1253–1334) of Ardabīl, head of the Sufi order of the Ṣafawiyyah.

Sirwan River on the border between Iran and Iraq in the area of Hawar, sacred to the Kakais.

Surah Chapters in the Quran.

Tashar In the Saranjam, a village in the area of Hawar.

Tawûsî Melek (Arabic) Peacock Angel.

Turkman Turkmen claim to be the third largest ethnic group in Iraq, residing almost exclusively in the north, in an arc of towns and villages stretching from Tal Afar, west of Mosul, through Mosul, Erbil, Altun Kopru, Kirkuk, Tuz Khurmatu, Kifri and Khaniqin. They are probably descended from Turkic garrisons or, in the Shi'a case, fugitives from early Ottoman control, although they consider themselves to be descendants of the earlier Seljuq Turks.

Ziggurat Ancient Mesopotamian temple in the shape of a pyramid on successive levels, which had a sanctuary at its top and was used to observe the stars.

Ziyara (Arabic) Pilgrimage.

Zoroastranism Religious movement reformed by Zoroaster between 1700–1000 BCE, perhaps in Balkh but taking as its base a much older Iranian religion as is expressed in Zend-Avesta. The name derives from the supreme God of the Good, Ahura Mazdā to whom the evil Angra Manyu is opposed. The main characteristic of the religion is fire-worship and it was the main religion with both the Achaemenids and Sassanids. It disappeared with the Arab-Muslim invasions. Followers of this religion can still be found in Iran, India and Iraq.

Notes

Introduction

1. The Kurdish Region revised its own constitution in 2009. A new one is under discussion as I write.
2. When I exposed this reality to some academics in the West, my findings were dismissed on the ground that they were not interested in what people said. They also were not interested in talking with people who did not speak English, not even using translators on the ground, adding that 'the elite speaks English'.
3. Gulan Café (2011).
4. USCIRF (2017).
5. McDowall (2000: 385).
6. For a detailed account of the causes and facts of the civil war between the Barzani and Talabani, see ibid., 387–91.
7. Ibid., 380.
8. Ibid., 381.

Chapter 1

1. In May 1916, when the First World War was still raging, a secret agreement was made between France and Great Britain to divide the dying Ottoman Empire. A line of division was arbitrarily drawn creating French and British areas of influence. All of Mesopotamia, including Baghdad, became a British protectorate.
2. A fascinating introduction to the people of the Zagros Mountains can be found in Balatti (2017).
3. Ibid.
4. Herodotus (2014: 93).
5. Ibid.
6. Ibid.
7. 1- Pīr Nariman Shahoaei, 2- Pīr Meani Kheatai, 3- Pīr Ahmed Paryshaai, 4- Pīr Tayar Kashani, 5- Pīr Nazdar Shirazi, 6- Pīr Ibrahim Jaf, 7- Pīr Mohamed Sgarazuri, 8- Pīr Ahmed Ganjaei, 9- Pīr Qabil Samarqandi, 10- Pīr Ismail Gulani, 11- Pīr shamsadden, 12- Pīr Rokndden Halabja, 13- Pīr Mekael Dawdani, 14- Pīr Nali Murdini, 15- Pīr Taher Asfahani, 16- Pīr Alamdar Khutni, 17- Pīr Haedar kurdi, 18- Pīr Kamal

Mamolani, 19- Pīr Alias Moriasi, 20- Pīr Faeroz Hindi, 21- Pīr Hayas Magribi, 22- Pīr Nakartani, 23- Pīr Rastgo Karadagi, 24- Pīr Hasan Istambuli, 25- Pīr Kamar Srwaqumashi, 26- Pīr Taki Banmbui, 27- Pīr Nari balamuai, 28- Pīr Ahmed Lurstani, 29- Pīr Tajadden Parsi, 30- Pīr Hasan Kurasani, 31- Pīr Mahmud bagdadi, 32- Pīr Aziz Basraui, 33- Pīr Ibrahim Turazi, 34- Pīr Sulaiman Ardalani, 35- Pīr Yaqub Kalati, 36- Pīr Khaliq Ardabili, 37- Pīr Mansur Shshtari, 38- Pīr Ali Shaqaqi, 39- Pīr Malk Goran, 40- Pīr Mamal Mahidshi, 41- Pīr Naser Bakhtyari, 42- Pīr Aisa baskani, 43- Pīr KHalil Musali, 44- Pīr Jafaar Karazi, 45- Pīr Hamzai Khurkaei, 46- Pīr Tamaz Krmani, 47- Pīr Taemur Aurumi, 48- this is missing 49- Pīr Qubad Diwani, 50- Pīr Kazam Knguri, 51- Pīr Daniar Dalahuei, 52- Pīr Safar Qalacha, 53- Pīr Musa miana, 54- Pīr Sura handala, 55- Pīr Neamatalah Tabardari, 56- Pīr Sadiq Mazindarani, 57- Pīr Haidar Glmidani, 58- Pīr Hayat Machini, 59- Pīr Dalawar Darashishi, 60- Pīr Qanun Shami, 61- Pīr Hatam Hamadani, 62- Pīr Abas Karzani, 63- Pīr Mlwan Kaabi, 64- Pīr Fatali Sahana, 65- Pīr Azadden Hudana, 66- Pīr Muamin Hasan Abadi, 67- Pīr Farand Lahuri, 68- Pīr Ahsham Barbari, 69- Pīr Mardan Hurini, 70- Pīr Daiar Shrari, 71- Pīr Baba Gib Hawari, 72- Pīr Rostam Zibaai.

8   For a more detailed description of Yarsan/Kakai mythology, see Kreyenbroek and Kanakis (2020).
9   The translation of this section of the Saranjam included in Edmonds' paper has been provided by Adel Kakay in 2020.
10 Yoga Sūtras, 3: 18.
11 The tale refers to the emāmah, 'black' for Shia and 'white' for Sunnis.
12 Dinsmore (2002).
13 Baban (2008: 10–24).
14 Baba in Arabic and Bawa in Kakai language mean father.
15 Morton (2006: 8).
16 Plutarch (2008: 345–6).
17 Morton (2006: 9).
18 Pelosi (2010: 7).
19 Ibid., 30.
20 Interview with Rashid Luqman, October 2020.
21 Mir-Hosseini (1996), cited by Kreyenbroek and Kanakis (2020: 35).
22 Shilani (2021).
23 In their book, *God First and Last* (2020) Kreyenbroek and Kanakis, talking about the Iraqi community, mention that their level of emancipation still did not reach that of the Yezidis.
24 Song (2011).
25 Ibid.
26 Ibid.
27 Anonymous interview, October 2019.

28 Interview with Kakai representative, September 2020.
29 Interview with Farhad al-Kake, Director of Chraw Organization for Documentation, Erbil, 20 June 2020.
30 Shafaq (2020).
31 Interview with Farhad al-Kake, Director of Chraw Organization for Documentation, Erbil, 20 June 2020.
32 Ibid.
33 The Babylonian Brigades are composed of Christians and were born after 2014. They always claimed to fight against ISIS; however, their connection with Shi'ite militias, including Hashd al-Shaabi, has been recorded. The Chaldean Church has publicly distanced itself from these militias and from their leader, Ryan al Kildani. See *Independent Catholic News* (2019).
34 Interview with Farhad al-Kake, Director of Chraw Organization for Documentation, Erbil, 20 June 2020.

Chapter 2

1 'This landscape is the great garden of the Bible, the earthly paradise of Adam and Eve. In the distance, I saw Noah, Abraham, Jonah, Alexander the Great, Saint Thomas and Marco Polo walking on the road to Mosul' [my translation].
2 Chaldeans are historically associated with the Assyrian Church of the East, also called the Nestorian Church. They fully united with Rome in 1778. Currently, Chaldeans are the most numerous Christian community in northern Iraq.
3 References to the history of the Tomb of Prophet Nahum in Alqosh can be found on the webpage of Mesopotamia Heritage (n.d. a).
4 Ibid.
5 Interview with Father Ghazwan, Alqosh, 16 April 2019.
6 In Fiey (1965: 395).
7 English translation of the inscription in Harrak (2010), Réf. AO.01.09, photo p. 189, text p. 418.
8 According to tradition, Mar Mikha was one of the holy fathers of Alqosh in the fourth century, at a time when Christianity was already settled there. The very first church of Mar Mikha had been founded at that time to host its relics. The fame of the local saint was such that every family in Alqosh had to give the name 'Mikha' to one of their baby boys. See Mesopotamia Heritage (n.d. a).
9 Wallis Budge (1902).
10 Ibid.
11 Harrak (2001: 168–89).
12 Wallis Budge (1902).

13 Ibid.
14 Ibid.
15 Becker (2006: 77–97).
16 Penn (2015).
17 Theophanes Confessor ([815] 1997), 310–11/442–43. See also Kaegi (2012: 18) and Stoyanov (2011: 61).
18 Walker (2006: 3–5/20).
19 In his book, *A State of Mixture*, Payne notes that:

> The History of Karka and History of Mar Qardagh hagiographers went beyond the account in the Book of Genesis to make Nimrod the primordial source of kingship in northern Mesopotamia, from whose patrilineage legitimate political power flowed. On the basis of the Chronicle of Eusebius and the Hebrew Bible, and likely in dialogue with local oral accounts, these hagiographies recast Nimrod as an Assyrian, joining two ancient historical traditions that had previously been distinct.
>
> 2015: 149

20 Ibid., 66/52.
21 Ibid.
22 Ibid.
23 Harrak (2010).
24 Description from the *Encyclopedia Britannica*.
25 Amir Harrak, in his study, notes:

> Funerary inscriptions with the speech in the first person are rather rare in Syriac Christianity, though they are widely known in the Classical and Near Eastern worlds. The earliest case is the Aramaic inscription of Agbar, the priest of the moon-god in Nerab (near Aleppo), dated to the 7th century BC. In it he says: 'On the day of my death, my mouth was not shut from (saying) words, and with my own eyes I saw my children of the fourth generation weeping for me.'
>
> Fiey 1965

26 Extract from the epitaph about Patriarch Audo. See Fiey (1965: 549). Also see Harrak (2010) for the detail of all dedicatory inscriptions, particularly funeral inscriptions of the Monastery of Our Lady of the Seeds.
27 Mesopotamia Heritage (n.d. b).
28 Bas Snelders offers a very detailed description and artistic analysis of this specific wall painting, establishing links with Byzantine art. Discussing the representation of the personification of the River Jordan without a beard, he states that similar ones can be found 'in the Cappella Palatina in Palermo (mid-twelfth century, the Church of St George in Kurbinovo (1191) in Macedonia, and in several wall paintings in Cappadocia, where he is frequently shown blowing a horn' (Snelders 2010: 6).

29 Jonah, 4: 11.
30 Seven visits to the Mosque of Nabi Younis are equivalent to a pilgrimage to Mecca.
31 Everyone in the city knows the story of this prophet. In Mosul, parents make their offspring believe that if they are well behaved, they will be able to see the whale bathing in the Tigris. And when a child who is a little less credulous than the others doubts, the adults explain to him that the best proof that the whale still swims in the river is that no one has ever found his grave. As a child, I, too, was shocked by this story.
32 Anonymous interviewee, Alqosh, April 2018.
33 Ibid.
34 Anonymous interviewee, October 2020.
35 The Sabean-Mandaeans' religion is a form of Gnosticism, descended from ancient Mesopotamian worship. Their central prophet is John the Baptist and they practise baptism through immersion in flowing water. Sabean-Mandaean faith bars the use of violence or the carrying of weapons. It is difficult to establish an exact number of Sabean-Mandaeans in Iraq, but they are estimated to be around 120,000. Within Iraqi society, Sabean-Mandaeans are much appreciated as refined goldsmiths.
36 Cave (2006).See at: https://www.nytimes.com/2006/09/04/world/middleeast/04dora.html.
37 AINA (2007).
38 Ibid.
39 See at: http://www.aina.org/releases/2007053195824.htm.
40 Anonymous interviewees.
41 The Shlomo Organization for Documentation is an independent, non-profit organization based in Erbil. It began its activities in January 2016, and its mission is to monitor and document violations and crimes committed by ISIS against Christians and other religious minorities in Iraq and Syria. Its aim is to submit the documents to national and international authorities to prevent the recurrence of the crimes.
42 Williams (2016).
43 Ibid.
44 Halsall (1996).
45 Wasserstein (2017b).
46 Ibid.
47 Interview with Father Salar Bodag, Teleskof, October 2019.
48 Ibid.
49 Ibid.
50 Anonymous interviewee, Teleskof, October 2019.
51 *The Citadel: Fascinations of the Ancient Erbil, Heart of Iraqi Kurdistan*, Catalogue of the Photography Exhibition, Institute of the Italian Encyclopaedia, Rome, 4–14 November 2014.

52 Cuneiform tablet, Hecht Museum, Haifa; from MacGinnis (2014).
53 Stele, Louvre, Parigi, AO 2666; from MacGinnis (ibid.).
54 Esarhaddon Cylinder Kalah A, BritishMuseum, London, BM 131129; from MacGinnis (ibid.).
55 Herodotus (2014), *Histories*, V. 52.
56 By K. Kris Hirst (2018).
57 In the Anabasis of Alexander, Arrian lists Persian forces on the ground: 'The number of Dareius' forces was given as 40,000 horses, 1,000,000-foot, 200 scythe-chariots, a few elephants, the Indians on this side of the Indus having some fifteen. With this army, Dareius had encamped at Gaugamela by the River Bumodus, about 600 stades from the city of Arbela, in a position level on all sides. For what few uneven parts for cavalry there had been, the Persians had long ago made convenient both for chariot-driving and for cavalry to ride over.
58 Dio Cassius, *Roman History*, LXXIX.1.
59 Mellon Saint-Laurent (2015).
60 The *Acts of Thomas* is an early third-century apocryphal narrative present in the missionary narrative of the Syriac tradition that attributes the conversion of India to Saint Thomas. It is divided into thirteen chapters which contain Saint Thomas' travels and miracles.
61 Mellon Saint-Laurent (2015).
62 To abandon a garden, but a tree also that we have known since our childhood. But also, the smell of a road, the colour of a door, all that make a man's life.
63 Interview with Archbishop Bashar Warda, Erbil, April 2019.
64 Ibid.
65 This interview is part of the recording for the BBC World Service programme, 'The Last Christians in Iraq?', which I presented and which was produced by Eve Streeter in April 2019.
66 Ibid.
67 Yazda (n.d.).
68 Ibid.
69 'The installation was all the more difficult as this building of refugees quickly took on the appearance of a kind of Noah's Ark. I absolutely wanted to make room for several Yezidi families' [my translation].
70 Not helping a few families who survived this massacre was becoming an accomplice of evil.
71 We have the same enemy and we both wear a white habit.
72 Vatican News (2019).
73 Ibid.
74 Tornielli (2021).
75 A village where Muslim shepherds used to sell the wool to the Christians who weaved it.

76 Paul Moses (2009).
77 Arnald of Sarrant (2010: 15).
78 Paul VI (1965).
79 Ibid.
80 Konrad-Adenauer-Stiftung (KAS) (2018).
81 Ibid.

Chapter 3

1   For a more detailed description of Yezidis' culture and religion, see Açikyildiz (2014). See also Kreyenbroek (2009).
2   Hartman (1995): 192.
3   Kreyenbroek (1995).
4   Açikyildiz (2014).
5   Fuccaro (1999: 10).
6   See Açikyildiz (2014) for a detailed reconstruction of the history of the Yezidis.
7   Guest (1993: 67).
8   Ibid., 135–7.
9   Feierstein (2014).
10 Ingrams (1983).
11 Fulanain (2010: 18).
12 Ibid., 29–30.
13 Ibid.
14 Efrati (2015: 135).
15 Ali (2018: 113).
16 For a better understanding of the interaction between federalism, secession and the need for international recognition in the Kurdish region, see Danilovic (2019).
17 Galbraith (2007: 140).
18 In his book, *Iraq: From War to a New Authoritarianism*, Toby Dodge (2012) explains the failure of the central government in Baghdad and the rise of Maliki into power.
19 Article 13(1).
20 Institute for International Law and Human Rights (2011: 22).
21 Human Rights Watch (2017).
22 Part of this section has been published in Corticelli (2021), 'Survival: The Case of Yezidi Women', in Sara E. Brown and Stephen D. Smith (eds), *The Routledge Handbook of Religion, Mass Atrocity, and Genocide*, (London and New York: Routledge).
23 In 'Rape during War is not Inevitable', Elisabeth J. Wood (2012) explains how, in different conflicts, sexual violence could be controlled if not completely prevented by

the same perpetrators. The Salvadorian insurgency, for example, has successfully prohibited the use of sexual violence against civilians. Also, the Israeli–Palestinian conflict saw a very limited use of sexual violence.

24 Warren (2018: ix).
25 Bouchet-Saulnier (2013).
26 UN International Residual Mechanism for Criminal Tribunals (n.d.).
27 UN International Criminal Tribunal for the Former Yugoslavia (n.d.).See at: https://www.icty.org/en/features/crimes-sexual-violence/landmark-cases.
28 On 5 September 1981, Law 442 cancelled honour killing and shotgun marriage from the Italian penal code. Until then, men who killed wives, daughters or sisters who had caused them 'dishonor', benefitted from a large penalty discount.
29 Memory of persecution is at the core of Yezidi culture. From various interviews, I managed to learn that they were victims of 72 genocides. During the Ottoman Empire, due to their religious beliefs, Yezidis were persecuted both by Ottomans and by Kurdish tribes. For more detailed information about the persecutions suffered by Yezidis, see Açikyildiz's (2014).
30 Mahmoud (2017).
31 For a better understanding of ISIS's ideology, see Fawaz (2016).
32 See, among others, Nalle (2011).
33 See, for example, Portelli (2003).
34 For a general introduction to the genocides committed in the former Yugoslavia and Rwanda, see chapters 8 and 9 in Jones (2011).
35 Ibid.
36 Interview with Khadhir Domle, Yezidi activist, Erbil, 2018. See also Callimachi (2015).
37 Quoted by Michaeel Najeeb (2017). Father Michaeel Najeeb is currently Archbishop of Mosul. At the time of the attack, he was living in Qaraqosh and organized the rescue of the Christian heritage held in Qaraqosh Monastery.
38 Omtzigt and Ochab (2019).
39 An analysis of the relationship between rape and shame has also been tackled by UN advisors. For example, during a meeting in 2017, Adama Dieng stated that: 'Aggressors understand that this crime attacks individual and collective identity, social relationships and status' (UN Meeting Coverage and Press Releases 2017). The consequence of this is that victims find it very difficult to return to their own community. This topic is also explored in, Kizilhan, Steger and Noll-Hussong (2020).
40 The study of the impact of the organization of local civil society in Iraq and in the Kurdish region is still pretty much uncharted territory and deserves more attention. However, during my fieldwork, I had the opportunity to experience how important their work is in particular in advocating for minorities' rights.
41 Murad (2018).

42 The inclusion into Yezidi society of children born from the rapes inflicted by ISIS militants is still a point of contention. Yezidi women who had children or were made pregnant during their captivity have been forced to give up their children if they wanted to be reintegrated into the community. Yezidi authorities made very clear that 'no Yezidi child from an ISIS father would be accepted into a Yezidi home for any period of time' (Greaser 2018: 6).

Chapter 4

1 Mahmoud (2011).
2 Ibid.
3 Mardini (2020: 1).
4 Ignatius (2014).
5 Associated Press Archive Video (2016a,b).
6 Sowell (2020: 124).
7 Peterson (2017).
8 al-Jamas (2019).
9 Leezenberg (2019: 197–8).
10 Michael Knights writes on this regard that: 'From the outset, however, the key leader in the PMF was Abu Mahdi al-Muhandis, the most inveterate opponent of the United States among the Special Group leaders, and al-Muhandis worked assiduously to develop the PMF into an organization that was neither subject to full prime ministerial command nor subordinate to the conventional security forces' (2019: 2).
11 Ibid.
12 Interview with Father Behnam Benoka on 19 April 2021.
13 See Spyer (2019). 'Iraqi Government Fails to Rein in Iraqi-Backed Militias in Nineveh Province: Implications for Israel', *The Jerusalem Institute of Strategy and Security*, 7 October 2019, available at https://jiss.org.il/en/spyer-iraqi-government-fails-to-rein-in-iran-backed-militias/ (accessed 10 June 2021). See also European Asylum Support Office (2020). See Knights, Malik and Jawad al-Tamimi (2020).

Chapter 5

1 A video of Francis Fukuyama's intervention is available (2017).
2 This privilege granted to the KDP and not to the PUK reveals the way Baghdad weakened the two Kurdish parties with the purpose of sharpening their differences.
3 For further information, see Jafar (2007).

4 Interview with Masoud Barzani (2014).
5 A copy of the KRG constitution is available at: www.krg.com (accessed 15 May 2021).
6 Article 121/4 of the Iraqi Constitution grants the regions the right to establish offices in embassies with the purpose of participating in diplomatic missions in order to follow cultural, social and developmental affairs (Iraq Government 2005).
7 Data reported in Manara Network (2001: 41).
8 Iraq Council of Ministers (2020).
9 Data reported in Manara Network (2001: 42).
10 Ibid.
11 Interview with Nozad Polis Hakim, Soraya Organization, Erbil, 20 December 2017.
12 Business people interviewed in 2016 advocated for a more flexible approach to training and development to improve the region's economy.
13 Assyrian Confederation of Europe (2017: 10).
14 It suits us even if no one has forgotten what they did to our great-grandparents and if we all know they have a secret agenda.
15 See at: https://youtube/zVqcmgAtjp8?t=18. Through interviews with witnesses and documents, this video shows the accusation of the minorities against the KRG. This accusation has also been confirmed in confidential interviews with members of the Assyrian/Christian community and the Yezidis held in Erbil between 2016 and 2018.
16 Ibid.
17 Assyrian Confederation of Europe (2017: 10).
18 Ibid.
19 Human Rights Watch (2009) and Voice of Free Assyrians (2016).
20 Member of the Kakai community interviewed in Erbil on 13 January 2018. This point will be discussed in more detail in Chapter 1 here on the Kakais.
21 Interview with Assyrian refugees in Jordan, December 2018.
22 Ibid.
23 Ibid.
24 Interview with Father Noel Kosso, Athens, 2018.
25 Interview with Sangor George Donabed, 23 July 2018, and Interview with Christian refugees in Jordan, 25 July 2018.
26 Interview with Christian representative, Ankawa, June 2016.
27 Ibid.
28 Assyrian Confederation of Europe (2017: 41–2).
29 Washington Kurdish Institute (2017).
30 Interview with Christian refugees in Jordan, 25 July 2018.
31 Kurdish Draft Constitution, 2009.
32 Interview with a former resident of Batnaya, December 2018.
33 Assyrian Policy Institute (2018).

34 Interview with Omed A. Massor, Erbil, 7 June 2017.
35 Interview with Christian refugee from Batnaya, 25 July 2018.
36 Ibid.
37 Interview with Sangor George Donabed, 23 July 2018, and with Interview with Christian refugees in Jordan, 25 July 2018.
38 Anonymous refugee from Bartalla, Ankawa, 12 June 2017.
39 It is not the purpose of this report to analyse the reality of the refugee camps. More information about the costs of the refugees crisis can be found in the report by the World Bank Group (2015).
40 Iraq/3RP 2016/2017; Multi/Sector Needs Assessment (MSNA) of Syrian refugees living in host communities, April 2015 & Multi/Cluster Needs Assessment for Internally Displaced Persons Outside of Camps in Iraq, October 2015.
41 Freedom House (2019).
42 UN (2017).

Conclusion

1 The translation of the Saranjam Chawdar was provided by Luqman Rashid.
2 See Minority Rights (2021).
3 Vatican News (2021).

Bibliography

Açikyildiz, Birgül (2014), *The Yezidis: The History of a Community, Culture and Religion*, London: I.B. Tauris.
Ahmed, Badeeah Hassan (2019), *A Cave in the Clouds*, Toronto: Annick Press.
al-Ali, Nadje and Nicola Pratt (2011), 'Between Nationalism and Women's Rights: The Kurdish Women's Movement in Iraq', *Middle Eastern Journal of Culture and Communication*, 4 (3): 337–53.
al-Jamas, Raad (2019), 'Finding Homes in Ruin, Destitute Iraqis Return to Camps', Agence France-Presse (AFP), 24 August.
Ali, Zahra (2018), *Women and Gender in Iraq: Between Nation-Building and Fragmentation*, Cambridge: Cambridge University Press.
Alinia, Minoo (2013), *Honor and Violence against Women in Iraqi Kurdistan*, New York: Palgrave Macmillan.
Anonymous (n.d.), *The Book of Treasures*.
Aprim, Fred (2004), 'El-Qosh (Alqosh), Yimma d'Athor (The Mother of Assyria)', *Assyrian Education Network*, 22 September. Available at: https://www.atour.com/education/20040922a.html (accessed 20 October 2020).
Arnald of Sarrant (2010), *Chronicle of the Twenty-Four Generals of the Order of the Friars Minor [1369–1374], Section 1*, Malta: TAU Franciscan Communications.
Associated Press Archive (2016a), *Iraqi Sunni Militia*, Video, 10 August.
Associated Press Archive Video (2016b), 'Hajj Ali – 9 August 2016', AP Video, Story Number: 4049828, 10 August.
Assyrian Confederation of Europe (ACE) (2017), *Erasing Assyrians: How the KRG Abuses Human Rights, Undermines Democracy, and Conquers Minority Homelands*, 25 September, Washington, DC: Assyrian Confederation of Europe.
Assyrian International News Agency (AINA) (2007), Editorial, 'Mounting Fears of Assyrian Genocide in Iraq', 31 May. Available at: http://www.aina.org/releases/2007053195824.htm (accessed 18 February 2021).
Assyrian Policy Institute (2018), *Iraq's Stolen Elections*, Washington, DC: Assyrian Policy Institute.
Aziz, S. (2014), 'The Kurdish Regional Government Elections: A Critical Evaluation', *Insight Turkey*, 16: 67–76.
Baban, Taha (2008), *Alam al-Kurd al-Morab*, Erbil: Aras Publisher.
Bader, Fr. Rif'at. (2020), *Vatican News*, 15 December. Available at: https://www.vaticannews.va/en/church/news/2020-12/pope-visit-iraq-rif-at-bader-background.html (accessed 10 February 2021).

Balatti, S. (2017), *Mountain Peoples in the Ancient Near East: The Case of the Zagros in the First Millennium BCE*, Wiesbaden: Harrassowitz Verlag.

Bartov, Omer and Phyllis Mack, eds (2001), *In God's Name: Genocide and Religion in the Twentieth Century*, New York and Oxford: Berghahn Books.

Barzani, Masoud (2014), Interview with Masoud Barzani, July. Available at: http://www.al-monitor.com/pulse/originals/2014/07/iraq-kurdistan-region-barzani-interview-crisis-independence.html# (accessed 15 May 2021).

Becker, Adam H. (2006), *The School of Nisibis and the Development of Scholastic Culture in Late Antique Mesopotamia*, 77–97, Philadelphia, PA: University of Pennsylvania Press.

Begikhani, N. (2010), *Honour-Based Violence (HBV) and Honour-Based Killings in Iraqi Kurdistan and in the Kurdish Diaspora in the UK*, Bristol: Roehampton University, Kurdish Women's Rights Watch, Bristol University.

Bengio, O. (2012), *The Kurds of Iraq: Building a State within a State*, Boulder, CO: Lynne Rienner.

Bouchet-Saulnier, Françoise (2013), *The Practical Guide to Humanitarian Law*, Lanham, MD: Rowman & Littlefield Publishers.

Brock, Sebastian P. and Susan Ashbrook Harvey, introd. and trans. (2008), *Holy Women of the Syrian Orient*, https://hdl-handle-net.uoelibrary.idm.oclc.org/2027/heb.94258, Los Angeles and Berkeley, CA: University of California Press.

Brown, Peter (1971), 'The Rise and Function of the Holy Man in Late Antiquity', *Journal of Roman Studies*, 61: 80–101.

Burton, Neel (2009), *Plato's Shadow: A Primer on Plato*, Oxford: Acheron Press.

Callimachi, Rukmini (2015), 'ISIS Enshrines a Theology of Rape', *The New York Times*, 13 August. Available at: https://www.nytimes.com/2015/08/14/world/middleeast/ISIS-enshrines-a-theology-of-rape.html (accessed 5 June 2021).

Castellino, Joshua and Kathleen A. Cavanaugh (2013), *Minority Rights in the Middle East*. Oxford: Oxford University Press.

Cave, Damien (2006), 'Troops Cut Death, but not Fear, in Baghdad Zone', 4 September. Available at: https://www.nytimes.com/2006/09/04/world/middleeast/04dora.html (accessed 20 January 2021).

Civil Development Organization (CDO) (2012), *The Minorities in Iraq: Seeking Justice, Equality and the Fear for the Future*, Sulaymaniyah: Civil Development Organization.

Corticelli, Maria Rita (2021), 'Survival: The Case of Yezidi Women', in Sara E. Brown and Stephen D. Smith (eds), *The Routledge Handbook of Religion, Mass Atrocity, and Genocide*, 383–90, London and New York: Routledge.

D'Costa, Bina (2018), 'Rape Survivors Bearing Witness in War and Peace in Bangladesh', in Elisssa Bemporad and Joyce W. Warren (eds), *Woman and Genocide: Survivors, Victims, Perpetrators*, 159–90, Bloomington, IN: Indiana University Press.

Danilovic, Alex (2014), *Iraqi Federalism and the Kurds: Learning to Live Together*, London: Ashgate Publisher.

Danilovic, Alex (2019), *Federalism, Secession, and International Recognition Regime: Iraqi Kurdistan*, London: Routledge.
Dinsmore, Guy (2002), 'The Enduring Pain of Halabja', *Financial Times*, 10 July.
Dodge, Toby (2012), *Iraq: From War to a New Authoritarianism*, London: International Institute for Strategic Studies.
Edmonds, C. J. (1957), *Kurds, Turks and Arabs: Politics, Travel and Research in North-Eastern Iraq 1919–1925*, Oxford: Oxford University Press.
Edmonds, C. J. (1969), 'The Beliefs and Practices of the Ahl-i Ḥaqq, of Iraq', *Iran: Journal of the British Institute of Persian Studies*, 7: 89–101.
Efrati, Noga (2015), *Women in Iraq: Past Meets Present*, New York: Columbia University Press.
European Asylum Support Office (EASO) (2020), *Iraq: Security Situation*, Country of Origin Information Report, October, Grand Harbour Valletta: EASO.
Failyon, Al (2012), *History and Destructive Citizenship*, Erbil: Aras Publishers.
Fanon, Franz (1967), *Black Skin, White Mask*, London: Pluto Press.
Fawaz, George (2016), *ISIS: A History*, Princeton, NJ: Princeton University Press.
Feierstein, Daniel (2014), *Genocide as Social Practice: Reorganizing Society under the Nazis and Argentina's Military Juntas*, New Brunswick, NJ: Rutgers University Press.
Fiey, J. M. (1965), *Assyrie Chrétienne: Contribution a l'étude de l'histoire et de la géographie ecclésiastique et monastiques du nord de l'Iraq*, Vol. 2, Beyrouth: Imprimerie Catholique.
Freedom House (2019), *World Report 2019 – Iraq*, Washington, DC: Freedom House. Available at: available at: https://freedomhouse.org/report/freedom-world/2019/Iraq (accessed 12 April 2021).
Fuccaro, Nelida (1999), *The Other Kurds*, London: I.B. Tauris.
Fukuyama, Francis (2017) Sulaimani Forum: An Interview with Francis Fukuyama, 10 March. Available at: https://www.youtube.com/watch?v=aUkRuNhIV18 (accessed 18 April 2021).
Fulanain (2010) *The Tribes of the Marsh Arabs of Iraq: The World of Haji Rikkan*, London: Routledge.
Galbraith, Peter (2007), *The End of Iraq: How American Incompetence Created a War without End*, London: Simon & Schuster.
Goodnick-Westenholz, Joan, Yossi Maurey and Edwin Seroussi, eds (2014), *Music in Antiquity: The Near East and the Mediterranean*, Berlin and Boston, MA: Walter de Gruyter GmbH.
Greaser, Jordan (2018), *Attitudes of Sinjari Yezidis in Iraq Regarding the Rape of Yezidi Women and the Babies Born from Rape during the ISIS Genocide*, Lincoln, NB: University of Nebraska Press.
The Guardian (2014), 'Islamic State Destroys Ancient Mosul Mosque, the Third in a Week', 28 July. Available at: www.theguardian.com (accessed 16 September 2020).
Guest, Jordan (1993), *Survival among the Kurds*, London: Kegan Paul International.

Gulan Café (2011), حرق وتدمير اماكن المساج وبيع المشروبات (Burning and Destroying Massage Parlours and Alcohol Shops). Available at: http://www.facebook.com/GulanCafe http://gulancafe.com/ (accessed 2 December 2011).

Gunter, M. (2011), 'Economic Opportunities in Iraqi Kurdistan', *Middle East Policy*, 18 (2): 102–9.

Gunter, M. (2013), 'The Kurdish Spring', *Third World Quarterly*, 32 (9): 441–57.

Halliday, Fred (2005), *The Middle East in International Relations*, Cambridge: Cambridge University Press.

Halsall, Paul (1996), Internet Medieval Sourcebook, January. Available at: https://history.hanover.edu/courses/excerpts/211umar.html (accessed 30 June 2021).

Harrak, A. (2001), 'Tales about Sennacherib: The Contribution of the Syriac Sources', in P. M. M. Daviau, J. W. Wevers and M. Weigl (eds), *The World of the Aramaeans III: Studies in Language and Literature in Honour of Paul-Eugène Dion*, Vol. 3, 168–89, Sheffield: Sheffield Academic Press.

Harrak, Amir (2010), *Syriac and Garshuni Inscriptions of Iraq (Répertoire des inscriptions syriaques, 2)*, Paris: Académie des Inscriptions et Belles-Lettres.

Harrak, Amir (2014), *The Christian–Muslim Symbiosis of Mosul and Its End*. Available at: https://www.oasiscenter.eu/en/the-christian-muslim-symbiosis-of-mosul-now-coming-to-an-end (accessed 12 February 2020).

Hartman, Geoffrey H. (1995), 'Learning from Survivors: The Yale Testimony Project', *Holocaust and Genocide Studies*, 9 (2): 192–207.

Herodotus (2014), *The Histories*, London: Penguin.

Hirst, K. Kris (2018), *The Royal Road of the Achaemenids*. Available at: https://www.thoughtco.com/royal-road-of-the-achaemenids-172590 (accessed 27 March 2020).

HRW (2017), 'Iraq: Parliament Rejects Marriage for 8-Year-Old Girls', 17 December. Available at: https://www.hrw.org/news/2017/12/17/iraq-parliament-rejects-marriage-8-year-old-girls (accessed 12 March 2021).

Huffman, Carl, ed. (2014), *A History of Pythagoreanism*, Cambridge: Cambridge University Press.

Human Rights Watch (HRW) (2009), *On Vulnerable Ground: Violence against Minority Communities in Nineveh Province's Disputed Territories*, 10 November, New York: HRW.

Hussein, Mahmood (2017), 'UNESCO', *Unesco*, 15 April. Available at: https://en.unesco.org/courier/2017-april-june.koran-between-text-and-context (accessed 2 January 2021).

Ibrahim, Hawkar, Verena Ertl, Claudia Catani, Azad Ali Ismail and Frank Neuner (2018), 'Trauma and Perceived Social Rejection among Yazidi Women and Girls Who Survived Enslavement and Genocide', *BMC Med.*, 16 (1): 1–2.

Ignatius, David (2014), 'Iraq and the U.S. are Losing Ground to the Islamic State', *Washington Post*, 23 October.

Ihsan, Mohammed (2017), *Nation Building in Kurdistan: Memory, Genocide and Human Rights*, London: Routledge.

Independent Catholic News (2019), 'Iraq: Chaldean Church Repeats Complete Rejection of So-Called "Christian Militias"', 25 July. Available at: https://www.indcatholicnews.com/news/37554 (accessed 3 July 2020).

Ingrams, Doreen (1983), *The Awakened: Women in Iraq*, London: Third World Centre.

Institute for International Law and Human Rights (2011), *Minorities and the Law in Iraq*, Washington, DC: Institute for International Law and Human Rights.

Investment Board, KRG (2006), Kurdistan Investment Board. Available at: https://gov.krd/molsa-en/activities/categories/activities/ (20 March 2020).

Iraq Council of Ministers (2020), 'Iraq Constitution of 2005'. Available at: http://www.Parliament.iq/manshurat/dastorar.pdf (accessed 25 October 2020).

Iraq Government (n.d.), Iraq Constitution. Available at: http://www.iraqinationality.gov.iq/attach/iraqi_constitution.pdf.

Iraq Government (2005), 'Iraqi Constitution'. Available at: https://gds.gov.iq (accessed 20 April 2020); and https://www.constituteproject.org/constitution/Iraq_2005.pdf?lang=en (accessed 4 January 2021).

Jafar, M. (2007), 'Iraqi Faylee Kurds and Their Role in the Iraqi Kurdish National Movement', Faylee Kurds Democratic Union (FKDU), September. Available at: http://www.faylee.org/english/studies/doc3.php (accessed 30 April 2021).

Jones, Adam (2011), *Genocide: A Comprehensive Introduction*, London and New York: Routledge.

Kimball, Sam (2017), *Iraq's Shabaks Return to Devastated Homes in Battle against IS*, 11 May 2017. Available at: https://www.middleeasteye.net/features/iraqs-shabaks-return-devastated-homes-battle-against (accessed 25 May 2020).

Kizilhan, J. I., F. Steger and M. Noll-Hussong (2020), 'Shame, Dissociative Seizures and Their Correlation among Traumatized Yazidi with Experience of Sexual Violence', *British Journal of Psychiatry*, 216 (3): 138–43.

Knights, Michael (2020), 'Iran's Expanding Militia Army in Iraq: The New Special Groups', *CTC Sentinel*, 12 (7): 1–12.

Knights, Michael, Hamdi Malik and Aymenn Jawad al-Tamimi (2020) *Honored, Not Contained: The Future of Iraq's Popular Mobilization Forces*, March, Washington, DC: Washington Institute of Near East Policy.

Konrad-Adenauer-Stiftung (KAS) (2018), *Minority Representation in the KRI*, August 2018. Available at: www.kas.de and www.kas.de/syrien-irak (accessed 30 August 2018).

Kreyenbroek, Philip G. (1995), *Yezidism: Its Background, Observances and Textual Tradition*, Lewiston, NY: Lampeter.

Kreyenbroek, Philip G. (2009), *Yezidism in Europe: Different Generations Speak about their Religion*, Iranica, Wiesbaden: Harrassowitz Verlag.

Kreyenbroek, Philip G. and Yiannis Kanakis (2020), *'God First and Last': Religious Traditions and Music of the Yaresan of Guran*, Vol. 1: *Religious Traditions*, Leipzig: Harrassowitz Verlag.

KRG (2012), *National Strategy to Confront Violence against Women in Kurdistan*, Governmental Report, Erbil: Kurdish Regional Government (KRG).

KRG, Joint Crises Coordination Center (2017), *Baghdad's Flights Embargo on KRI's Airports has Directly Affected Millions of People across Kurdistan Region of Iraq*, Erbil: KRG.

Kurdish Regional Government (KRG) KRG Constitution. Available at: www.krg.com (accessed 15 May 2021).

Leezenberg, Michiel (2019), 'The Shabak: Between Secular Nationalisms and Sectarian Violence', in Bayar Mustafa Sevdeen and Thomas Schmidinger (eds), *Beyond ISIS: History and Future of Minorities in Iraq*, 197–206. London: Transnational Press.

Ludwig, Theodore (2005), *The Sacred Paths of the East*, Upper Saddle River, NJ: Prentice Hall.

McDowall, D. (2000), *A Modern History of the Kurds*, London: I.B. Tauris.

McGee, Thomas (2018), 'Saving the Survivors: Yezidi Women, Islamic State and the German Admissions Programme', *Kurdish Studies*, 6 (1): 85–109.

MacGinnis, John (2014), *A City from the Dawn of History: Erbil in the Cuneiform Sources*, Cambridge: Cambridge University Press.

Mahmoud, Hussein (2017), *The Koran: Between Text and Context*, UNESCO. Available at: https://en.unesco.org/courier/2017-april-june/koran-between-text-and-context (accessed 2 January 2021).

Malesevic, S. (2013), *Nation-States and Nationalisms*, Cambridge: Polity Press.

Manara Network (2001), *A Review of the Implementation of the UN Convention on the Rights of the Child*.

Mansfield, S. (2014), *The Miracle of the Kurds: A Remarkable Story of Hope Reborn in Northern Iraq*, Brentwood: Worthy Publisher.

Mardini, Ramzy (2020), 'Preventing the Next Insurgency: A Pathway for Reintegrating Iraq's Sunni Population', in Aaron Stein (ed.), *Iraq in Transition: Competing Actors and Complicated Politics*, 77–97, Philadelphia, PA: Foreign Policy Research Institute.

Mellon Saint-Laurent, Jeanne-Nicole (2015), *Missionary Stories and the Formation of the Syriac Churches*, Berkeley, CA: University of California Press.

Mellon Saint-Laurent, Jeanne-Nicole, David A. Michelson, Fr. Ugo Zannetti and Claude Detienne, eds (2016), *Bibliotheca Hagiographica Syriaca*. Available at: http://syriaca.org/bhse/index.html (accessed 8 September 2020).

MERI Economic Forum (2016), 'The Future of the Middle East: Challenges and Opportunities', Conference, Erbil, Kurdistan Region of Iraq, 25–27 October.

Mesopotamia Heritage (n.d. a), Available at: https://www.mesopotamiaheritage.org/en/monuments/la-tombe-du-prophete-nahoum/ (30 April 2021).

Mesopotamia Heritage (n.d. b), Available at: https://www.mesopotamiaheritage.org/en/lassociation/ (accessed 30 April 2021).

Michael the Syrian (1899–1924), *Chronicles*, Jean-Baptiste Chabot.

Minority Rights (2021) 'Why Iraq Must Support New Bill which Redresses the Suffering of Yezidi Women', 6 February. Available at: https://minorityrights.org/2021/02/06/iraq-yezidi-women/ (accessed 12 August 2021).

Minorsky, Vladimir (1921), *Notes sur la secte des Ahlé-Haqq*, Paris: Ernest Leroux.

Mohammed, Herish Khali and Francis Owtram (2014), 'Paradiplomacy of Regional Governments in International Relations: The Foreign Relations of the Kurdistan Regional Government (2003–2010)', *Iran and the Caucasus*, 18 (1): 65–84.
Morton, M.Q. (2006), *In the Heart of the Desert*, Aylesford: Green Mountain Press.
Moses, Paul (2009), *The Saint and the Sultan: The Crusades, Islam and Francis of Assisi's Mission of Peace*, New York: Doubleday Religion.
Murad, Nadia (2017), *The Last Girl*, London: Virago Press.
Murad, Nadia (2018), Nobel Lecture. Available at: https://www.nobelprize.org/prizes/peace/2018/murad/55705-nadia-murad-nobel-lecture-2/ (accessed 13 April 2021).
Najeeb, Michaeel (2017), *Sauver les livres et les hommes*, Paris: Grasset.
Nakash, Yitzhak (1994), *The Shi'is of Iraq*, Princeton, NJ: Princeton University Press.
Nalle, Sara (2011), *The Spanish Inquisition*, Oxford: Oxford University Press.
Natali, D. (2010), *The Kurdish Quasi-State: Development and Dependency in Post-Gulf War Iraq*, New York: Syracuse University Press.
Omarkhali, Khanna (2016), 'Transformation in the Yezidi Tradition after the ISIS Attacks: An Interview with Ilhan Kizilhan', *Kurdish Studies*, 4 (2): 148–54.
Omtzigt, Pieter and Evelina U. Ochab (2019), 'Bringing Daesh to Justice: What the International Community Can Do', *Journal of Genocide Research*, 21 (1): 71–82.
Patton, Douglas (1982), 'A History of the Atabegs of Mosul and Their Relationship with the Ulama A.H. 521–600/A.D. 1127–1262', PhD dissertation, New York University.
Paul VI (1965), *Nostra Aetate*, 'La Santa Sede', *Vatican.va*., 28 October. Available at: http://www.vatican.va/archive/hist_councils/ii_vatican_council/documents/vat-ii_decl_19651028_nostra-aetate_en.html (accessed 20 March 2021).
Payne, Richard E. (2015), *A State of Mixture: Christians, Zoroastrians and Iranian Political Culture in Late Antiquity*, Berkeley, CA: University of California Press.
Pelosi, Francesco (2010), *Plato on Music, Soul and Body*, trans. Sophie Henderson, Cambridge: Cambridge University Press.
Penn, Michael Philip (2015), *When Christians First Met Muslims: A Sourcebook of the Earliest Syriac Writings on Islam*, Oakland, CA: University of California Press.
Peterson, Scott (2017), 'How Sunnis' Post-ISIS Crisis is Leading Some to a New Iraqi Nationalism', *Christian Science Monitor*, 27 December.
Plato, *Timaeus*.
Plutarch (2008), *Greek Lives*, Oxford: Oxford University Press.
Portelli, Alessandro (2003), *The Order has Been Carried Out*, New York: Palgrave Macmillan.
Rahimi, B. and P. Eshaghi (2019), 'Introduction', in Babak Rahimi and Peyman Eshaghi (eds), *Muslim Pilgrimage in the Modern World*, 3, Chapel Hill, NC: University of North Carolina.
Rasche, Stephen (2020), *The Disappearing People: The Tragic Fate of Christians in the Middle East*, New York: Posthill Press.
Risley, Amy (2015), *Civil Societies Organizations, Advocacy and Policy Making in Latin American Democracies*, Basingstoke: Palgrave MacMillan.

Robinson, C. F. (2000), *Empire and Elites after Muslim Conquest: The Transformation of Northern Mesopotamia*, Cambridge: Cambridge University Press.

Rubin, Alissa (2007), *Nazik al-Malaika, 83, Poet Widely Known in Arab World, is Dead*, 27 June. Available at: https://www.nytimes.com/2007/06/27/arts/27malaika.html (accessed 15 October 2020).

Sa'ad, Salloum (2013), *Minorities in Iraq: Memory, Identity and Challenges*, Baghdad: Masarat for Cultural and Media Development.

Sam, Dagher (2010), 'Bombs Hit School Buses in North Iraq', *New York Times*, 2 May, 10.

Sarafian, A. (2001), 'The Absorption of Armenian Women and Children into Muslim Households as a Structural Component of Armenian Genocide', in Bartov, Omer and Phyllis Mack (eds), *In God's Name: Genocide and Religion in the Twentieth Century*, 209–21, New York and Oxford: Berghahn Books.

Schwarz, R. (2011), *War and State Building in the Middle East*, Gainsville, FL: University Press of Florida.

Shafaq (2020), تقارير-وتحليلات/مقابلة-سنكاوي-داعش-اخترقت-فصائل-عراقية-لضرب-الكورد-وثائق/ (Reports, Analyses/Interview – Sinkawi – ISIS Hacked Iraqi Tribes to Hit the Kurds Documents), 21 May. Available at: https://shafaq.com/en (accessed 3 July 2020).

Shamsadin, Abbas (2017), *Al-Maraqid al-Muzayfa* [*Faked Shrines*], Baghdad.

Sharabi, Hisham (1992), *Neopatriarchy: A Theory of Distorted Change in Arab Society*, Oxford: Oxford University Press.

Shilani, Mustafa (2021), 'Top Kurdistan Region Official Honors Kakai Religious Observance', *Kurdistan News*, 27 January. Available at: https://www.kurdistan24.net/en/story/23843-Top-Kurdistan-Region-official-honors-Kakai-religious-observance (accessed 15 March 2021).

Snelders, Bas (2010), *Identity and Christian–Muslim Inteaction: Medieval Art of the Syrian Orthodox from the Mosul Area*, Orientalia Lovaniensia Analecta, 198, Leuven: Peeters.

Song, C. S. (2011), *At the Beginning Were Stories, Not Texts*, Cambridge: James Clarke.

Sowell, Kirk H. (2020), 'Continuity and Change in Iraq's Sunni Politics: Sunni Arab Political Trends, Factions and Personality since 2014', in Aaron Stein (ed.), *Iraq in Transition: Competing Actors and Complicated Politics*, 98–124, Philadelphia, PA: Foreign Policy Research Institute, 11 December.

Spyer, Jonathan (2019), 'Iraqi Government Fails to Rein in Iraqi-Backed Militias in Nineveh Province: Implications for Israel', *Jerusalem Institute of Strategy and Security*, 7 October. Available at: https://jiss.org.il/en/spyer-iraqi-government-fails-to-rein-in-iran-backed-militias/ (accessed 10 June 2021).

Stansfield, G. (2003), *Iraqi Kurdistan: Political Development and Emergent Democracy*, London: Routledge.

Stein, Aaron (2020), 'Introduction', in Aaron Stein (ed.), *Iraq in Transition: Competing Actors and Complicated Politics*, 1–3, Philadelphia, PA: Foreign Policy Research Institute.

Taie, al-Khalid (2020), *Iraq's Shabak Community Calls for Holding Extremists Accountable*, 28 August. Available at: https://diyaruna.com/en_GB/articles/cnmi_di/features/2020/08/28/feature-01 (20 September 2020).

Theophanes Confessor ([815] 1997), *The Chronicle of Theophanes Confessor, Byzantine and Near Eastern History AD 284–813*, trans. with Introduction and Commentary by Cyril Mango and Roger Scott with the assistance of Geoffrey Greatrex, Oxford: Clarendon Press.

Tilly, C. (1975), *The Formation of National States in Western Europe*, Princeton, NJ: Princeton University Press.

Tornielli, Andrea (2021), 'The Pope in Iraq: Starting over from Abraham to Recognise One Another as Brothers', *Vatican News*, 2 March. Available at: https://www.vaticannews.va/en/vatican-city/news/2021-03/pope-iraq-abraham-brothers.html (accessed 15 March 2021).

Tripp, Charles (2014), *A History of Iraq*, Cambridge: Cambridge University Press.

UN (2014), *Immediate Response Plan Phase II (IRP2) for Internally Displaced People in the Kurdistan Region of Iraq*, Washington, DC: UN.

UN (2016), *'They Came to Destroy': ISIS Crimes against the Yazidis*, Human Rights Council, New York: United Nations.

UN (2017), 'UNAMI Acknowledges Kurdistan Region's Government Statement Announcing Respect for the Federal Court Ruling on Unity of Iraq', 15 November. Available at: https://reliefweb.int/report/iraq/unami-acknowledges-kurdistan-region-s-government-statement-announcing-respect-federal (accessed 12 April 2021).

UN Assistance Mission for Iraq (UNAMI) (2017), *UNAMI Acknowledges Kurdistan Region's Government Statement Announcing Respect for the Federal Court Rulin on Unity of Iraq*, Report, 15 November. Available at: https://reliefweb.int/report/iraq/unami-acknowledges-kurdistan-region-s-government-statement-announcing-respect-federal (accessed 12 April 2021).

UN International Criminal Tribunal for the Former Yugoslavia (n.d.), *Land Mark Cases*. Available at: https://www.icty.org/en/features/crimes-sexual-violence/landmark-cases (accessed 10 September 2021).

UN International Residual Mechanism for Criminal Tribunals (n.d.), *The ICTR in Brief*. Available at: https://unictr.irmct.org/en/tribunal (accessed 10 September 2021).

UN Meeting Coverage and Press Releases (2017), Meeting SC/12819, *Shame, Stigma Integral to Logic of Sexual Violence as War Tactic*, Special Adviser Tells Security Council, as Speakers Demand Recognition for Survivors, 15 May. Available at: https://www.un.org/press/en/2017/sc12819.doc.htm (accessed 5 June 2021).

United Nations (UN) (2001), *A Review of the Implementation of the UN Convention on the Rights of the Child*, Report, Washington, DC: United Nations.

United States Commission on International Religious Freedom (USCIRF) (2017), *Wilting in the Kurdish Sun: The Hopes and Fears of Religious Minorities in Northern Iraq*, prepared for the USCIRF by Crispin M. I. Smith and Vartan Shadarevian, May–August 2016, Washington, DC: USCIRF.

Vatican News (2019), 'Document on Human Fraternity for World Peace and Living Together', 4 February. Available at: https://www.vaticannews.va/en/pope/news/2019-02/pope-francis-uae-declaration-with-al-azhar-grand-imam.html (accessed 15 March 2021).

Vatican News (2021), 'Meeting with the Bishops', Pope Francis, Bishops, Priests, Religious, Consecrated Persons, Seminarians, Catechists, in the Cathedral at Sayidat al-Nejat, 5 March. Available at: https://www.youtube.com/watch?v=P8wrbnCgSS4 (accessed 15 April 2021).

Voice of Free Assyrians (2016), 'Assyrians Disarmed and Abandoned to ISIS by Peshmerga', 12 April. Available at: https://www.youtube.com/watch?v=zVqcmgAtjp8&t=18s (accessed 15 March 2021).

Walker, Joel Thomas (2006), *The Legend of Mar Qardagh*, Berkeley, CA: University of California Press.

Wallis Budge, E. A. (1902) *The Histories of Rabban Hôrmîzd the Persian and Rabban Bar-'idtâ*, London: Luzac.

Wallis Budge, E. A., trans. (2018), *The Book of the Cave of Treasures*, London: Aziloth Books.

Wallis Budge, E. A. (2020), *The Babylonian Story of the Deluge as Told by Assyrian Tablets from Nineveh*, Manila: Arcani Press.

Warren, Joyce W. (2018), 'Preface', in Elissa Bemporad and Joyce W. Warren (eds), *Women and Genocide: Survivors, Victims, Perpetrators*, ix–xiv, Bloomington, IN: Indiana University Press.

Washington Kurdish Institute (2017), 'Interview with Loay Mikhael, the Representative of the Christian Chaldean Syriac Assyrian Popular Council to Washington', 25 July. Available at: https://dckurd.org/2017/07/25/interview-with-loay-mikhael-the-representative-of-the-christian-chaldean-syriac-assyrian-popular-council-to-washington/ (accessed 12 August 2018).

Wasserstein, David J. (2017a), *Black Banners of ISIS: The Roots of the New Caliphate*, New Haven, CT: Yale University Press.

Wasserstein, David J. (2017b), *ISIS, Christianity, and the Pact of Umar*, 16 August. Available at: http://blog.yalebooks.com/2017/08/16/ISIS-christianity-and-the-pact-of-umar (accessed 4 January 2019).

Williams, Daniel (2016), *Forsaken: The Persecution of Christians in Today's Middle East*, New York and London: OR Books.

Wood, Elisabeth J. (2012), 'Rape during War is not Inevitable: Variation in Wartime Sexual Violence', in Morten Bergsmo, Alf Butenschøn Skre and Elisabeth J. Wood (eds), *Understanding and Proving International Sex Crimes*, 389–419. Beijing: Torkel Opsahl Academic EPublisher.

World Bank Group (2015), *The Kurdistan Region of Iraq: Assessing the Economic and Social Impact of the Syrian Conflict and ISIS*, New York: World Bank.

Yazda (n.d.), Available at: https://www.yazda.org/post/yazda-is-registering-students-for-scholarships-to-study-ba-at-the-catholic-university-in-erbil (accessed 6 June 2021).

Yerevan, S. (2020), 'Without Diversifying Its Rentier Economy, Pessimism among Kurdish Youth Will Increas', 13 October. Available at: https://www.washingtoninstitute.org/policy-analysis/without-diversifying-its-rentier-economy-pessimism-among-kurdish-youth-will (accessed 10 November 2020).

Zeeuw de, Hans (2019), *Tanbûr Long-Necked Lutes along the Silk Road and Beyond*, Oxford: Archeopress.

Zhmud, Leonid (2019), 'The Papyrological Tradition of Pythagoras and the Pythagoreans', in Christian Vassallo (ed.), *Presocratic and Papyrological Tradition: A Philosophical Appraisal of Sources*, 111–46, Berlin and Boston, MA: De Gruyter.

Index

Abadeen 24
Abba Abraham of Risha monastery 12
Abbas Shamsadin 24
Abd al-Karīm Qāsim 8
Abednego 24
Abraham 5, 18
    Abrahamic religions 14
Abu Dhabi 18
Achaemenian 13
Adiabene 25
Adur Gushnasp at Takht-e-Suleyman 13
Ahl-e Haqq 21
Akkadian 22
Akum Kak Remi 22
Al-Azhar Ahmed el-Tayeb 18
Alexander the Great 22
Al-Hamdaniya University 17
Al-Qaida 26
Alqosh 19
    Our Lady of the Seeds, Monastery 65, 71
    Qeshta d'Maran 47
    Rabban Hôrmîzd Monastery 51, 53, 58, 64, 65, 66
    Yimma d'Athor 47
    Yimma d'Mathwatha 47; see Alqosh
Amadiya 13
Amar-Sin 16
Amida 12
Ankawa 17
    St Joseph Church 85
Apostles
    Acts 12
Arabic
    poetry 7
Aramaic
    Language 11
    Sureth 11
Ardashir 17
Argentina
    Military Junta 7
Arrapha 5
Ashura 9

Ashur-dan I 16
Askar Goptapa 24
Assyrian
    Chaldeans 18
    Assyrian Christians 21
    Assyrian Confederation of Europe 10
    Assyrian Democratic Movement 21
Athenophanes 25
Avesta 14
Ayatollah Khomeini 5

Ba'adrie 97, 99
Ba'ath Part, 7, 11–12, 43, 101, 107, 123, 131, 138, 139–40, 157
Baba Gurgur 28, 29
Baba Sheikh 88, 118–20
Babylon 15–16, 44
Badeeah Hassan Ahmed 101–2, 112
Baghdad 8–10, 12, 27, 36, 42–3, 46, 71–5, 89, 110, 117, 123, 127, 132, 137–9, 141–2, 144, 149, 152, 161, 165.
    Chamber of Commerce 139
    Dora 72–4
    Our Lady of Salvation Assyrian Catholic Church 71
    Saint Elia Chaldean Catholic Church 72
    Saint Peter and Paul Chaldean Catholic Seminary 72
    Sayidat al-Nejat Cathedral 165
Bakr al-Baghdadi 70, 117
Balisan 28
Bangladesh 114, 115
    government 114
Baqosfa 78
Bar Shakko 67
Bar-'idta monastery 51
Barham Salih 89, 137
Barhebraeus 67, 68
Bartalla 6, 68, 78, 88, 133–4, 158
Basrah 21, 57
Batnaya 71, 74, 157

Bawa Gurgur 28–9
Bawa Mahmi 27–8
BBC World Service 27, 30, 36, 45, 48
Berossus 51
Beth Nuhadra, Dohuk 45
Bezkîn monastery 52–3
Bible 56, 60, 67
Birangona 114
Burhan Hatam Muhammed 42
Bush George W. 109

Canadian Addax Petroleum 145
Caracalla 82, 83
Catholic University 86
Chaldeans 2, 45, 88, 94, 156
Chraw Organization for Documentation 5, 42, 125, 165
Christian Chaldean Syriac Assyrian Popular Council 155
Christian communities
    Abyssinia 56
    Egypt 55
    Mesopotamia 55
    Nubia 55
    Palestine 55
Christians
    Arab 45
    Iraqi 45
    Kurdish 45
    Persian 45
    Syriac 45
    Turkish 45
Christology 63
Church
    Assyrian of the East 49–50, 53–5, 58–9, 63, 93
    Dyophysite 54
    Miaphysite 54
    Nestorian 45
    Syrian Orthodox 45
coexistence 2, 4, 7–9, 41, 61, 75, 77, 89–90, 95, 108, 122, 125, 135, 157, 165–6
Colonel Taufiq Wahby 20
Constantine, Emperor 84
Corinthians
    letter 92
Customary Law 105
Cyrus, King 15, 16, 56, 82

Damascus 69
    Great Mosque 69
Damietta 91
Dawūd 18, 30, 33
Deir Mar Barsauma monastery 68
dhimmi 76–7
Dio Cassius 83
divination 24, 35
Diyala Province 36, 38, 43, 82
Diyar Bakir 63
Diyarbakyr 100–1
Dohok 8, 125, 159
    Dohuk Governorate 7
Doquq 42

Edessa 49, 58, 82
Edmonds, Cecil J. 4, 11, 18–22, 26
Eil Qushti 47
Eil-Kushtu 47
Elamite, empire 15
Emmanuel II Patriarc of Babylon 50
Enuma Elish 49
Equal Franchise Act 108
Erbil 5–6, 8, 13, 29–30, 39, 40, 42–3, 45–6, 59, 61, 67, 80–2, 85–90, 94, 124–5, 127, 130, 132, 137, 142, 144, 146, 148–50, 152, 154, 156–7, 159–60, 164–5
    Archdiocese 85
Esarhaddon, King 60, 81
Eski Kalak 130
Esrāfil 21
Estangela
    calligraphy 63
Ezrā'il 21

Fakhr al-Din 'Abd al Masih 67
First World War 13, 28, 105, 130
Fosse Ardeatine 99–100
France 88, 143, 146
Francis, Pope 89–91, 93, 137, 163–5
Frantz Fanon 112
Fukuyama Francis 137, 140, 147
Fulanain 105

Garmawa Refugee Camp 7, 126, 12–19
Garshuni
    inscriptions 63

Gaugamela 82
Gawra 81
General Federation of Iraqi Women 109
Geneva Convention 114
genocide
    Armenian 77
    Assyrian 64
    Convention 116, 117
    Kurdish 12
German Federal state of Baden
    Württemberg 118
Germany 88, 116–19, 146
Gnostics 9, 22–3
Goran Party 146, 161
Gorani Kurdish 7, 14, 17, 20, 130
Grace Monica 105
Grand Ayatollah Ali al-Sistani 89–90
Great Britain 28, 88
Gyndes 15–16, 82

Halabja 11, 13, 19, 25–6, 140
Handel 31
Hashd al-Shaabi 42–4, 78, 88, 132–3, 160
Hattusa 82
Hawar 11, 15–16, 18–19, 20–1, 24,
    26–7, 34
    Saraw Dudara Temple 18
    Shirnawa Mountain 18, 25
Heraclius, emperor 59
Herodotus 15, 82
Hittite, empire 13
Holocaust 99, 116
Honorius III, Pope 91
Hormizd 50
Human Rights Watch 152

International Criminal Tribunal for
    Rwanda 114
International Criminal Tribunal for the
    Former Yugoslavia 114
Iran 4–5, 11, 13–15, 17, 19, 26, 30, 34–5, 37,
    43, 64, 80, 82, 90, 108, 127, 131,
    133–4, 141, 146, 161
Iraq 1–10, 12–14, 17–20, 25–7, 30, 34–5,
    37, 39, 40–7, 50–1, 61–2, 66, 71,
    75–6, 83, 87, 89–91, 93–4, 101,
    107–10, 115, 117–19, 121–9, 131,
    133, 135, 137, 139, 140–6, 148–50,
    152–6, 160–1, 164–5, 166

Iraqi Personal Status Law 112
Iraqi Petroleum Company 28–9
Îsâ bar-Isha'ya' Diacon 51
Išhtar 81, 82
Islam 8–9, 18, 22, 24, 34–5, 37, 42, 54, 57–8,
    60, 62–3, 69, 74, 77, 91–2, 100–1,
    116, 124–5, 131, 144, 156, 164
Islamic State of Iraq and Syria 1, 4–8, 10,
    12, 24, 3–7, 39–43, 46–8, 66, 69,
    70–2, 74–8, 80, 85–90, 94–5, 97–8,
    101–3, 109, 112, 115–29, 131–2, 134,
    141, 144, 148, 150–1, 154–5, 157–61,
    163–5
Izates II 83

Jacobites 51–3, 55
Jalal Talabani 10, 138, 140
Jamkhānes 35
jams 35
Jazira
    principality 100
Jebrā'il 21
Jesus 13, 35, 49, 55, 79, 84, 92
Jews 29, 47, 60, 69, 72, 76–8
John the Ephesus 54–5
Jonah, Prophet 69–70
Joseph VI, Patriarch 64
Joseph Emmanuel II Toma, Patriarch 64
Joseph VI Audo, 1 Patriarch 64
Judaism 83

Kabarli 152
kafir 37, 124
Kakai Chraw Organization for
    Documentation 5, 42, 125, 165
Kakais 1–2, 4–5, 10–24, 26–8, 30–1, 33–5,
    38, 41–4, 94, 100, 130, 149, 152, 161,
    163, 165
Kalar 36, 130
KaliGaKuzna 16
Karamless 78
Karbala 35, 131
Kaven Golestan 26
Kaywan 28
Kermanshah Province 17
Keykawis, Median ruler 14
Keyxesrew, Median ruler 14
Khanaqin 13, 27, 34, 36, 37, 39, 42–3
Khopushkia Province 13

Khusro II, Sassanid ruler 59
Kirkuk 8, 11, 24, 28–30, 34, 36, 42, 45, 49, 59, 67, 82, 124–5, 139, 144, 146, 152, 160–1
   Karkā d-Beth Slōkh 59
Kocho 101–2, 164
Kulabor 152
Kurdish Region 7, 9–12, 30, 43, 46, 75, 94, 110–11, 119, 124–5, 129, 132, 137–8, 141–2, 145–7, 149–51, 157, 159–61, 165
   Kurdistan Regional Government 8–9, 34, 36, 40, 42–3, 47, 80, 111–12, 129, 142, 144, 148, 164–5
Kurdistan Democratic Party 10
Kurdistan Development Corporation 146
Kurds 7–8, 10–11, 13–14, 18, 26, 38, 43, 64–5, 71, 73, 100–1, 111, 115, 123, 137–40, 141–4, 148, 150, 152, 154, 159, 161
   Faylee, 139
Kuwait 108

Lalish 1, 6, 22, 98, 101–2, 119
League of Defence of Women's Rights 108
Licinius 84
Loay Mikhael 155

Macedonians 35, 82
Mahar 106
Mahmood Uthman 10
Mahmoud Sankawi 42
Malik Margaret George 11
Mandeans 9, 10, 73, 76, 152
Manichaeism 83
Maqamas 34
Mar Addai II, Patriarch 74
Mar Mattai Monastery 52
Mar Mikha 48, 49–51
Mar Qardagh 59, 60–1, 83
Mar Toma Audo 64
Marano Cave 18, 26
Mardin 101
Massoud Barzani 10, 140–1, 151
Matrad 152
Matti Warda 6, 11
Mawla 24
Meshach 29
Mesopotamia 1–2, 45, 50, 53–4, 56, 59–60, 63, 67, 80–2, 115

Michael Gunter 137, 145–6, 148
Michael Quentin Morton 28–9
Mikā'il 21
Mir-Hosseini 34
Mohammed, Prophet 13, 21–2, 35, 58, 62, 65
Mohammed Pasha of Rawanduz 65
Mongols 54, 65, 67
Moses 13, 33, 69
Mosul 6–9, 24, 39, 40, 45–7, 49–51
   Al-Nuri Mosque 9
   Church of Mar Ahudemmeh 68
   Holy Spirit Church 71
   Mashad al-Nabi Jirjis – St. George Church 69
   Nabi Younis 70
Mozart 37
Mulla Uthman al-Aziz 11
Murad Nadia 99, 101, 103, 112, 117, 121, 150
Murîds 97
Mustafa Barzani 138–9

Nabard Naser Fatehulla 42
Nahum 47, 48, 50
Najaf 89, 131
Nargiza 24
Nazar Abdul Karim Faizal al-Khazraji 26
Naziha al-Dulaimi 108
Nazik al-Malaika 104, 105, 106
Nazis 102
Nebuchadnezzar 29
Nineveh 4, 8, 45–6, 48, 60, 70, 72, 74, 81–2
   Nineveh Plain 4, 6, 9, 12, 15, 49, 51, 58, 65, 69, 71, 73, 75, 78, 86, 88, 90, 130–4, 146–52, 154, 156, 159
Noah 51
Nouri al-Maliki 110

Pact of Omar 76–7
Parthia 82
Patriotic Union of Kurdistan 10, 93–4, 111, 138, 140, 147–8, 152, 161
Paul Bremen 110
Paul VI, Pope 92
Paulos II Shiekho, Patriarch 64
Peacock Angel 97
Peshmerga 11, 37, 39, 42, 78, 143, 150–2, 154
Peter Galbraith 110
Pīrdwer 17–18

Pius XI, Pope 50
Plato 13, 31, 32
Plutarch 29
Pythagoras 31

Qaraqosh 6, 9, 68, 78, 86, 88–9, 91, 133
   Bakhdida 86
   Church of Mart Shmuni 68
Qawltas 18
Quintilianus 31
Quran 70

Reincarnation 23
Roman
   Roman empire 54
Rome 47, 63, 82, 84, 99, 117
   Statute 87
Rowanduz 101
Ryan al-Kildani 44

Sabis 94
Saddam Hussein 2–3, 7, 10–12, 24–6, 43–4, 71, 73, 80, 95, 101, 107–11, 119, 123, 126, 131, 133–4, 137, 140–1, 143, 153, 161
Safa Abdullah Ali al-Kake 36
Saint Francis of Assisi 91–2
Saint Paul 92
Saint Thomas 45, 47, 54–5, 84
SajNar 17
Šamši-Bēl 81
Saranjam 5, 9, 14–19, 21–4, 28, 30–1, 33, 35, 163
Sardis 16
Sarlî 82
Sassanid Empire 59–60, 62
Savafids 100
Second World War 47, 102, 107–8, 113, 116, 143
Seleucids 60
Sennacherib, King 49, 61
Sextus Empiricus 31
Sha Koshin 35
Shabak 7, 12, 86, 94, 100, 123, 125, 130–5, 152, 164
Shadrach 29
Shams al-Din al-Ba'shiqi 67
Shamshi-Adad I 81
Shapur II 59, 61

Shara d'Rabban Hurmiz 64
Shari'a law 9, 110, 144
Sheikhan 100
Shias 72, 115
Shlomo Organization 6, 11
Sinjar 36, 100–1, 129
Sirwan River 15–17
Siyosinan 26
Sofi Rashid 18–21
Solomon Bishop of Perâth Maishân 56
Strabo 82
Stuart Edwin Hedgcock 105–7
Sufaia 152
Sulaymaniyah 8, 13, 25, 30, 34, 36, 38, 73, 100, 125, 137
Sultan Malik al-Kamil 91
Sultan Sahaq 16–19, 22, 26, 33
Sumerian, empire 15
   dynasty 81
   epic creation 49
Sunnis 7, 71–3, 110, 115, 123–9, 131–2, 134, 149–50, 154
   caliphate 116
   Shabak 2
   Sunni-Shia war 37
Supreme Council of Women's Affairs 144
Sykes-Picot Agreement 101, 105
Syriac
   inscriptions 63
   Language and literature 49, 51, 53, 55–6, 58–9, 63, 84, 97
   manuscripts 55
   Orthodox Church 49, 54, 62, 85
   traditions 56, 83, 91, 155, 156
Syrian
   refugees 159

Takzara 19–20
Tappouni, Monsignor 88
Tashar 16, 17
Tasûsî Melek 97
Teleskof 69, 78–9, 154
   Church of St George 78–9, 134
Thebes 48
Tigris 80, 82
Timaeus 31–2
Transitional Administrative Law 109
Tribal Criminal and Civil Disputes Regulations 105

Tulaban 152
Turkey 63, 137, 141, 146, 161
Turkish Petroleum Company 29
Turkmans 11
Turner William 29
Tuz-Khurmatu 29

Umar ibn Khattab 76
Umayyads 62
United Arab Emirates 146
United Kingdom 142, 146
United Nations
    United Nations Development Program 10
    United Nations Genocide Convention 116, 118
    United Nations Refugee Agency 126
United States Department of Defense 109
Ur 90
    Ziggurat 90

Vatican 63, 89, 92, 165
    Council 18

Wallis Badge 51, 55, 56–7, 69
Wardak 152
World Bank Group 146, 160

Xenophon 82

Yarsanism 13
    Yarsans 13, 17, 34, 43
Yezidis 1–2, 6, 10, 12, 22, 27, 87–8, 94, 97, 98, 99–104, 113, 115, 117–19, 121, 129–30, 149–50, 152, 160–1, 162, 164–5
Youhanna Hirmuz, Patriarch 63
Youhanna Sulaqa, Patriarch 63
Yuhanon Bar Nagarre, Monastery 67

Zab river 39, 81, 82
Zagros mountains 1, 4, 9, 13, 15, 80
Zakho 8
Zalim River 25
Zangal 152
Zoroastrian 14, 59–61, 95
Zoroastrianism 23, 83

www.ingramcontent.com/pod-product-compliance
Lightning Source LLC
Chambersburg PA
CBHW061827300426
44115CB00013B/2277